Race and Class
in the Southwest

Race and Class in the Southwest

A Theory of Racial Inequality

Mario Barrera

UNIVERSITY OF NOTRE DAME PRESS

NOTRE DAME ~ LONDON

Copyright © 1979 by
University of Notre Dame Press
Notre Dame, Indiana 46556

9 8 7 6 5 4 3 2

Library of Congress Cataloging in Publication Data

Barrera, Mario.
  Race and class in the Southwest.

  Bibliography: p.
  Includes index.
  1. Mexican Americans—Southwest, New—Social conditions.
2. Southwest, New—Social conditions. 3. Southwest,
New—Race relations. 4. United States—Race relations.
I. Title.
F790.M5B37   301.45′16′872079   78-62970
ISBN 0-268-01600-3
ISBN 0-268-01601-1 pbk.

Manufactured in the United States of America

To my parents
   Pedro and Elena

and to S, M, and T
   for their support, moral and otherwise

Contents

Contents

Acknowledgments

A GREAT NUMBER of people have contributed directly or indirectly to the development of this book. Carlos Muñoz, currently at work on his much-anticipated study of the Chicano student movement, has been a constant intellectual companion. Ernesto Galarza has served as the very model of the committed scholar, as meticulous in his research as he is passionate in his advocacy. Robert Blauner has helped me clarify my thoughts on the merits of the internal colonial model. Rudy Torres and Danny Moreno have provided a continuing stream of insights on Chicanos in the labor market, and have at times accompanied me during the last few years on my periodic escapes from the social isolation of research and writing. Tomás Almaguer has engaged me in an on-going debate that has always been stimulating if not always harmonious; I owe much to his tough-mindedness. Julian Samora and Jorge Bustamante have provided inspiration not only through their publications on immigration but through their suggestions and guidance. I am grateful to two of my former instructors, Michael Rogin and Warren Ilchman, for their encouragement.

For their written or verbal comments on earlier versions of some of these chapters I am indebted to Clark Knowlton, Gil Cárdenas, Howard Sherman, and a number of the "new generation" of Chicano historians, especially Carlos Cortés, Ricardo Romo, Alberto Camarillo, Mario García, Luis Arroyo, Alex Saragoza, and Victor Nelson Cisneros. I would also like to acknowledge the help of several research assistants, particularly Jim Johnson.

Three of my former students have made indispensable contributions by collaborating with me on various research projects; they are Art Luján, Geralda Villalpando, and Richard Llata. There are many other students I would like to acknowledge, but space does not permit.

The development of the National Association for Chicano Studies (NACS) since 1972 has been a great help to me, in that it put me in touch with other Chicano researchers throughout the nation. Several of the chapters in this book were originally presented as papers at the annual conferences of this association. I particularly want to express my appreciation to the Southern California *foco* (local chapter) of NACS, to which I belonged for five years. I have also benefitted from the many critical and at times heated discussions that have taken place with the members of the Chicano Political Economy Collective (CHIPEC) at Berkeley, a truly unique group: Tomás Almaguer, Luis Arroyo, Jorge Chapa, Patricia Chávez, Regino Chávez, Elena Flores, Guadalupe Fríaz, Hisauro Garza, Felipe Gonzales, Andrés Jiménez, David Montejano, and Larry Trujillo.

At a critical point in the writing of this manuscript I was fortunate enough to be able to spend a year at UCLA's Center for Chicano Studies, headed by Juan Gómez-Quiñones. The support of the Center and its fine library was of great help. I also appreciate the secretarial support I have received through Berkeley's Chicano Studies Program.

The Appendix of this book originally appeared in a longer article in the *Review of Radical Political Economics,* whose editors have graciously consented to having it reprinted here in a re-edited version.

CHAPTER I

Introduction

AT THE CONCLUSION of the Mexican American War in 1848, the United States added a vast and potentially rich territory to its possessions. This territory, while by no means densely settled, was certainly not unpopulated. In addition to numerous Native American groups, the area that is now called the Southwest contained a number of former Mexican citizens who, in terms of their origin, were part Indian, part Spanish, and part African. Separated by vast reaches of terrain and internally divided by class distinctions, this Spanish-speaking population nevertheless had a certain common identity which has persisted up to the present day. This group has responded at different times and in different places to various designations. Mexican American, Mexican, Latin American, Hispano, and Latino are some of the more common variations, Chicano being the most recent. Neither the variety of labels, however, nor the undeniable heterogeneity of this group should conceal the very real sense of a common origin and a common fate. The concept of "La Raza," probably the most generally accepted self-designation (and properly understood as "the people" rather than "the race") best expresses this feeling of unity.

While one major source of this group identity is a cultural heritage with certain core common elements, another and very important source has been the collective perception of injustice based on a fundamental and persistent condition of group inequality with respect to the "Anglos" in American society (the term "Anglos" as used by Chicanos refers to all Americans not members of a racial minority, and not just to those who trace their origin to the British Isles). The perception of injustice has been the motive for innumerable planned as well as spontaneous political activities on the part of Chicanos, from guerrilla warfare in the last century to agricultural workers' strikes, community control movements, party-building, and urban uprisings in the present one. The condition of inequality which underlies the perceptions of injustice has been the subject of innumerable government and academic studies, which have, however, made little dent in the problem.

In recent years these interlinked phenomena of inequality and group identity have taken on a new urgency because of changing demographic patterns in the Southwest. Whereas in the past most Chicano political activi-

1

ties have been contained because of the minority status of this group, the combination of a high birthrate and a continued high rate of immigration from Mexico now threatens, or promises, to bring about a Chicano majority in several states in the not too distant future. These trends have raised the specter of a "Chicano Quebec" in the Southwest in the minds of many observers.

The question of Chicano inequality, of course, is one aspect of the broader question of racial inequality in the United States. How are we to understand the causes of this condition, perhaps the most profound and divisive social problem that this country has had to face? Briefly, three kinds of answers have been provided by analysts of inequality: (1) they're to blame, (2) we're to blame, (3) the system is to blame. In more formal terminology, these three types of explanations may be called deficiency theories, bias theories, and structural discrimination theories.

Deficiency theories hold that racial minorities are poor and powerless because of some deficiency in the group itself. The classic racist theories, for example, advance the argument that non-White racial groups are characterized by biological deficiencies, such as inferior intelligence. More modern deficiency theories name the family or the culture as the culprit.

Bias theories typically place the responsibility for inequality on racial prejudice. Gunnar Myrdal, in his *An American Dilemma,* developed a prototype of this theory. He felt that prejudice produced discrimination, that discrimination kept minorities subordinate, and that a vicious circle was set up when the perception of subordination by subsequent generations reinforced the stereotype of minority unworthiness that had created the situation in the first place. The Kerner Commission and its condemnation of "White racism" is a recent example of this type of theory in the wake of the racial unrest of the mid-1960s.

A third type of racial inequality theory focuses on *structural discrimination*. Like bias theory, it places an emphasis on prejudice and discrimination, but with some major differences. Structural theory stresses *institutionalized* patterns of discrimination based on individuals' prejudiced attitudes. Examples of such institutionalized discrimination are dual labor markets (discussed more fully in later chapters) and school segregation and tracking. Political gerrymandering and other forms of systematic political manipulation are other examples.

While I favor a variety of structural discrimination theory called colonial theory, this tradition shares with the others a neglect of the class dimension in American society. From my reading of Southwestern economic history (presented below in chapters 2, 3, 4 and 5), an understanding of racial inequality is incomplete without taking into account class dynamics. In the concluding chapter, therefore, I make the attempt to integrate this with other elements in order to produce what I hope will be a new, improved structural theory.

ON HISTORY AND THEORY

The approach that I have followed is that of an extended historical and interdisciplinary case study. Unfortunately, American scholarship tends to suffer from a division between history and theoretical social science. The kind of approach that was followed by such nineteenth-century writers as Karl Marx and Max Weber is studied in the universities but never followed, as far as combining historical materials with a systematic theoretical framework. One does not need to be as ambitious as Marx and Weber to take up this kind of approach and to attempt a work which is more integrative than fragmented.

A historical approach allows us to see the persistence of patterns as well as changes over time. The changing historical conditions provide a kind of natural variation that allows us to see which factors make a difference in racial inequality and which do not. Naturally occurring historical variation can provide what might be seen as "crucial experiments" that tend to verify one kind of theoretical explanation over others. To give one example, taken from the following material: if wartime labor shortages in the United States provide racial minorities with opportunities for occupational mobility, and if minorities take advantage of those opportunities and perform satisfactorily in their new roles, theories that explain occupational inequality on the basis of cultural or other deficiencies, rather than on the structure of opportunities, tend to be undermined. While no one instance is decisive, a number of cases which point in a consistent direction eventually add up to persuasive evidence for one theory.

A historical approach also allows us to see commonalities in the experience of different groups. For example, it appears that Chicanos in the second half of the nineteenth century were concentrated in certain occupations in which Blacks were also concentrated in other parts of the country, for example, agriculture, railroads, lumber. It also appears that both groups suffered downward mobility during the same period. That these patterns could be repeated in different sections of the country for different racial groups seems to indicate that the sources of the patterns lay not in regional characteristics or in factors peculiar to a racial group, but in broader national characteristics, a type of explanation consistent with structural theory.

Historical investigation can also clarify chains of causation which are not obvious through studies confined to one time period. For example, studies which attribute occupational stratification to educational deficiencies among racial minorities are seriously misleading in that they do not take into account the historical conditions under which the pattern of segregated and inferior schooling for minorities was established. If it can be shown that such patterns were deliberately instituted and that the interests of certain groups, such as agricultural and industrial employers, were involved in their establishment, a very different light is thrown on the pattern of racial inequality.

The study that follows is part of a broad school of Chicano scholarship that has emerged in the last few years. Under the stimulus of the social activism of the 1960s and early 1970s, a number of relatively young Chicano scholars have begun systematic research into several areas. While there had been significant earlier studies, they remained the work of isolated scholars pursuing particular research topics. Only in the last few years has there emerged what might be termed a generation of Chicano scholars, many of whom are dealing with a set of interrelated topics such as labor, economics, community institutions, social relations, and politics. Numerous articles and dissertations on these topics have now been completed, and I have drawn heavily on them in the present study. One of the hopeful signs in this research is that considerable exchange has taken place between researchers trained in history and in the social sciences.

TERMINOLOGY

The term "Chicano" is used here in the demographic sense rather than in regard to conscious political identification. It refers to persons of Mexican origin who reside permanently in the United States and thus is synonymous with "Mexican American." The term "Mexican" or "Mexicano" when used to refer to persons in the Southwest, means persons from Mexico who are in the United States temporarily or on an irregular status. Given legal and social complexities, there is no clear dividing line between Chicanos and Mexicanos. They live in the same communities and generally do the same kind of work. Unless otherwise specified, "Chicano" will often refer to both groups. In the past, many writers have used "Mexican" to refer to both groups.

The term "Anglo" will refer to all Caucasian residents of the United States. This is the common meaning of the term as used in the Southwest, illogical as that may seem to some.

Racial and ethnic terms are often mixed together in discussions of discrimination, and the results can be confusing. I use "ethnic" to describe cultural factors such as language, customs, or religion where these characteristics are used to identify a group or to serve as the basis of group identity. "Race" refers to physical characteristics, such as skin color, when these characteristics are used in a similar manner. Both sets of characteristics are, of course, subject to social definition, and have different meanings in different settings. The term "minority" refers to a racial minority. Chicanos are a minority group which is defined partly on the basis of racial characteristics and partly on the basis of ethnic characteristics.

ORGANIZATION

In chapter 2 I describe the circumstances that gave rise to the unequal position of Chicanos. The political penetration of the United States into the area now referred to as the Southwest was preceded by economic penetration, and economic motives were central to that conquest. Indeed, I argue that the conquest of the Southwest can only be understood as an expression of a dynamic and expansive American capitalism, itself part of a broader historical current that propelled European societies into what is now called the Third World. The bulk of the writings on the Mexican American War has seriously misplaced the emphasis in dealing with motivation or has dealt with it in terms of vague phrases such as "Manifest Destiny," without looking for an underlying structure of interests. I deal with the motivations behind the war in detail because I consider that the interests represented in that military conquest have figured importantly in all the subsequent history of Chicanos. In the second section of the chapter I indicate one of these continuities by describing the displacement of Chicanos from the land, which occurred after the war. From the historical literature it seems clear that the interests that primarily benefited from this land transfer were not those of the average American citizen, moving into that area, but those of the land speculators, developers, and large companies that rapidly came to dominate the economy of the Southwest.

Chapter 3 deals with the establishment of a subordinate labor force in the Southwest, which included but was by no means limited to Chicanos and Mexicanos. Here I introduce the concept of a colonial labor force by listing five ways in which racial minorities were treated unequally in the work force. The structure of this labor force was shaped by large employers in the Southwest, especially the mining companies, transcontinental railroads, and large agricultural concerns that employed the bulk of the racial minorities. This chapter is the key link in the structure of the book. It describes how the shaping of the Chicano work force, and thus the role of Chicanos in the economy, was influenced by the displacement from the land, which in turn was an expression of the constellation of forces that had produced the Mexican American War. At the same time, the formation of a racially subordinate labor force in the nineteenth century provided the structure and the baseline which has influenced the entire twentieth-century experience of the Chicano.

In chapter 4 I describe the changes in the situation of the Chicano in the first three decades of the present century. The Chicano population expanded greatly as a result of large waves of immigration from Mexico, but the immigrants found themselves fitted into the economic and social structure that had been developed earlier. The Chicano presence in the urban areas also expanded during this period, but the milieu provided only a variation of the unequal economic status to which Chicanos and other minorities had been relegated. Since there is more literature for this period, it is possible to give a fuller description of the small but significant group of Chicano white-collar workers and "middle class" elements that were present in the cities.

Chapter 5 covers the contemporary period, from the Great Depression to the present. Chicanos during this period have suffered considerable economic buffeting because of changes in the labor market. During periods of economic prosperity and labor shortage, such as the Second World War and the Korean War, Chicanos have been able to gain a better foothold in urban industrial occupations. During periods of economic downturn and labor surplus, such as the Depression, after the Korean War, and in the 1970s, efforts have been made to reduce social and economic strains by deporting or repatriating part of the combined and intermixed Chicano and Mexican population to Mexico. At the same time, the greater interpenetration of polity and economy since the Depression has acted in various ways to provide a very gradual economic upgrading of Chicano workers and thus a mild lessening of economic inequality. The chapter concludes with a discussion of the possible emergence of a sector of the Chicano population which is permanently marginal, in that its labor is no longer necessary to the economy.

Chapter 6, the first of two theoretical chapters, deals with the role of the state in creating and perpetuating the unequal situation of Chicanos. I review several different concepts of the role of the state in situations of class conflict: the pluralist, power elite, Marxist instrumentalist, and Marxist structuralist. The Marxist structuralist version appears to account better for the role the state has played with respect to such aspects of Chicano history as the expropriation of the land and the regulation of the labor supply in the Southwest.

The concluding chapter (7) summarizes the argument and provides a more formal presentation of the theory which underlies the book, and which is introduced in chapters 3 and 4. The theories of racial inequality that were mentioned above are described in more detail, and the strengths and limitations of each are discussed. The concept of colonialism is examined in some detail. I also review certain aspects of Marxist writing on race and class structure to evaluate what this tradition has to offer for the analysis of racial inequality. Certain elements of Marxist analysis are then combined with colonial concepts to arrive at a theory of racial inequality in the United States.

The appendix ("The Case of International Harvester") consists of information on the racial minority labor practices of a major industrial employer, International Harvester. This is a case study at the microeconomic level of the class and racial dynamics that are discussed at a more general level in the rest of the work.

CHAPTER 2

The Nineteenth Century, Part I:
Conquest and Dispossession

Westward the course of Empire wends its Way.

—slogan favored by
William Blackmore,
British land speculator
in the Southwest

IN THE NINETEENTH CENTURY the area that is now the Southwest was incorporated into the United States through a war of conquest. With the Southwest came a population of former Mexican citizens who were now granted American citizenship by the Treaty of Guadalupe Hidalgo. These were the original Chicanos. During the remainder of the century a social and economic structure crystallized in the Southwest in which Chicanos and other racial minorities were established in a subordinate status. It is into this structure that succeeding generations of Chicanos have been fitted during the twentieth century, with some modifications.

There were certain key developments affecting the Chicano's social and economic status in the nineteenth century. The first of these was the Mexican American War. In considering this topic, my main concern has been with the identification of the interests that motivated that war, since such an analysis has an important bearing on subsequent developments. The second key factor was the displacement of Chicanos from the land in the various areas of the Southwest. The third was the emergence of a labor system in which Chicanos and other minorities constituted a clearly subordinate segment, which I call a colonial labor force. It is my contention that the processes affecting the land and labor showed important continuities with the interests underlying the Mexican American War. A consideration of all three developments reveals an intricate interplay between class and race factors in the Southwest.

This chapter deals with the first two of these three topics, the war and the land. The next chapter outlines the development of the colonial labor system.

7

EVENTS UP TO 1848

The Spanish settlements in the area that is now the Southwest date from the late sixteenth and early seventeenth centuries. The earliest settlements were in the area now known as New Mexico, where Santa Fe was founded in 1609. Over the next 200 years there were additional settlements, and by the early nineteenth century there were three main areas of concentration: the New Mexico territory, southern and southeastern Texas, and the California coast. With the independence of Mexico in 1821, these areas became part of the new Mexican republic. These territories were thinly populated and relatively isolated from each other and from the major centers of Mexican population. The bulk of the population was *mestizo,* a mixture of Mexican Indian, European, and African stocks, and the predominant economic activities were mining, ranching, and agriculture. Vast areas of the Southwest were still controlled by various Native American groups, such as the Apaches, Pueblos, Navajos and Comanches.

It was during the first half of the nineteenth century that regular contacts were made between merchants and traders of the United States and the people of northern Mexico. Regular trade between St. Louis and northern New Mexico was initiated with the blazing of the Santa Fe Trail in 1822, leading to a lively trade in furs, silver, and other goods. One result was the weakening of the economic ties between northern New Mexico and the rest of Mexico, as the area came more into the orbit of the Missouri merchants (Lamar, 1970, p. 48). By the 1840s there was a sizable number of American businessmen in the cities of Taos and Santa Fe, whose economic activities were paralleled by their efforts to increase their political influence. In addition to trading, Anglos in New Mexico engaged in land speculation.

In California, Yankee maritime traders had established a presence going back to the late eighteenth century, built around their interests in sea-otter furs and whaling. During the 1820s an important trade developed around the exchange of California cattle products (the hide-and-tallow trade) for manufactured goods from New England (Billington, 1974, p. 474). In 1830 an overland route was established from Santa Fe to California which became known as the Old Spanish Trail. In addition to the exchange of California primary products for American processed goods, the trail served as a conduit for commodities brought to the California coast from Asia. In a recent paper, Almaguer has emphasized the manner in which these developments linked California to the United States and the broader world-economy (Almaguer, 1977).

The penetration of Texas by settlers from the United States was more thorough than in the other areas of northern Mexico. Here the Spanish and later the Mexican governments had made vigorous attempts to populate the

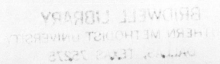

area through a series of land grants, some of which had gone to Anglo colonizers. The most famous of these was the Austin Colony, but there were others. While the Mexican government realized to some extent the dangers of settling the area with non-Mexicans, there was considerable danger in allowing this territory to remain very thinly populated. In any case, by the 1830s only the area around and south of San Antonio could be said to be distinctly Mexican in character (Meinig, 1969, pp. 35ff.).

The main economic activities in the Texas area were subsistence agriculture and cattle raising, although, starting in the 1820s, cotton became increasingly important. Eastern Texas in particular had very close economic ties with Louisiana and looked much more to the United States than to Mexico as far as trade was concerned.

It was in Texas, of course, that the first major political development took place that foreshadowed the incorporation of northern Mexico into the United States. There was a history of unrest and tension between the Anglo settlers in Texas and the Mexican government, as exemplified in the short-lived Fredonia Revolt in 1826. There was also a long-standing effort by the United States to purchase the Texas area from Mexico. As presidents, both John Quincy Adams and Andrew Jackson made offers to the Mexican government for the acquisition of Texas, and these overtures made Mexico suspicious of American intentions toward the area.

Mexican anxieties had also been aggravated by the continued influx of Anglo settlers (many of them ''illegal aliens''), which resulted by 1830 in a ratio of some 25,000 Anglos to 4,000 Spanish-speaking Mexicans in that area (Meier and Rivera, 1972, p. 58). As a result, there had been sporadic attempts by Mexico to curb Anglo-American influence in Texas. In 1830, for example, the Mexican government passed a Colonization Law which prohibited the importation of more slaves into Texas and also attempted to cut off further Anglo settlement. Texas at this time was part of the state of Coahuila-Texas. The law was ineffective and was repealed in 1833, but it indicates the concern of Mexican officials over the situation.

Specific economic interests were clearly involved in the conflict. On the one hand, many of the Anglo settlers were interested in cotton cultivation and desired the free importation of slaves to work in the cotton fields. Mexico had abolished slavery, and its policy toward the movement of slaves into Texas was ambivalent but obviously negative. In addition, Anglos with commercial interests wanted to engage in free trade with the United States, and resented Mexican efforts to enforce the national customs laws (Meier and Rivera, 1972, p. 59).

The decisive revolt for an independent Texas came about during a period of considerable internal conflict within Mexico. Federalists and Centralists were contesting for national power, with the Centralists, led by Santa

Anna, gaining the upper hand. Resistance to the Centralist regime broke out in several provinces, and it was in this context that the conflict in Texas was converted into a revolt among the Anglo settlers against any form of Mexican authority over the area. With the success of the revolt, the Republic of Texas was established in 1836. During the course of the armed conflict the official position of the United States was neutrality, but considerable support for the separatist cause flowed into Texas unofficially.

The new authorities in Texas promptly sought to be annexed to the United States, but annexation was rejected by the United States because of complications over the issue of slavery. Texas would have come in as slave territory, and the entire issue thus became embroiled in the American sectional conflict as well as in the competition between the two major parties, the Democrats and the Whigs. Texas thus remained a republic until 1845, during which time the Anglo population greatly increased through immigration.

The subject of the annexation of Texas came up again in 1844, and when annexation was rejected by the Congress the issue became important in the presidential campaign of 1844. In this campaign the Democratic candidate, James K. Polk, ran on a strongly annexationist platform and defeated the more ambivalent Whig nominee, Henry Clay. With the results of the election known, the outgoing president, Tyler, managed to get a joint resolution through Congress providing for the addition of Texas to the union. This act led Mexico, which had never formally recognized the independence of Texas, to break off diplomatic relations with the United States. In this charged atmosphere it became increasingly clear that Polk had broader territorial ambitions.

Shortly after the annexation of Texas, an American emissary, Slidell, was sent to Mexico to settle the Texas matter, but also to attempt to purchase the areas of New Mexico and California. With the failure of the Slidell Mission, the stage was set for the outbreak of hostilities. Polk had ordered American troops into Texas, and these had advanced to the Rio Grande, although the southern area between the Nueces River and the Rio Grande had always been a contested area between Texas and Mexico, in which there were no Texas settlements. In April 1846 the United States blockaded the mouth of the Rio Grande, which historian Glenn Price points out constituted an act of war even if the river had been the agreed-upon international boundary (Price, 1967, p. 153). In that same month an armed clash between Mexico and American troops along the river provided the incident which quickly led the United States to declare war against Mexico. Polk's war message to Congress was based on the claim that Mexican troops had invaded the territory of the United States and attacked American forces. But Price argues that Polk had concluded that his territorial aims could not be achieved peacefully, and that he had thus engaged in a series of actions designed to provoke an incident that could be used to stir up popular support for war.

The Mexican American War which resulted from these events lasted from 1846 to 1848, and the Treaty of Guadalupe Hidalgo, signed in the latter year, added a vast territory to the United States. Mexico lost one-third of its territory and the United States gained an area that was to become the states of California, New Mexico, Arizona, Nevada, Utah, and part of Colorado, as well as all of Texas. The former citizens of Mexico who remained in this area became American citizens and constituted the original Chicanos. In light of the preceding discussion, their incorporation into the United States must be seen as the product of an imperial war.

The interests that underlay the conquest of the Southwest have been a subject of considerable debate among historians, and a number of motivations have been put forth which need to be reviewed and assessed. One interpretation that has enjoyed considerable popularity is that Southern slaveowners were instrumental in instigating the conflict. According to this argument, they stood to gain in that the Southwest would provide room for expansion of cotton agriculture. Also, the addition of more slave states would aid the Southern planters in their conflict with Northern industrialists for control of the government (see Rhodes, 1907, p. 79). That political considerations led many in the South to push for the annexation of Texas is admitted even by those who play down the Southern conspiracy thesis (for example, see Boucher, 1921, p. 22). The economic argument also makes sense, in that cotton agriculture, as it was practiced at the time, tended to exhaust the land rapidly, and there was a continuous move westward from the old cotton states in search of more land suitable for plantations. The fact that most Southern planters were Democrats and that the national administration was Democratic also seems to add weight to this thesis.

However, the limitations of the argument need to be carefully noted. In the first place, there seems to be a consensus among historians that Polk did not act as a sectional president, in spite of his Southern origins. Rather, his thinking seems to have run primarily along national lines. In addition, it was already clear at the time of the Mexican American War that most of the Southwest was not suitable for cotton agriculture. Southerners, clearly, had little to gain from seeing more free territory enter the Union, and it was this consideration that led them to oppose the trend toward the annexation of all of Mexico that developed once the Mexican American War was under way (Fuller, 1969). Thus, while it seems clear that Southerners were active in pushing the demand for Texas, their interests do not explain the acquisition by the United States of the rest of the Southwest as well.

A second explanation for the expansion of the United States into the

Southwest has been couched in terms of Manifest Destiny. This explanation is the most widely held among historians, including Mexican American historians. According to this explanation, Anglo-Americans were possessed of a vision of history in which they were divinely chosen to populate the North American continent and to bring the blessings of democracy and progress to this area. Their expansion into the Southwest was simply an expression of this conviction.

  While it is true that there was strong popular support for expansionism in the United States, especially in the West and in some portions of the Northeast, various considerations severely limit the usefulness of Manifest Destiny as a fundamental motive for expansion into the Southwest. It may be more accurate to say that the fervor behind the idea of Manifest Destiny was the product of a campaign of ideological manipulation. Such a hypothesis is reinforced by the timing of the phenomenon:

> The date at which the doctrine emerged as a force to be reckoned with in politics is important to ascertain. . . . It can be ascertained only approximately, for many facets were present in this complex phenomenon and some of them came into prominence sooner than others. Some editorial voices proclaiming the full doctrine were heard already during the campaign of 1844. They were voices crying in the wilderness. The date when the full chorus proclaimed the doctrine came after the election, as late even as the closing months of the Tyler administration. It came after the annexation of Texas had emerged as a good prospect in politics. [Merk, 1963, p. 41]

The suddenness with which the doctrine emerged and spread inevitably arouses suspicions, as does the fact that the annexation of Texas was a contested political issue and that one of the major parties, the Democratic party, was strongly identified with the issue. As Merk points out, "In party affiliation, journals of Manifest Destiny views were Democratic. Organs of the Polk administration were strongly represented among them" (Merk, 1963, p. 35). From Merk's account, there was a large-scale selling effort by many newspapers for the doctrine.

A second major objection to Manifest Destiny as a fundamental explanation is that the doctrine was too vague and diffuse to serve as an adequate explanation of the expansion. It does not explain why certain areas were taken over and others were not. As Merk points out, "In some minds it meant expansion over the region to the Pacific; in others, over the North American continent; in others, over the hemisphere" (Merk, 1963, p. 24). Historian Norman Graebner puts it this way:

> Manifest destiny persists as a popular term in American historical literature to explain the expansion of the United States to continent-wide

dimensions in the 1840's. Like most broad generalizations, it does not bear close scrutiny. . . . The concept of manifest destiny, as a democratic expression, represented an expanding, not a confining or limiting, force. As an ideal, it was not easily defined in terms of precise territorial limits. . . . Some suggested that American laws be extended to include the downtrodden peons of South America. . . . In their enthusiasm to extend the ''area of freedom,'' many even looked beyond the continental limits to Cuba, the Sandwich Islands, the far-flung regions of the Pacific, and even to the Old World itself. This was a magnificent vision for a democratic purpose, but it hardly explains the sweep of the United States across the continent. [Graebner, 1955, pp. 217–18]

As others have pointed out, the concept of Manifest Destiny fit in very well with the All-of-Mexico movement, but all of Mexico was not taken.

Another objection to this type of explanation can be raised in terms of a general theory of history. Materialist theories in particular argue (and I would agree) that political movements are motivated fundamentally by interests rather than disembodied ideas. Ideas and concepts which ''catch on'' enter into political debate largely as expressions or justifications of specific interests, rather than as free-floating concepts and doctrines. In the case at hand, elites in the form of politicians and journalists played a major part in popularizing the doctrine, and the role of interests does not appear to be too difficult to identify.

In summary, then, Manifest Destiny was essentially a manipulated appeal and an attempt to secure broad popular support for an expansionist policy of particular benefit to certain political and economic interests. The specific nature of those interests will become clearer as we examine other explanations.

Some writers have argued that the incorporation of the Southwest into the United States should be understood in terms of economic and commercial interests of various types. To assess this argument we have to look at the three major areas of the Southwest: Texas, California, and New Mexico (which at that time included what is now Arizona). In the case of Texas (described above) there was clearly a desire on the part of cotton-growing interests in expanding into that area. California, however, appears to be the key to understanding commercial interests in expansion. The interest in California was particularly keen among the merchant and manufacturing interests of the American Northeast, generally represented in the Whig party. According to Robert Cleland,

A second reason for the belief that the annexation of California was not a slavery measure is the fact that the movement found its strongest popular favor in the north. Most of the contemporary newspaper and magazine articles which advocated the acquisition of this portion of

Mexican territory first appeared in New York or New England. [Cleland, 1914–15, p. 250]

Cleland also notes an 1846 article in the *American Review* ("Text Book of the Whig Party") detailing the rich resources of California and urging its immediate annexation, provided it could be done peacefully. He goes on to state:

Yet the interest with which the commercial states of the north regarded the future of California was unquestionably greater than that of any other section of the country, with the possible exception of the extreme west. For it was natural that those who had important trade relations not merely with California, but with India, China, and the Sandwich Islands, beside extensive whale fisheries, should of all others desire most eagerly a harbor and territory on the Pacific. [Cleland, 1914–51, p. 251]

The thesis that ports on the Pacific were the most important factor in explaining the conquest of the Southwest has been extensively developed by Norman Graebner. According to him,

The essential fact [is] that the expansion of the United States was a unified, purposeful, precise movement that was ever limited to specific maritime objectives. It was the Pacific Ocean that determined the territorial goals of all American presidents from John Quincy Adams to Polk. From the beginning, travelers, traders, and officials who concerned themselves with the coastal regions had their eyes trained on ports. The goal of American policy was to control the great harbors of San Francisco, San Diego, and Juan de Fuca Strait. With their acquisition, expansion on the coastline ceased. [Graebner, 1955, pp. v–vi]

Two of these three Pacific ports were in the California territory. The other was in the Oregon territory, which the United States acquired at about the same time after a contest with Great Britain. San Diego at that time was the center of the hide trade. San Francisco was also involved in that trade, and was seen as a major future trade link with Asia. In his message to Congress in December 1847, Polk declared that the California ports "would afford shelter for our navy, for our numerous whale ships, and other merchant vessels employed in the Pacific ocean, [and] would in a short period become the marts of an extensive and profitable commerce with China, and other countries of the East" (quoted in Graebner, 1955, p. 225).

American interest in New Mexico can also be interpreted in economic terms. For one thing, the New Mexico area served as an overland route between California on the one hand and Texas and the American Midwest on the other. Significant trade routes crossed this territory and had been in existence for some time. Santa Fe served as the overland link between California and St. Louis in a trade route that followed the Old Spanish Trail. Over this route passed manufactured goods, silver, livestock, and commodities from Asia (Billington, 1974, p. 477). Howard Lamar, in speaking of the New Mexico conquest, puts the matter this way:

> It was not an expression of land hunger or slavery extension; and it was only partly prompted by that vaguer expansionist sentiment called Manifest Destiny. Rather, American conquest meant regularizing and securing rich trade and safe transportation routes for a previously erratic, uncertain enterprise. It was, in short, a conquest of merchants who worried little about extending the glories of free government to their captive customers. [Lamar, 1970, p. 63]

The evidence thus seems clearly to support the argument that the American intrusion into the Southwest was motivated by several important economic considerations, perhaps most importantly in California. One objection that has been raised to this thesis has to do with the role of the Whigs in the national debate with regard to American expansionism during that period. While both Whigs and Democrats represented commercial interests, the Whigs were preeminently the party of Northeastern merchants and manufacturers, and they were for the most part vociferous critics of Polk and the conduct of the Mexican American War. From this fact some critics have argued against the kind of emphasis Graebner and Cleland have given to California and its ports as a motivation for the war. According to these critics, if that thesis was correct the Whigs should have been enthusiastic supporters of the war, since they represented economic interests that stood to benefit from it (see Zwelling, 1970).

There are several answers to this criticism. Whigs were not opposed to the acquisition of California, but they apparently felt that it could be done without necessarily resorting to war (Merk, 1963, p. 39). Whigs were also critical of the war for other reasons. They were not enthusiastic about the acquisition of Texas because of the slavery question and their fears of creating splits within their party and within the nation (ibid., p. 153). It should also be kept in mind that the war provided an issue which the Whigs were trying to turn to partisan advantage (Graebner, 1955, pp. 171–72, 188). At any rate, as Graebner has pointed out, Whig congressmen continued to vote financial support for the war while trying to make political hay by criticizing Polk's conduct of it. That this was a sound political strategy was indicated by their political gains in the elections of 1848.

Another interpretation of the Mexican American War that is sometimes found in the historical literature has to do with the pioneer movement. According to this view, the Anglo pioneers who had moved into the northern provinces of Mexico constituted an important force behind the American annexation of this area, acting as a kind of latter-day Trojan Horse. In assessing this argument, it seems fair to say that Anglo settlers played an important role in Texas, but were not a major force elsewhere. These settlers had of course been the prime movers behind the splitting of Texas from Mexico and the establishment of the Texas Republic, and this paved the way for the incorporation of Texas into the United States. However, there was only a sprinkling of Anglo settlers in California and the New Mexico area, and they did not play a central role in the Mexican American War.

Yet another factor that entered into the American move into the Southwest was the role played by foreign countries, especially England. England, seeing the United States as a potentially formidable competitor economically and politically, was doing what it could to limit American influence on the North American continent and to increase its own. While contesting the Oregon territory with the United States, England was attempting to prevent the annexation of Texas and was supporting the Mexican government in its efforts to hold on to the rest of its northern provinces. England apparently considered that an independent Texas would constitute a receptive market for British goods, as well as an ally in limiting American growth and power. At the same time, England was interested in exercising as much control as possible over the Pacific coast and its ports, although it was in no position to think of taking over California. The maneuvers and ambitions of Britain were well known in Washington, and were undoubtedly a source of anxiety to national policymakers. In attempting to assess the role this factor played, however, it may be best to quote a historian's opinion:

> The degree to which Polk's moves to acquire California were influenced by concern over British designs can be—and have been—easily exaggerated, for he was wise enough to realize that the jingoistic ambitions of a few English empire-builders did not constitute official policy. He was also aware, however, that those ambitions provided him an effective tool to manipulate American opinion toward favoring peaceful annexation, and Polk used that tool well. [Billington, 1974, p. 485]

Another dimension to American expansion into the Southwest is curiously missing or seriously underemphasized by historians. In the various interpretations that have been written there is rarely a discussion of the dynamics and level of development of the American economy as a whole during this period. It may be that a closer examination of this dimension will further clarify the motivations behind the Mexican American War.

The American economy during the first half of the nineteenth century was marked by a distinct regional pattern. The South, which had been a diversified agricultural area, was becoming more and more specialized as a cotton-growing region. The West was primarily a grower of foodstuffs. The Northeast, an area of incipient manufacturing, also provided important services in shipping and trade. According to the classic account by Douglass C. North (North, 1966), prior to the 1830s it was not clear that the United States would be able to develop into a major industrial country. The internal market was not highly developed, and the export sector was less than dynamic. The urban areas were relatively small, and the West was relatively isolated from the Northeast by natural geographic barriers. Starting around 1830, however, there was a major expansion in the value of the goods the United States was able to export. The earnings derived from exports then became the key factor in the economic development of the country, and particularly in manufacturing and regional integration. Of the various components that went into the export trade, cotton was by far the leading element.

The effects of this growth in exporting were many and interrelated. With growth in the demand for cotton, more land in the South was devoted to that crop, and the search for land suitable for cotton cultivation was intensified. However, a great deal of the cotton earnings flowed to the Northeast, since that region provided the services to finance, transport, and market the South's cotton. Some of these resources went into the establishment of a textile industry in the Northeast, and this in turn led to the development of an industry that produced machinery, first for the textile industry and then more generally. With the growth of urban industrial centers, the demand for Western-grown foods increased, and this stimulated the economy of the West and accelerated the development of transportation links between the Northeast and the West. As North notes, "it was industrialization in the Northeast and the opening up of the West and Far West which was primarily responsible for the growth of the 1840's and 1850's" (North, 1966, p. 71).

From this perspective, some of the interests and motivations reviewed above take on added significance. The boom in the demand for cotton and the key role this played in the economy of the entire country help explain the strong interest in Texas. The interest of the Southern ruling class in that area was also stimulated by the economic and population gains being made in the Northeast and West, since this tended to undercut their relative power at the national level. The booming economy of that period also heightened the interest of Northeastern commercial elites in California, with its ports and its potential role in future trade with Asia. The New Mexico territory, with its natural resources and its trade routes, also took on added significance. At the same time, the fact that the United States was more and more becoming an economic competitor helps explain England's concern with limiting American territorial growth, and made the United States even more eager to establish the base for its future role as a major world power.

The other side of the coin is that the economic and technological growth of the period made it possible for the United States to act on its ambitions. As Frederick Merk puts it,

The steam engine had come into its own in river, ocean, and land travel. From distant territories to the center of government travel time by water had been sensationally reduced. On land railroads had proved themselves practical. But even more remarkable than the actual achievements of these agencies in contracting space was the stimulus given to the expansion of thought. In the mid-1840's projects to build transcontinental railroads to the Pacific by northern, central, and southern routes were on the lips of all. [Merk, 1963, pp. 51–52]

In summary, then, a variety of interests can be seen to have played a role in the American penetration into the Southwest, some of major importance and some distinctly secondary. But at the heart of the phenomenon were a number of economic interests closely tied to the dynamic expansion of American capitalism from the 1830s on. These interests included those of Southern agricultural capitalists, based on the plantation system, but more importantly those of the Northern industrialists and men of commerce who were on the ascendance nationally.

THE LAND

With the termination of the Mexican American War, a process of transferring Southwestern land from Mexican American to Anglo hands was set in motion—in spite of provisions in the Treaty of Guadalupe Hidalgo guaranteeing the new citizens the security of their property. The pace of dispossession varied from area to area because of a variety of factors, but the general trend was everywhere consistent. Still, it would be an oversimplification to deal with this topic in strictly ethnic or racial terms. Class factors strongly influenced the process, as I emphasize in the following account. Given the uneven pace of land transfer, it is necessary to look at developments by geographic area.

California

In 1851 the U.S. Congress passed a Land Law that established a commission to review the validity of claims to the land in California based on grants made during the Spanish and Mexican periods. Attention has usually focused on the resulting adversary process, and the conflict over the land has been perceived as pitting the native Spanish-speaking Californios, as the land-grant claimants, against Anglo settlers who were often squatters on the land. While this was an important part of what was going on, several complicating factors need to be added to the picture.

On the Californio side, account needs to be taken of the fact that landownership in California had been highly unequal. Much of the desirable California land was held in the form of land grants that had been made by the

Spanish and Mexican governments. Among the Californios was a small class of large landowners and a much larger group of people who lived on a more modest scale. Among these were agricultural laborers, small farmers, servants, artisans, and small merchants. Laborers were the majority and were very poor. Thus all Californios did not have the same immediate stake in the question of who should control the land. According to Leonard Pitt, reports in 1849 showed that 200 California families owned 14 million acres (Pitt, 1970, p. 86).

There are complications as well on the Anglo side. In the first place, not all of the land grants had been made to Californios. There was a group of Anglos who had been recipients of grants prior to the Mexican American War. Among them were such well-known figures as Abel Stearns and John C. Fremont. Many of the Anglo landholders of this period were in the central valley of California, but several of the most important were in southern California (Robinson, 1948, pp. 63–64). Many of these men blended into Californio culture and had intermarried with Californios.

Another complicating factor arises from the fact of land transference through mechanisms that had little to do with the Land Commission. According to Paul Gates, "before 1851, 42 percent of the claims were in the hands of non-Mexicans and in the years thereafter an increasing number were lost to the hard-driving, better-financed Americans who began to develop their grants" (Gates, 1975, p. 159). Richard Morefield comments on this situation as follows:

> The process [of land transfer] had begun as soon as the first foreigner had set foot in California. . . . A breakdown of the figures gives an idea of how much of the land had already passed from [Californio] control. Of the 813 cases presented to the Commission, 521 were confirmed by the time the Commission adjourned in 1856; this number was raised to 604 by successful appeals to the courts. Of these 604 cases only 330 were confirmed to Californians of Mexican descent. [Morefield, 1971, p. 26]

This transfer was not being made to small Anglo settlers, as Gates makes clear:

> When sales were made, it was to new men with financial backing who were able to develop some portions of their purchases, even to lay out towns and cities on them. Thus, the early non-Mexican owners of great ranchos such as Thomas O. Larkin, John Bidwell, William A. Dana, Nicholas Den, W. E. P. Hartness, and Abel Stearns were joined by a group of new millionaires whose wealth had been or was being made in banking, shipping, the cattle trade, mining, and railroads. This new group became owners of numerous ranchos or parts of ranchos running into hundreds of thousands of acres. [Gates, 1975, p. 159]

Thus while it was true that Californios were being displaced from the land, many Californios owned no land from which to be displaced. While it was true that Anglos were taking over the land, some had been there earlier, and the new masters of the land were increasingly likely to be men of means rather than the average Anglo newcomer.

The process of displacing the Californios from the land was more rapid in northern than in southern California. The reason for this is that the Gold Rush in northern California attracted large numbers of Anglos into that area during and after 1848. With the influx of Anglos, land values in northern California skyrocketed (Gates, 1962, p. 100). Pitt and others have discussed various factors that facilitated the transfer of land. One was that the requirements for proof of ownership under American law were different and more stringent than under Mexican law. The Land Law of 1851 put the burden of proof squarely on the shoulders of the land-grant claimants. In addition, unfamiliarity with American law and the English language put many of the claimants at the mercy of Anglo lawyers, many of whom had designs on the land (Pitt, 1970, pp. 91, 97; Cleland, 1951, p. 39). Gates notes that "a fairly common practice was for lawyers prosecuting claims to charge a contingent fee of one quarter of the land if successful" (Gates, 1958, p. 235). The shortage of capital often forced the claimants to pay their lawyers entirely in land. The high legal fees and other costs led many landowners to borrow money at high interest rates, so that even if they won their case they frequently had to sell their land to meet their debts (Pitt, 1970, p. 1001; Cleland, 1951, p. 40; Robinson, 1948, p. 106). In addition, land claimants in northern California were faced with a particularly strong surge of squatters on their land. These settlers formed associations to exert political pressure on behalf of their interests. Not infrequently, they exercised intimidation and coercion on the grant claimants (Pitt, 1970, pp. 95ff.).

> In the north of California . . . the basis of landownership had changed drastically by 1856. Through armed struggle, legislation, litigation, financial manipulation, outright purchase, and innumerable other tactics, Yankees had obtained a good deal of interest in the land. The transfer of property destroyed the irenic vision provided by the Treaty of Guadalupe Hidalgo, which guaranteed the Californios the "free enjoyment of their liberty and property"—an obligation that did not worry many Yankees. [Ibid., p. 103]

The process operated at a slower pace in southern California, largely because the northern area was more dynamic economically in the first two decades following the Mexican American War. In the south there were few newcomers to speed the transfer of land. Other factors, however, intervened. The Gold Rush and population increase in the north stimulated the cattle industry of the south, which boomed in the early 1850s. But the boom was short-lived. By 1856 the cattle industry had peaked and started to decline (Cleland, 1951, p. 110). Overexpansion and poor investment practices had undermined the stability of the cattle ranches, and a severe drought in the 1860s brought about the downfall of many Californio rancheros (ibid., pp. 130ff.).

> Before the catastrophe, practically all land parcels worth more than $10,000 had still been in the hands of old families; by 1870, these families held barely one-quarter. A mean and brassy sky thus did in the south of California what lawyers and squatters had accomplished in the north—the forced breakup of baronial holdings, their transfer to new owners, and the rise of a way of life other than ranching. [Pitt, 1970, p. 248]

The finishing touches were added by the events associated with the coming of the railroads of southern California in the late 1870s and early 1880s. With the railroads came a monumental land boom that largely completed the erosion of the California-held lands. The immigration of large numbers of Anglos reduced the Californios in the southern part of the state to a small minority, as it had earlier in the north. Combined with the other factors cited above, the economic expansion of the 1880s reduced the Californios' holdings to a small fraction of their former possessions.

The situation of the Californios in San Diego County has been described by García (1975a) and Hughes (1975). Hughes stresses the role of legal fees and associated court costs in eroding the financial position of San Diego landowners. Land taxes also played an important role here, as in other parts of southern California.

> Since state laws exempted much of the northern mining industry, the brunt of the property tax fell on the large property owners of southern California who were primarily Californios. Most of the state's population resided in the North and worked in the mines or in related occupations. Their representatives dominated state government and attempted to use taxation to break up the large land holdings. [Hughes, 1975, p. 18]

In the Santa Barbara area, important changes in landownership took place during the 1860s, according to a study by Camarillo (1975a, 1975b). The downturn in the fortunes of the pastoral economy seems to have played an important role here as well. A comparison of censuses taken in 1860 and 1870 shows a dramatic decline in the number of Spanish-surname rancheros and farmers in the Santa Barbara area during that period (Camarillo, 1975a, p. 6).

In summary, a number of factors had gone into the process that resulted in dispossession from the land of the Californio elite and some small farmers.

Among these were:

> Imposition of a different legal system with different standards of proof of ownership
>
> Placing the burden of proof on the land-grant claimant to demonstrate that the claim was legitimate
>
> Legal chicanery by Anglo lawyers dealing with culturally different clients
>
> Manipulations of the tax system on land
>
> High legal fees and court costs, combined with a shortage of capital and the necessity to borrow money at high interest rates (see Cleland, 1951, p. 114; Pitt, 1970, p. 100)
>
> Coercion and intimidation (e.g., on the part of squatters)
>
> Anti-Californio biases by elected and appointed government officials
>
> Natural calamities, such as drought
>
> Overextension of the cattle industry following the boom of the 1850s

All this is not to say that legitimate transfers of land through proper sales at fair prices did not take place. Nevertheless, a distinct discriminatory aspect was present, not only in the attitudes of individuals but in the effects of the institutional mechanisms that were set up to deal with the problem. While "institutional racism" is a relatively recent concept, it should be applied to the situation in California with respect to the land in the nineteenth century.

At the same time, the conflict between the interests of the Californio landowners and the Anglo newcomers should not obscure the fact that racial divisions were only part of the story. As mentioned earlier, Anglos found themselves on both sides of the conflicts over land, as many land-grant claimants were Anglos. In addition, there appears to have been a considerable amount of intra-Anglo class conflict over the land. Paul Gates has documented the process from 1860 to 1900 through which agricultural capitalists accumulated large holdings at the expense of small settlers.

> Statistics of the number of new farms being created in California between 1860 and 1900—55,826—offer little support for the notion that the great ranchos were being subdivided into many small farms. During this period 147,000 homestead and preemption applications were filed. These might have led to small farms but did not for, as is seen later, many were filed by men acting as dummies for large engrossers. . . . Prominent Californians seemed determined to bring about the greatest possible concentration of land in large ownerships and bent their energies to shape state and federal legislation to contribute to that end while paying lip service to the small-family-farm concept. From the election of John C. Fremont as its first senator in 1850 . . . the state was represented in Washington by men closely identified with the great landowners and railroad tycoons. . . .

Much unhappiness was expressed at the speed with which the 500,000 acres were grabbed up by capitalists who were accused of making their entries on lands being improved by settlers who were waiting for the enactment of a free homestead measure. . . . Meetings of squatters were held at which "raging excitement" was expressed at the land speculators who had entered land on which settlers had commenced their homestead. [Gates, 1975, pp. 160–61, 163]

Or as Pitt puts it:

No set pattern emerges in these land transformations, but the eroded claims of the original claimants washed away steadily and flowed into the hands of the newcomers—financiers, railroad developers, town promoters, cooperative colonizers, and irrigation companies. [Pitt, 1970, p. 275]

In the long run, then, the main beneficiaries of the displacement of Californios from the land were those who had the financial resources and the political clout to reconcentrate the land in their own hands. The benefits were disproportionately appropriated by the same class of Anglo capitalists, speculators, and financiers whose interests had most strongly motivated the Mexican American War.

New Mexico

During the nineteenth century the bulk of the Chicano population of the Southwest was concentrated in New Mexico. Here, as in California, settlement of the land had taken place through Spanish and Mexican grants. In the southern part of the state, the common pattern was haciendas established by grantees who became patrons and brought in settlers to do the work. The haciendas were largely self-sufficient and were usually organized around a system of debt peonage. The haciendas grew their own food and were also engaged in pastoral activities. Sheep were the main export. Trade was carried on largely with Mexico, until the Santa Fe Trail was opened and American economic penetration of the area began.

The northern part of the state was characterized by "communal" villages which were organized on the basis of grants that had been given to the community as a whole. Here homesteads and farming lands were owned privately, whereas grazing and other land was owned in common and grazing and water rights were assigned by community councils (Zeleny, 1944, p. 68). Economic life revolved around subsistence agriculture and sheep raising. There was little manufacturing in the area. Northern New Mexico was more densely settled by Hispanos than the southern area.

The pace of Anglo economic penetration in New Mexico was more like that of southern than northern California, and the tempo of land transfer was correspondingly slow, although steady. In the mid-nineteenth century the economic penetration took the form of movement into agriculture and expansion of the commercial sector.

Initially, the Anglo conquest of New Mexico resulted in a limited expansion of the area occupied by the Spanish-speaking New Mexicans, or Hispanos. The reason for this is that the American military presence served to decimate the nomadic Indians who had previously resisted encroachments on their territory (Meinig, 1971, p. 32). The Hispano expansion, however, was halted in the 1870s as Anglo cattlemen and farmers increasingly moved into the area. As Meinig puts it:

> The Hispano hold upon much of their newly acquired country was necessarily thin, discontinuous, and at times no more than seasonal. The vanguard of their herders was often repelled and confined to the poorer lands, the outermost of their settlements were often soon enclaved within Anglo cattle country. The actual stabilization of the patterns of the two peoples was a long and complicated process which resulted neither in simple areal boundaries nor simple contrasts in activities (increasingly, Hispano shepherds tended Anglo-owned flocks), but it was a process which relentlessly strengthened the dominance of the one over the other. [Ibid., pp. 34–35]

As in southern California, the coming of the transcontinental railroads had a significant impact in New Mexico. New Mexico was fully connected with the transcontinental system in the late 1870s and early 1880s, and with the transportation system came an economic boom and an influx of Anglos. "The notion of migration to New Mexico was boosted by promoters of development of the West and by financial interests in the East which stood to profit by such migration" (Zeleny, 1944, p. 143). The 1880s saw a rapid increase in the number of Anglo-owned cattle companies (Westphall, 1965, p. 56). With the economic boom and the movement of Anglos into the state, the pressure on the land increased. From that point on, the process of land transfer accelerated. According to Zeleny, the process went faster in the southern part of the state, where the hacienda pattern had been dominant. Presumably, the denser Hispano population in the north and the pattern of communal holdings acted to retard the transfer to some extent (Zeleny, 1944, pp. 186–87).

Clark Knowlton has provided a detailed list of the mechanisms by which the transfer of land took place in the New Mexico area. In general, the processes were much like those in California. Only two or three aspects of the transfer process warrant a more extended discussion, and one of them has to do with the impact of land taxes. Knowlton notes that under the Mexican system the land had been free of taxation—taxes were levied on the products of the land rather than on the land itself. "In an area where the income from agriculture fluctuates irregularly according to climatic conditions, a fixed land tax in bad years places heavy burdens upon farmers and ranchers. A small Spanish-American subsistence farmer living in the villages was singularly unprepared to adjust to a fixed land-tax system. Cultivating his land to feed his family, he seldom ever possessed enough actual cash to pay taxes requiring money payments'' (Knowlton, 1967, p. 7). According to New Mexico law, anyone can pay delinquent taxes on land and receive a title to that land. ''Probably no other Anglo-American measure has had a harsher impact upon Spanish-American property than the fixed land tax'' (ibid.). Knowlton argues that the county land tax was also subject to extensive fraud and manipulation, to the detriment of the Hispano population. McWilliams notes the same phenomenon:

> In many cases, the Spanish-Americans could not pay land taxes of $1.50 an acre, or more, levied against grazing lands. Anglo-Americans would then buy up the lands at tax sales and promptly have the land tax reduced to thirty or forty cents an acre. [McWilliams, 1968, p. 77]

In many cases it appears that the new owners of the land engaged in an unwarranted enlargement of the grant boundaries.

> A number of grants have had their boundaries stretched and areas marvelously expanded. But this has been done mostly by Yankee and English purchasers and not by the original Mexican owners. Where boundaries were made by natural landmarks, such as a ''white rock,'' a ''red hill,'' or a ''lone tree,'' another rock, hill or tree of like description could always be found a league or two farther off, and claimed to be the original landmark described in the grant documents. [Wilbur F. Stone, associate justice of the Court of Private Land Claims, cited in Westphall, 1973, p. 36]

In New Mexico, also, the role of the government and its use of land became an important factor—increasingly so toward the end of the century. Without compensation, the National Forest Service has taken millions of acres from the northern villages for the creation of national forests. Hispanos must now pay grazing fees on land that once belonged to the villages (Knowlton, 1967, p. 10).

> The creation of forest reserves by the Federal Government has likewise withdrawn large portions of the public domain from free grazing lands of the Spanish-Americans. The Santa Fe National Forest was created in 1892, and the Cibola and Carson National Forests were established in 1906 ... they combined with other factors in confining the Spanish-Americans to a smaller and smaller land base. Grants made by the government to railroads during the period of their construction also withdrew substantial portions of the public domain from the free use of the old residents. [Zeleny, 1944, p. 171]

Malcolm Ebright has described the process in relation to the San Joaquin del Rio de Chama grant in northern New Mexico, originally made in 1808 to a group of Mexican families:

> There was never any serious question regarding the validity of the grant nor of the nature of the grant as one made to a community. The only real question which the U.S. officials who were responsible for its adjudication asked was, how big was it. In 1861 when approximately 400 of the grantees and their heirs petitioned for confirmation of the grant, its size was estimated at 184,320 acres. But when surveyed in 1878 it turned out to contain 472,736 acres. It appears that the rejection of 471,314 acres of the grant, most of which eventually wound up in the Santa Fe National Forest, was based on the simple fact that the grant was too big and would unreasonably deplete the U.S. public domain. [Ebright, 1976, p. 3]

Of course, even if a different determination had been made by the court, there was no guarantee that the land would remain under the control of the villagers, given the various processes that were acting to concentrate the land in the hands of large companies and land speculators.

It was not until 1891 that a Court of Private Land Claims was established for New Mexico. Prior to that time, conflicts over claims were handled by the state surveyor general, subject to congressional confirmation. The Court of Private Land Claims was empowered to deal with all Spanish and Mexican land claims in the areas of New Mexico, Colorado, and Arizona. Because of the biases of the rules and procedures the court was to follow, similar to those of the California Land Commission, the results were highly disadvantageous to the Hispanos.

> The court [of Private Land Claims] was set up with five judges selected from other parts of the United States, a United States Attorney, and other court officials. The members of the court were Anglo-American legal officials with little knowledge of Spanish and Mexican law and no knowledge of Spanish-American land-owning customs. Court decisions were based upon a rigid interpretation of Anglo legal precepts. [Knowlton, 1967, p. 6]

> In the years from 1891 until 1904, when the Court was disbanded, decisions were made settling the currently urgent land claims. In this time about two-thirds of the claims examined were rejected; the court confirmed the grants to 2,051,526 acres, and rejected claims to 33,439,493 acres. . . . The stipulation that no grant be confirmed unless there was strict legal authority in the granting powers was the basis for the rejection of many claims. . . . The decisive action taken by the court in its years of activity actually relegated the Spanish-Americans to a position of greater disadvantage than they had occupied prior to its

establishment. . . . The conflicts over land were turned over to a sup-
posedly impersonal third party, the Court, which technically fulfilled
the Anglo-American conception of "justice" but at the same time proceeded to fix the Spanish-American in a position of subordination.
[Zeleny, 1944, pp. 166–67]

The result was that eventually Anglos came to own four-fifths of the
former grant areas (Brayer, 1974, p. 19; Meier and Rivera, 1972, p. 107).
The loss of the community lands, from an original 2 million acres to 300,000
by 1930, was a major blow to the economic viability of the villages (Harper,
Córdova, and Oberg, 1943, p. 62).

The emphasis in the litigation decisions was clearly on ascertaining if
there was legal authority in the original granting process. Although this
may seem a proper norm of justice, it must be emphasized it was a norm
of Anglo justice being applied to the *traditional legal process of
another* sovereign state (either Spain or Mexico) which functioned in a
different cultural and legal framework. Moreover, it applied current
norms to a previous circumstance, which to the Mexican Americans
could reasonably be considered an ex post facto application. It can
certainly be argued that the determination of legitimacy in the granting
process was an important aspect of the legal question, but the overriding
importance placed on this single norm, relative to the reasonableness of
the acceptance of the original grantors and the appropriate communities
or individuals of the legality of the grants by their traditional expressions of legality (occupation and use) and the long time lag between
the grants and their validity determination seems a clear bias against the
Mexican Americans. [Jim Johnson, 1975, memo prepared for this
study]

A number of the grants in New Mexico had been made under terms in
which the members of the local community were to use the land under the
condition of usufruct. "It is the nature of usufruct that it is a perpetual right
attached to the land, a right effective not only against the owner of the land,
but also against all others. Usufruct can be owned in common, but the owners
do not possess the land; they possess the right to use it" (Rock, 1976, p. 54).
The right is intended to be perpetual, as long as the grantees live up to their
obligations to maintain the land. This right was supposed to be protected by
the Treaty of Guadalupe Hidalgo, but the courts of New Mexico have refused
to depart from a rigid adherence to Anglo legal norms in deciding land grant
cases, and these norms do not include the right of usufruct (ibid., pp. 56–61).

At the same time, there is evidence that violence and intimidation
played a considerable role in the economic changes that were taking place.
"Hand in hand with the vast expropriation of lands went a wave of violence
and terrorism which caused many Hispanos to leave the San Luis Valley.

Family histories in the San Juan Basin relate incidents of covert shootings and public lynchings over land and political control'' (Swadesh, 1974, p. 80; see also Ganaway, 1944, p. 102).

As in the case of California, dispossession from the land was largely effected through the "normal workings" of the institutions which were set up by Anglo society. The process illustrates the way in which institutional discrimination can operate in an apparently color-blind manner.

> The situation of the Spanish-Americans was made even more difficult by the establishment of only two federal land offices in New Mexico during much of the territorial period. . . . The very existence of these offices, let alone their functions, was unknown to the Spanish-American village population. On the other hand, the Americans, who lived in the larger urban centers of the Territory, possessed far better means of traveling and of communicating with each other and with the land offices. As political alliances were established, often with the personnel of the land office, they were able to note which land grants were registered and which were not and thus to take appropriate action to register many unregistered grants in their own names. [Knowlton, 1967, p. 6]

The overall result was a steady decline in the economic and political fortunes of the Hispanos, with the land playing a key role.

> The struggle between the Spanish-Americans and Anglo-Americans taking place in New Mexico during this period was one in which the defeat of the Spanish-Americans was pre-ordained because of certain critical advantages which the Anglo-Americans possessed. In the struggle economic and political factors were inter-related in such a manner as to produce a shift in power from the hands of the numerically preponderant Spanish-American group to those of the invading Anglos. (Zeleny, 1944, p. 159]

> The accommodation which was effected in the economic sphere through land displacement and competition resulted essentially in a relationship of superordination and subordination between the two competing ethnic groups. [Ibid., p. 196]

The loss of lands by the Hispanos is only one aspect of the situation, however. If anything, the class dimension to the economic penetration and transfer of land in New Mexico was even more apparent than in other parts of the Southwest. Zeleny notes that

> New Mexico did not at first attract many of the regular settler class, but rather was a field for exploitation by American commercial enterprise and American and European capital. [Ibid., p. 159]

The activities of the Santa Fe Ring and its various component rings in the nineteenth century exemplify this class dimension. The ring consisted of a group of Anglo merchants, lawyers, bankers, politicians, and ranchers who dominated the territory during the last two decades of the century. With headquarters in Santa Fe, they exercised great influence in the territorial and national capitals. While engaged in every facet of commercial and political life, the biggest impact of the ring was probably in manipulating the land and concentrating it in their hands through a variety of sharp practices (Larson, 1968, pp. 137ff.; see also Lamar, 1970, chap. 6).

Frances Swadesh has provided us with a description of the manner in which Thomas Catron, one of the leaders of the ring, gained control of the large Tierra Amarilla grant. According to this account, his methods included the manufacture of evidence, collecting large legal fees in the form of land, and defrauding the original grant claimants (Swadesh, 1974, pp. 84–85). By the 1880s, he was one of the largest landowners in the United States, with the Tierra Amarilla grant alone totaling some 600,000 acres. In the process of developing this area, Hispano communities were disrupted and much of the land was "clean cut" by lumber companies (ibid., pp. 88–89). Brayer's extended account of the activities of the British capitalist and speculator, William Blackmore, in gaining control over several grants in the northern New Mexico–southern Colorado area also highlights the class dimension in the transfer of land titles.

One of the more interesting aspects of this process stands out clearly in the Santa Fe Ring, which was able to exercise power effectively because of the alliance it forged with the wealthy Hispano elite, the *ricos* (McWilliams, 1948, p. 122; Knowlton, 1967, p. 5; Larson, 1968, p. 144). In effect, there was an interethnic class alliance, which, however, was dominated by the Anglos. Actually, such an alliance had long been in existence. Brayer has described the manner in which Cornelio Vigil and Ceran St. Vrain, prominent residents of Taos, combined to petition Governor Armijo for a substantial grant of land in 1843. The grant was made in that same year. Within two months, the two recipients of the grant had deeded a one-sixth interest to Armijo, to Donanciano Vigil (Armijo's territorial secretary), and to Charles Bent and Eugene Leitensdorfer, important merchants and traders (Brayer, 1974, pp. 127–29).

In another example, Guadalupe Miranda and Charles Beaubien were placed in possession of a large grant of northern New Mexico land in 1841 by Governor Armijo. The curate of Taos, Father Martínez, protested that much of the land belonged to the people of Taos and had long been used as common grazing land, but to no avail (Keleher, 1964, pp. 13–15).

The role of the ricos in the post–Mexican American War period was to provide their Anglo partners with political support through their influence with the Hispano population. In return, they hoped to be safeguarded to some extent in retaining control of their lands (Zeleny, 1944, p. 160). In the long run, however, the bargain turned out badly for many of the ricos. Rodman Paul has given us an assessment of the effects of the alliance on the Hispano elite:

> Whether Hispanos really were the big gainers from the operations of either the Ring or the early business houses may be doubted. One suspects that their Anglo associates were too resourceful for that. And in any event, while some of the Hispano upper class were prospering, many of their cousins ... were losing ownership of the land that had been the traditional basis of their power. So at best only a portion of even the favored class were better off at the end of the century than they had been in 1848. [Paul, 1971, p. 39]

Another aspect of the class dimension as it affected the land (already seen in California) was class conflict within the Anglo population. Keleher provides a vivid account of the formation on the Maxwell land grant of groups of Anglo settlers determined to wage a struggle against the promoters and capitalists who had gained control of the grant. In the end, their efforts were largely unsuccessful (Keleher, 1964, pp. 84–107). Westphall has documented the fraudulent manipulation of the land by land and cattle companies, along the same lines as the practices described by Gates for California (Westphall, 1965, pp. 64, 81, 100ff.).

In summary, it is possible to see in New Mexico, even more clearly than in California, the interrelated nature of ethnic and class factors in the dispossession of the land and its reconcentration in the hands of an Anglo-dominated economic and political elite.

Texas

Texas differs from the other areas of the Southwest in that here there was a pattern of extensive Anglo settlement of the land. A substantial amount of land had been granted to Anglos through the Mexican government's *empresario* grants, particularly in southeastern Texas.

Perhaps in part because of this, little has been written about the displacement of Mexicans and Chicanos from the land in this region. Yet this process appears to have started quite early. During the war that resulted in the independent Republic of Texas in 1836, Spanish-speaking residents were apparently driven out of certain areas, notably in Bexar County, where San Antonio is located (Meinig, 1969, p. 46). Joseph Nance adds that Texas Anglo raiders "forced the abandonment of many of the Mexican ranches between the Neuces and the Rio Grande" in the late 1830s (Nance, 1963, p. 547). Meinig notes that "east of Victoria nearly all of the few Hispanos who had not fled in 1836 were harassed and driven out in 1845 or shortly thereafter" (Meinig, 1969, p. 55).

The process continued after the termination of the Mexican American

War. Speaking of south central Texas, Meinig states that "by 1860 the Anglos had gotten control, by fair means or foul, of nearly every ranch worth having north of the Neuces" (Meinig, 1969, p. 54). As in other areas, force and fraud were not the only mechanisms used to facilitate the transfer of land. The Texas historian Fehrenbach describes the situation in this way, with an unconscious touch of irony:

> There is some truth that many Mexican landowners, especially the small ones, were robbed in south Texas by force, intimidation, or chicanery. But what is usually ignored is the fact that the hacendado class, as a class, was stripped of property perfectly legally, according to the highest traditions of U.S. law. [Fehrenbach, 1968, p. 510]

The Espíritu Santo grant in the Rio Grande Valley provides one example of a Chicano-held grant that was validated by the courts but in which the land was lost because of the prohibitive costs of the litigation (Acuña, 1972, pp. 43–44). "The imposition of American law infuriated most Mexican landowners. They had to defend their ancient titles in court, and they lost either way, either to their own lawyers or to the claimants" (Fehrenbach, 1968, p. 511). Acuña notes that an 1860 census showed that 263 Texans owned over $100,000 in real property, and that only two of these were Chicanos (Acuña, 1972, p. 44).

Paul Taylor has provided us with a more intensive look at the situation in the southern Gulf Coast county of Neuces. He states that by 1835 all of the county had been granted in large tracts to Mexicans, who used the area for cattle. By 1859 all but one of the grants had passed to Anglo hands (Taylor, 1971, p. 179). The process of transfer started in 1840, through sales. Taylor addresses himself to whether the sales could be considered fair and free:

> When the Mexicans first sold to Americans they were under stress to sell. They were not simply individual holders of property selling of their free will; they were selling *because they were Mexicans* who, in a time of chaos, could no longer occupy their land, and who saw the imminent American military and political domination. . . . It was under the pressure of these conditions that the grants passed to Americans, who as bargainers took advantage of them in varying degrees. (Ibid., pp. 182–83]

Taylor's insights into the psychological pressure on the Mexican landholders undoubtedly apply to other areas of the Southwest as well.

As in other parts of the Southwest, land transfer in Texas was strongly affected by the economy. The boom in cattle that followed the American Civil War led to greater pressure on the land, as did the economic development stimulated by the coming of the railroads. According to Meier and Rivera, "as a result of the cattle boom after the Civil War . . . the loss of land by tejanos to Anglos was accelerated. In many cases these lands were acquired by forced sales for nonpayment of taxes, with Anglo speculators often obtaining tejano lands at only a few cents per acre" (Meier and Rivera, 1972, pp. 93–94).

Again, the class factor in this process needs to be emphasized. In spite of the fact that there was strong antispeculator sentiment in Texas, speculating in land was a major economic factor even before the establishment of the Republic of Texas. Several important land speculation ventures began in the early 1830s, including those of the notorious Galveston Bay and Texas Land Company. Such famous names as General (later Texas President) Sam Houston and Jim Bowie were closely linked with these activities (Hogan, 1946, pp. 83–85). According to Fehrenbach, "the land maps of virtually every central Texas county show that the best lands, with their precious water rights, passed into private ownership between ten and thirty years before these counties were settled by whites" (Fehrenbach, 1968, p. 283). Alwyn Barr, in his study of late nineteenth-century Texas, makes references to west Texas county-based land rings, and quotes Texas land commissioner Charles Rogan to the effect that

> while the laws were enacted ostensibly for the benefit of the actual settler, he has derived but little benefit from them. The chief beneficiaries have been land agents, speculators and bonus hunters, and finally the ranch men. [Barr, 1971, p. 84]

According to Barr, Rogan's "statement may well stand as a summary of Texas land policy for the last two decades of the nineteenth century" (Ibid., p. 84).

LAND TRANSFER IN THE SOUTHWEST

Perhaps the key point that emerges from this review of the land situation in the nineteenth century is that the subordinate status of Chicanos in the Southwest put them in a particularly vulnerable economic position. Anglo capitalists and land speculators were best able to take advantage of this vulnerability to dispossess Chicanos of the land they had previously controlled. Certain factors, such as class status, population density, or geographic isolation, had an effect on the pace of dispossession, but eventually it affected all or nearly all Chicanos.

While it is true that Anglo settlers were also adversely affected by the increasing concentration of land in the hands of large Anglo landowners, there was an important difference in degree. As Brayer has pointed out for New Mexico, Anglo settlers were better able to defend their claims to the land than Chicanos (Brayer, 1949, pp. 119–20n.). In addition, as Keleher notes, in

most cases the Anglo settlers did not have the same long-standing claim to the
land that most Chicanos had (Keleher, 1964, p. 23).

Anglo control of the political process appears to have been a key factor
in all this (political control is explored further in chapter 6). Zeleny describes
the situation in New Mexico:

> The land situation, and the control exercised by the Anglo-American
> officials in land decisions, were important factors in producing this shift
> in power. In the political field the Spanish-Americans, whose numerical
> superiority had given them an advantage in territorial politics, rapidly
> became the victims of corrupt American practices and machine politics.
> Politics in the territory were soon in the hands of a political com-
> bination . . . which succeeded in controlling appointments made through
> both the territorial and federal governments in New Mexico. [Zeleny,
> 1944, pp. 159–60]

The link between loss of political control and loss of the land has also
been recognized by other writers. Swadesh points out that "officials appointed by the federal government helped deprive the land grant heirs of their
rights" (Swadesh, 1974, p. 69), and Fehrenbach, writing of Texas, states that
"the law added injury to insult, because it failed to protect the Mexicans and
actually was the chief instrument of their dispossession" (Fehrenbach, 1968,
p. 510).

Dispossession from the land, in turn, depleted the economic base of
Chicanos and put them in an even less favorable position to exercise influence
over the political process. In addition, it had other far-ranging consequences,
including facilitating the emergence of a colonial labor system in the Southwest, based in large part on Chicano labor.

CHAPTER 3

The Nineteenth Century, Part II:
The Establishment of a
Colonial Labor System

> *For every empire built in Arizona upon a for-*
> *tune in high grade ore, ten empires were built*
> *by men who discovered low grade ores and a*
> *fortune in Mexican labor.*
>
> —Joseph Park

THE THIRD MAJOR DEVELOPMENT that affected Chicanos in the nineteenth century was the emergence of a racially stratified labor force in the Southwest. To put this situation in proper perspective, however, it is necessary to have some idea of how the American economy as a whole was developing during this period and how the economy of the Southwest fit into the picture.

THE ECONOMY

The major transformation in the American economy during the second half of the century was its industrialization. By the 1890s the manufacturing sector had expanded to the point that the United States was the leading industrial power in the world. In the words of Carl Degler, during this period "a nation of small property owners . . . became a nation in which most men had little or no connection with the land, were largely without property, and worked for other men" (Degler, 1967, p. 2).

Several factors had gone into this transformation. Important technological developments had resulted in a spreading use of machinery. The energy resources of the country had been greatly expanded. Substantial amounts of developmental capital had poured in from Europe, adding to the capital that was accumulated domestically. In addition, the Civil War resulted in consolidation of the national power of the northern industrial and commercial class, and it used this power to implement policies conducive to industrialization.

Associated with this industrialization were several other important

34

trends that helped to transform the social and economic map of the country. Urbanization was an important process throughout the country, particularly during and after the 1880s. Transportation and communication networks were rapidly expanded, with railroads playing an especially important role in establishing national economic links and lowering the cost of moving commodities. Immigration, especially from Europe, contributed to the growth of cities and to the emerging industrial labor force. During the latter part of the century the sources of immigration shifted from western and northern Europe to southern, central, and eastern Europe.

The concentration of economic power was another major trend with far-reaching consequences. Prior to the 1870s the American economy had been characterized by a large number of smaller firms. After that period the trend was toward larger and larger corporations. Economic concentration also took the forms of trusts, holding companies, and mergers. By the end of the century many important segments of the economy were dominated by one or a few corporations or trusts. During this period a number of labor organizations were formed, and major strikes and other forms of labor unrest became commonplace. Union organizing efforts were usually met with repression and harassment, and unions were not officially recognized as bargaining agents in American industry.

While industry gradually came to dominate the American economy in the second half of the nineteenth century, agriculture was also a dynamic sector. During this period vast areas were brought under cultivation for the first time, and agricultural productivity was sharply increased through the mechanization of farm work. The country also greatly expanded its output of metals and raw materials. The expansion into the Southwest was a major factor in both of these processes.

In the Southwest as a whole, the major economic trends can be discussed under three headings: agriculture and ranching, railroads, and mining.

Ranching activities centered on cattle and sheep. Cattle had been central to the California economy prior to the Mexican American War, and there was a cattle boom during the early 1850s as a result of the Gold Rush and the rapid increase in the California population. The boom was soon over, and subsequent droughts dealt heavy blows to the pastoral economy. After the 1850s the importance of cattle in California steadily declined. Texas also saw a cattle boom in the 1850s, but cattle remained an important part of its economy throughout the century. Originally centered in the eastern part of the state, the cattle business moved into west Texas after 1870 (Spratt, 1955, p. 87). After 1870 the sheep industry also gained a foothold in Texas. It was during the '70s that extensive fencing took place, and the traditional open range quickly disappeared. ''By the mid-1880's most of the rangeland had been fenced,

much of it had come under the control of large companies supplied with
Eastern and foreign capital, and railroads had replaced the great cattle trails''
(Meinig, 1969, p. 70). In New Mexico, sheep had been the major pastoral
activity during the Mexican period, and the sheep industry continued to expand after the American occupation, reaching a peak in the 1880s (Charles,
1940, p. 28). After 1860 the cattle companies, many from Texas, moved into
New Mexico. The New Mexico sheep industry also spilled over into
Colorado, and both there and in Arizona there was some development of
ranching during and after the 1860s.

Agriculture eventually came to be far more important than ranching,
and within the Southwest, Texas and California came to dominate agriculture.
In both states wheat and other grains were extensively cultivated from the
1850s on. In California, fruits and vegetables took on major significance in
the 1870s. In Texas, as Southern agriculturalists had foreseen before the
Mexican American War, cotton assumed a leading role from the 1870s to the
end of the century. By 1900 Texas cotton acreage surpassed the acreage
devoted to grains, and the value of cotton greatly surpassed the value of grains
(Spratt, 1955, p. 70). In other areas as well, agriculture made inroads, although the timing varied from area to area. In Arizona, for example, commercial agriculture largely dates from the 1870s.

Some general trends in agriculture during this period had a bearing on
the employment of labor. Mechanization of agriculture reduced the need for
labor in those crops which were most strongly affected, but this was not a
uniform process. Grains, such as wheat, were among the crops most susceptible to mechanization; fruits and vegetables were not. As areas like California
turned to growing these crops, their more intensive agriculture created a need
for more farm labor. Cotton also required a great deal of labor. The trend
toward commercial agriculture also had important implications. In the earlier
part of the century, much of the farming was subsistence farming, in which
the products were consumed by the farmers themselves. As the century wore
on, commercial farming gained in importance. The fruit and vegetable industry in California was largely commercial, and the Texas cotton crop was
entirely commercial. The trend, then, was toward specialized and commercial
farming, in which subsistence farming was transformed into production for
the market by large agricultural corporations. Whereas in subsistence farming
the farmers had worked for themselves, in commercial farming agricultural
laborers worked for wages.

It may also have been that the persistent trend during the latter part of
the nineteenth century toward lower farm prices (Fite and Reese, 1973, p.
286) had an effect on agricultural labor practices, but, if so, these implications
have not been brought out in the literature.

The impact of the transcontinental railroads on the American economy was nowhere more pronounced than in the Southwest. From 1869 to 1893 five railroads established transcontinental connections, and some of these routes passed through the Southwest. Spratt notes that more than half of the railroad mileage constructed in Texas during the century was built between 1875 and 1885 (Spratt, 1955, p. 26). Railroads had an impact on labor in two distinct manners. On the one hand they were major employers of labor. While they were being built they employed large numbers of construction workers; after they were built they required labor to run the trains and maintain the tracks and equipment. On the other hand, railroads had a major impact on the economy of the region, and in this way indirectly affected the demand for labor. The development of mining and agriculture depended heavily on the transportation provided by the railroads, and as these sectors boomed the need for labor increased accordingly. Railroads had other significant ramifications. By triggering land booms, they hastened the displacement of Chicanos from the land (as has been described above). The displaced Chicanos often entered the labor market as a consequence and out of sheer necessity, generally in very disadvantaged positions.

The extraction of natural resources was the third major economic sector in the Southwest during the latter part of the nineteenth century. While this category includes the lumber industry, which became more important as the century wore on, most of the extractive activities revolved around mining. California had the first great gold rush after the Mexican American War, and mining continued to play a part there for many years. Arizona silver mining had been developed during the 1850s, but had been interrupted by Indians in the '60s. During the 1870s mining was resumed in that area, and copper became increasingly important. In New Mexico mining had been established much earlier by Hispanos, but there was a resurgence of silver mining in the 1870s. Gold was discovered in Colorado in 1859, and silver and lead in the '70s, and copper assumed great importance later in the century.

The early gold and silver operations had been worked on a small scale, as in the placer mining associated with the gold rushes. Before long, however, mechanized and large-scale mining had replaced the small-time operators. By 1860 the California mining scene was dominated by heavily capitalized hard-rock mining, and the Arizona mines were extensively mechanized in the 1870s (Nash, 1964, p. 30; Park, 1961, p. 149). With this shift in technology, the self-employed miner gave way to the wage worker.

The three sectors described above were the most dynamic in the economy of the Southwest during the latter part of the century (see figure 1). Manufacturing developed more slowly here than in some areas of the United States. The manufacturing that gained a foothold did so primarily in California and Texas. In Texas, for example, manufacturing did not make an impact

FIGURE 1

THE SECOND HALF OF THE NINETEENTH CENTURY:
MAJOR ECONOMIC DEVELOPMENTS
IN THE SOUTHWEST (by State)

	California	Arizona	New Mexico	Colorado	Texas
1850s	Gold mining (placer) Grains (wheat, etc.) Cattle	Mining (silver)	Sheep		Grains (wheat, etc.) Cattle
1860s	Gold mining (hard-rock) Grains Cattle decline	Mining declines Ranching	Cattle Sheep	Gold mining Cattle	Cattle
1870s	Grains Fruits and vege- tables Railroads	Mining resumes (copper) Commercial farming Railroads	Cattle Sheep Mining (silver) Railroads	Sheep Mining (silver, lead) Railroads	Sheep Cattle (fencing) Cotton Railroads
1880s	Land boom Industry		Sheep Lumber Land values up		Cattle Cotton Industry
1890s				Mining (copper)	Cotton Lumber

until the last two decades of the century. In 1900 the industrial labor force of Texas comprised 1.6 percent of the state population, compared with 6 percent for the country as a whole (Spratt, 1955, p. 231). In Los Angeles, the number of industrial establishments increased from 1 in 1850 to over 170 in 1880, most involving small manufacturers (Griswold del Castillo, 1975, pp. 152, 155).

Urbanization was also having its impact in the Southwest, but at a slower pace than in the Northeast and Midwest. In Texas, the percentage of the population classified as urban increased from 5 to 17 percent from 1870 to 1900 (Spratt, 1955, p. 277). In California the process unfolded at a faster pace, particularly with the railroad-triggered boom of the 1880s. Many of California's urban communities trace their origins to that period. (Dumke, 1944). Many others, of course, had existed since the Spanish and Mexican eras, and experienced large increases in their populations.

Immigration into the Southwest was closely tied to all of these social and economic trends. Anglos, of course, flooded into the area, starting with the great California Gold Rush. Within a short period the Chicano population in northern California became a small minority. In southern California, Chicanos remained a majority until the 1870s, but by 1880 they are estimated to have constituted only some 25 percent of the population there. By 1890 this figure was down to 10 percent. (Meier and Rivera, 1972, p. 86). The California population as a whole increased from 100,000 in 1850 to 560,000 in 1870 (Nash, 1964, p. 65). In Texas, of course, Mexicans were a minority by the time of the Mexican American War, and they continued to lose ground after the war. Arizona remained sparsely settled, with a population of only 125,000 in 1900, the majority Anglo (Billington, 1974, p. 629). Only in New Mexico and south Texas did Chicanos remain a majority in the face of this Anglo population movement. Some immigration from Mexico took place during this period, into such areas as southern California (Meier and Rivera, 1972, p. 88). There was also some back-and-forth movement across the border in certain areas, such as the southern Arizona mining region. For the most part, however, the major waves of Mexican immigration did not come until the early twentieth century.

Many of the Anglos who were moving into the area were not, strictly speaking, Anglo in the narrow sense of the term. Many were recent arrivals from non-English-speaking countries of Europe, such as the many German settlers in San Antonio and central Texas. As will be brought out below, however, the experience of European immigrants in the Southeast differed considerably from that of immigrants from areas now referred to as the Third World. The Chinese and Japanese workers who immigrated to the Southwest in the nineteenth century were another important part of the population influx from other countries. They tended to concentrate along the West Coast.

THE COLONIAL LABOR SYSTEM

Closely linked to the economic developments described above was the emergence in the nineteenth-century Southwest of a segmented labor force which I refer to as a colonial labor system. This is the definition I propose of such a system:

A colonial labor system exists where the labor force is segmented along ethnic and/or racial lines, and one or more of the segments is systematically maintained in a subordinate position.

To be "subordinate" means to be disadvantaged with regard to the labor market or labor process in comparison with another group of workers. ("The labor market consists of those institutions which mediate, effect, or determine the purchase and sale of labor power; the labor process consists of the organization and conditioning of the activity of production itself. . . . Segmentation occurs when the labor market or labor process is divided into separate submarkets or subprocesses . . . distinguished by different characteristics, behavioral rules, and working conditions'' [Edwards, Reich, and Gordon, 1975, p. xi].) It should be made clear that ''segmentation'' is not absolute, and thus a colonial labor system is a matter of degree. Subordination can be greater or less, and the degree to which it is systematized can also vary.

It was by no means only Chicanos who were incorporated into the colonial labor system in the Southwest, although they are the only group that will be discussed in detail here. During the early stages of the formation of the labor system in the Southwest it was not uncommon to find Native Americans and Blacks experimented with as a subordinate work force. Apparently these experiments were not completely satisfactory, except for the use of Blacks on Texas plantations where the continuity with Southern institutions was very strong. In other parts of the Southwest, Asian labor took on major significance, especially in California. Lloyd Fisher notes that by 1880 the Chinese represented one-third of the agricultural labor force in California, and were the main source of seasonal and casual laborers (Fisher, 1953, p. 4). Chinese workers were also used in the mines, and were for a time the mainstay of the railroads in constructing their lines across the Southwest, always in the hardest and lowest-paying jobs. When Chinese immigration was banned by the Chinese Exclusion Act of 1882, Southwestern employers turned to the Japanese. The use of Japanese laborers in agriculture increased rapidly, until this source of labor was curtailed by the ''Gentlemen's Agreement'' with Japan in 1906. The large-scale importation of Mexican labor followed shortly thereafter.

There are five aspects of a colonial labor system that I have been able to identify, and they will be discussed under the following headings: labor repression, the dual wage system, occupational stratification, Chicanos as a reserve labor force, and the buffer role. In the discussion below I describe these aspects and review the evidence for their existence with respect to Chicanos in the nineteenth-century Southwest. Since there have been no systematic historical investigations of this topic, the evidence will necessarily be somewhat fragmentary.

Chicanos and Labor Repression

Robert Blauner has argued that the experience of racial minorities in the United States with various aspects of ''unfree labor'' (slavery, peonage) has been one of the key factors differentiating them from European immigrants (Blauner, 1972, chap. 2). More recently, David Montejano has applied the concept of ''labor repression'' to the experience of Chicano workers in Texas (Montejano, 1977). Basing his discussion on Barrington Moore's comparative analysis of the ways in which capitalism developed in different countries

(Moore, 1967), Montejano focuses on the use of non-market sanctions such as coercion and legal restrictions to limit the degree of freedom of Chicanos as compared to non-minority workers.

Such a system of labor repression clearly existed in the nineteenth-century Southwest, although it varied in degree of severity from place to place. One of the best examples of this practice was the system of debt peonage described by Joseph Park for the Arizona mines. The mines were well suited in some ways to this type of system since they were relatively isolated and the employers had substantial control over the workers. The key mechanism in this system was the company store. Miners had little choice but to buy the necessities of life at company stores, and by keeping the wages of Mexican and Chicano miners low enough and jacking the prices of goods high enough, the mine owners could keep them in a more or less perpetual state of debt and thus unable to leave (Park, 1961, pp. 56–60). This had the added advantage for the employers that they completely recovered the wages they paid these workers. The system was reinforced by the peonage laws which were in effect in New Mexico until 1867, but even after their repeal the system continued to operate in many places.

While not uncommon, the system did not become entrenched in the Arizona mining industry, apparently because it was not the most efficient in the long run. One factor is that the mines did not operate at the same level at all times. With their demand for labor fluctuating, there was little advantage to the mine owners in holding an idle labor force on the basis of their debts (ibid., p. 56).

According to Park, the system was not restricted to the mines, although it may have been more pronounced there. Apparently it was used in one form or another by Anglo employers on ranches, farms, and business establishments (ibid., pp. 64–65).

In another sense as well it could be said that Chicanos and other racial minorities have been subjected to a system of unfree labor:

> However mixed the motives of California employers, agricultural employment has been open to the Oriental, the Mexican, Filipino, and Negro, whereas much of industry has been closed to them. The result has been a form of segregation in which agricultural employers have clearly benefited from a labor force which has been relatively immobile [Fisher, 1953, p. 14]

This aspect of unfree labor has been more persistent over time than peonage.

The Dual Wage System

This practice consists of paying one wage to minority workers and another to nonminority workers who perform the same task. The frequent characterization of minority labor as "cheap labor" often refers to this practice.

Some of the best documentation of this aspect of colonial labor is again from the Arizona mines. Raphael Pumpelly, in an extended travel account, described the situation at the Santa Rita silver mines in the early 1870s. According to him, Mexican miners received from $12 a month to $1 per day, depending on their job, plus a weekly ration of flour. "American" miners received from $30 to $70 per month, plus board (Pumpelly, 1871, p. 32). Joseph Park has plotted the "Anglo" wage and the "Mexican" wage in the Arizona mines from 1860 to 1910, and according to his figures the gap in absolute terms increased during this period, although there was a tendency for both wage rates to rise (Park, 1961, table 6, p. 245). The system was not confined to the mines but was apparently general throughout the Arizona territory:

> A two-class socio-economic system had evolved by the late nineteenth century, which, despite the resentment it provoked among the Mexican population, had at least proved workable. The two-scale wage system had become traditional, and though a widening gap developed between Anglo-American and Mexican wages, the latter showed enough increase to offer Mexican families the promise of better living standards in the future. [Ibid., pp. 243–44]

Another highlighted point in Park's work is that the citizenship status of the minority worker was of little consequence in determining his work status:

> It is not actually important to distinguish between various groups of Mexican ancestry, for whether they were Mexican-Americans, resident Mexican aliens who may have lived in Arizona most of their lives, or Mexican nationals who had recently arrived, they were all treated largely the same, paid the "Mexican" wage, and usually assigned to jobs considered by Anglo-Americans as "Mexicans'" work. [Ibid., p. viii]

Chicanos and Mexicans, as well as other Latinos, thus generally found themselves in the same boat with respect to the wage system and other aspects of economic life. In a recent study, Andres Jiménez has emphasized the manner in which the Arizona mining companies segregated the "Mexican" and Anglo workers into virtually separate communities in many cases, a separation which made it easier for the companies to practice their discriminatory policies while fostering social divisions among their workers (Jiménez, 1977, p. 24).

In the California mines the situation was much the same. Pitt notes that Chicano and Mexican miners were recruited by the southern California hard-rock mines because they could pay them a lower wage than Anglos (Pitt,

1970, p. 59). Speaking of the situation around 1880, Lingenfelter states that "although the Mexican miner could still find a job in the mines of New Mexico, Arizona, and parts of California, even there he had to settle for discriminatory wages of only 50¢ to $1.50 a day, whereas his less experienced gringo brothers drew from $2 to $3" (Lingenfelter, 1974, p. 6).

Texas agriculture was also the beneficiary of Chicano "cheap labor." As cotton cultivation spread into south Texas in the latter part of the century, Chicano and Mexican labor came increasingly to be used for this crop. Paul Taylor quotes the Galveston *News* to the effect that "in those parts of the state where cheap Mexican labor can be secured for chopping and picking cotton . . . this staple can unquestionably be raised at a profit even when it can be raised 'at a cost' (i.e., at a loss) in other parts" (Taylor, 1971, p. 105). While there is no direct reference here to the wages paid non-Chicano labor, the implication is clear that a dual wage standard existed.

That the racially based dual wage was persistent in agriculture can be inferred from the following reference to California around the turn of the century:

> A report of the California State Labor Commission challenged the California Fruit Growers Association view on the subject of the inadequacy of Caucasian farm labor. Commissioner W. V. Stafford informed the press that Oriental wages were consistently below Caucasian wages for the same jobs. [Jones, 1970, p. 31]

Occupational Stratification

The third and almost surely the most significant aspect of colonial labor refers to the practice of classifying certain kinds of jobs as suited for minorities and others as suited for nonminorities. The result is that minority workers are concentrated in the least desirable occupations. Since this practice is informal, as are the others, it is often not an absolute principle. Nevertheless, the pattern that results is usually the most striking aspect of a segmented labor force.

Evidence of racially stratified labor can be cited for virtually all the important economic sectors of the nineteenth-century Southwest (reference has already been made to the use of Mexican labor in Texas cotton cultivation). As long as cotton had been confined to eastern Texas, the major labor supply had been Black. As the cotton-growing areas expanded into southern, central, and western Texas in the 1880s and 1890s, Mexicans and Chicanos dominated the field labor in those new areas. In some places these developments resulted in the displacement of White tenant farmers by Mexican day laborers' migrating into the area (McWilliams, 1968, pp. 170–71). In south Texas the work was done by resident Chicanos (Taylor, 1971, pp. 105–6). Agricultural employers were eager to hire Chicano laborers, thus being assured of an ample labor supply at low wages, as a Nueces County cotton planter testified in 1885:

> I have employed in cultivation almost entirely Mexican laborers, who I find work well, and readily learn to use our improved tools. Such labor is abundant along the Nueces river and can be secured at 75 cents a day, boarding themselves, and paying only for days of actual work. [Ibid., p. 81]

Joseph Park has described the situation in Arizona agriculture during the 1870s, illustrating the interaction between the dual wage structure and the stratification of occupations. Speaking of southeastern Arizona, he states that in this area

> all agricultural labor was done by Mexicans for fifteen dollars a month, plus the traditional ration of sixty pounds of flour, the wage having remained almost unchanged for two decades in this area. Due to the large number of Mexican workers available at this salary, there was no demand for Anglo-American laborers in agricultural work. [Park, 1961, p. 179]

Park also provides an insight into how some occupations came to be typed as subordinate occupations:

> This tendency toward a social division of occupations was becoming quite marked in areas of southern Arizona having a large Mexican population, and constitutes another distinction between this region and the intermountain zone, where the relatively lower number of Mexicans employed in mining, ranching and farming tended to free many types of common labor from the social stigma attached to them in southern Arizona. [Ibid., p. 180]

The tendency to classify some positions as suitable for Anglos and others as suitable only for minorities became even clearer as mechanization took place in the fields. With mechanization, many of the laborer positions were eliminated. New positions were created as operators of the new mechanical farm equipment, such as reapers and threshers, but these positions were filled with Anglos rather than Chicanos or other racial minorities (ibid., pp. 173–74).

A similar system of occupational classification by race prevailed in California agriculture. Testimony before a congressional committee outlined the situation shortly after the turn of the century in the California sugar industry:

> Of the total labor required in the industry, 10 per cent was factory labor and chiefly white-American, and 90 per cent was field labor which was practically 100 per cent foreign labor. In the northern California fields,

the field labor was almost exclusively Japanese; in Southern California, it was ¹/₅ Japanese and ⁴/₅ Mexican. [McWilliams, 1971, p. 87]

In ranching, Chicanos had a long history of working as cowboys on the cattle ranches and as sheepherders. After the American takeover, many of these workers continued in those occupations, with the difference that now there was an occupational distinction by race. On the Anglo-owned ranches the pattern was for the managers and overseers to be Anglos, while the average cowhand was Chicano (Taylor, 1971, p. 116; Meinig, 1969, p. 55). Both in New Mexico and Texas the *pastores,* or sheepherders, tended to be overwhelmingly Chicano (Taylor, 1971, p. 116; Charles, 1940, p. 29).

The railroads provided another sector with a marked racial division, or at least concentration, of labor. In the early years of railroad construction in the Southwest very extensive use was made of Chinese labor. During the 1880s, however, with this source of labor drying up, Chicanos and Mexicans came to dominate the categories of common labor on the rails, a situation that continued into the twentieth century. The Southern Pacific Railroad is particularly noted for its use of Chicano labor in the lowest-paid positions. By 1900 the Southern Pacific regularly employed some 4,500 Mexicans and Chicanos in California (McWilliams, 1968, pp. 168–69: Acuña, 1972, p. 93).

With their background in mining, it was natural for the Chicanos and Mexicans to be employed in this area. At the New Almaden mine in northern California (a producer of mercury used in the extraction of precious metals from its ores), it was estimated that five-eighths of the almost 2,000 miners were of Mexican background (McWilliams, 1968, p. 140). Mexican workers were found in mines from New Mexico to the California coast. In all locations, however, they were restricted to the hardest and most dangerous jobs (Pitt, 1970, p. 255). Meier and Rivera note the combination of dual wages and occupational stratification in New Mexico mines:

> A discriminatory dual wage system developed that favored Anglo miners by paying them at a higher rate than Mexican workers for the same type of work. Besides suffering from discriminatory wage practices, Mexican miners were restricted largely to menial and dangerous work, and they lived in segregated areas. [Meier and Rivera, 1972, p. 108]

As mining became mechanized, the pattern was for Anglos to operate the machinery while Chicanos did the manual labor (Park, 1961, pp. 151, 207; Morefield, 1971, p. 14).

All of the economic sectors described to this point—agriculture and ranching, railroads, and mining—were sectors in which the bulk of the work was done in non-urban areas. While those were the most dynamic sectors in the nineteenth-century Southwest, there was a steadily growing urban economy in which Chicanos were represented to some degree. There are few data on this aspect of the Chicano work experience, but a few clues can be found as to the existence or nonexistence of a segmented labor force in the cities.

Camarillo has done one of the few studies on Chicano labor in an urban area, in this case Santa Barbara. According to him,

> The limited seasonal employment in pastoral-related jobs and the meager income from miscellaneous employment forced the male head of household into the manual labor market of the construction-building industry of the city. Prior to 1868 the building trade in Santa Barbara was largely dependent upon Chicano masons and other workers who were experienced in adobe construction. By 1872, however, adobe construction had become obsolete in the expanding brick and board construction of the growing Anglo city. For two decades Chicano workers remained outside the construction trades personnel which consisted of Anglo skilled workers and Chinese unskilled laborers. Prior to the early 1890's building contractors imported the needed labor, Chinese and others, for private and city contracts. As the source of Chinese labor decreased the contractors began to rely more on local labor. By mid-decade Chicanos were increasingly identified as the street graders, ditch diggers, and general manual laborers at construction sites. As recurrent high unemployment prevailed in Santa Barbara throughout the 1890's, Chicano workers filled the manual laboring positions once occupied by transient non-Chicano workers. From then on, Chicanos supplied the primary source of manual day labor. A program in 1895 to hire residents for local county road work marked the institutionalization of the Chicano worker as the chief source of manual labor. [Camarillo, 1975a, pp. 18–19]

A study of San Antonio also indicates a pattern of occupational stratification by race in the nineteenth century. According to this study, the percentage of unskilled workers in 1870 broke down as follows: Mexican Americans 61 percent, Blacks 67 percent, native Whites 24 percent, and European immigrants 21 percent (Barr, 1970, p. 398).

A more detailed study of Los Angeles from 1844 to 1880 also indicates a very high concentration of Chicanos in the lowest occupational categories. During this period we find that laborers (including agricultural laborers) constituted 73 percent of the Chicano work force in 1844, 55 percent in 1850, 70 percent in 1860, 70 percent in 1870, and 65 percent in 1880 (Griswold del Castillo, 1975, p. 153). This study does not present the overall occupational distribution for Los Angeles, but the proportion of Chicano laborers appears high and remains so during the period. Laborers were only 26 percent of California's work force in 1880 (ibid., p. 156). The study also notes that Chicanos were able to participate in the growth of new industrial occupations in the city only in a marginal way, especially after 1860 (ibid., p. 155).

Chicanos as a Reserve Labor Force

It can be argued that it is useful for employers in a wage-labor system to have a group of workers who function in some ways as a reserve labor pool. There are at least two functions that such a group can perform. On the one hand, it can give elasticity to the labor force, so that as the demand for labor increases the work force can be expanded, without having to compete for labor and thus drive up wages. Secondly, a group of unemployed workers can be used by employers as leverage in bargaining with or controlling their workers. If workers can be easily replaced, as in a strike situation, their power is greatly reduced.

From the historical record it appears that minority labor functioned as a reserve labor force in the nineteenth-century Southwest. As described above, the presence in Texas and northern Mexico of a large number of available workers who could be employed at low wages because they had little alternative was an important factor in the expansion of cotton cultivation from its east Texas base. Likewise, the presence of Hispano villagers in New Mexico who could no longer make a living on their reduced land holdings made it easier for other kinds of industries to secure the labor they needed to develop in that area. More importantly, however, the existence of such a reserve labor force made it possible to develop in the Southwest a type of commercial agriculture that was in great need of specifically *seasonal* labor. While this reserve labor force was not always exclusively made up of racial minorities, it became increasingly so as time went on.

In California, the growth of the fruit and vegetable agribusiness in the 1870s illustrates this process. According to McWilliams, "what has long been termed the 'farm labor problem' in California may be said to date from the introduction of intensive farming with the attendant requirements for an abundance of cheap, skilled, mobile, and temporary labor" (McWilliams, 1971, p. 65). As one California grower put it with reference to Chinese labor, "Any desired force can be obtained without delay on a few hours' notice, which is of the greatest importance in picking of small fruits" (Jones, 1970, p. 26). Referring to Mexican labor, another grower stated: "I don't know where they come from. They just keep coming, year after year. When the work is finished, I do not know where they go. That is the condition of our country" (McWilliams, 1971, p. 87). Camarillo notes that as local employment became more difficult for Chicanos to obtain in the Santa Barbara area during the 1870s, "the Chicano work force began a pattern which has characterized various sectors of the Chicano working class to the present day—part-time, seasonal-migration work" (Camarillo, 1975a, p. 12).

In the case of the second potential function of a minority reserve labor force, I have been unable to find a great deal of evidence for the nineteenth century, although the practice was to become prevalent in the twentieth century. Park mentions the fact that mine operators around Globe, Arizona, used the availability of Mexican labor to exert a downward pressure on the wages of all miners in the 1890s, and that Mexican labor was also used to break miners' strikes around the turn of the century in Colorado and Arizona (Park, 1961, pp. 247, 249).

Minorities as Buffers

The final aspect of a colonial labor system is the use of minority workers as buffers or "shock absorbers" in times of economic dislocation. For example, in periods of high unemployment, minority workers can be laid off at a disproportionate rate. This is the essential concept behind the saying that minorities are "the last hired and the first fired." The advantage to the employer in such a system is that the impact of hard times is concentrated on the workers who are most vulnerable and least able to defend themselves, thereby lessening the discontent of the potentially more dangerous nonminority workers.

While Acuña claims that this practice was followed during difficult times in the Arizona mines (Acuña, 1972, p. 89), evidence is generally lacking for the nineteenth century. In all probability this is due more to the scarcity of detailed information on labor practices of the time than to the absence of the practice.

LAND AND LABOR

There was an important connection between the establishment of a colonial labor system and the displacement from the land that had preceded and partly overlapped it. In a way, what was going on in the Southwest was a variation on a theme closely associated with the coming of capitalism in many other areas. The changes which were brought about by the penetration of capitalistic enterprises into the area resulted in a displacement of the rural population from the land, or at the very least a considerable shrinkage of the land base on which the rural population depended. The displaced population was then available for employment in the new enterprises. While this theme has not generally been emphasized in the literature on the Southwest, the connection was clearly perceived by some writers. In a description of the development of the Middle Rio Grande Valley in New Mexico, we find the following passage:

> The laying of railroad tracks in the Middle Valley in the 1880's opened the area to industrial development: mining, lumbering, commercial agriculture and the building and maintenance of the railroads themselves demanded a labor supply. The other developments which were creating

an inadequate land base for the Spanish-Americans provided a stimulus for many of them to leave their villages and to become wage-workers in new industries that were being built up. Some remained around the mining and lumbering camps as a permanent laboring class; others returned to their villages. [Harper, Córdova, and Oberg, 1943, p. 64]

DOWNWARD MOBILITY

In a sense, the displacement from the land can be seen as part of a broader movement of downward mobility for the Chicano population that took place after the Mexican American War. According to Camarillo's study of Santa Barbara, Chicanos in that area experienced a general phenomenon of downward economic mobility which was tied to the dislocation of the traditional economy (Camarillo, 1975b, chap. 4). The same was true for the Hispanos of northern New Mexico. Griswold's data for Los Angeles show a decline in the number of skilled Chicano workers after 1860, as the goods they produced came increasingly into competition with manufactured goods (Griswold del Castillo, 1975, pp. 154–55). As noted, Chicanos were not able to gain much foothold in the new occupations being created in the city. According to the same study, "there appears a dramatic decline in the overall property holdings of employed Chicanos during these years [1850–70]. As a whole, the Chicano community was becoming poorer since the average wealth of all occupational levels declined" (ibid., pp. 157–58). The author notes that a study of an Eastern city showed considerable upward property mobility among White workers during the same period (Griswold del Castillo, 1974, p. 97).

RACE AND ETHNICITY

The system of colonial labor appears to have been based on racial rather than ethnic distinctions. On the subordinate side were all the racial minorities in the Southwest at that time: Native Americans, Asians, Blacks, and Chicanos and other Latinos. On the other side were all the White groups, regardless of ethnicity. At the time, of course, there was quite a variety of White ethnic groups—Germans, French, Irish, Scandinavians, and so on. This is not to say that the division was neatly dichotomous—there are scattered references in historical works to distinctions among the racial minorities. In certain times and places, for example, it appears that Native Americans, Chinese, or Blacks occupied positions in the colonial labor system even lower than Chicanos. On the whole, however, these distinctions were minor and transient in nature; the main dividing line was drawn between the racial minorities and the Anglos, broadly defined. In the economic sectors described above, for example, little or no distinction was made in the way the various White ethnic groups were treated as workers.

Another line of evidence points to the same conclusion. In a study of occupational mobility in San Antonio from 1870 to 1900, Alwyn Barr found that rates of upward and downward occupational mobility for European immigrants (mostly German) compared very favorably with those for native Whites, whereas Mexican Americans and Blacks were in distinctly disadvantaged positions (Barr, 1970, pp. 400–401).

THE ROLE OF EMPLOYER AND WORKER INTERESTS

The colonial labor system was created in the Southwest, as in other parts of the United States, because it served the interests of employers to do so. Some of the quotes below make it clear that agricultural employers knew very well what they were doing and why they were doing it. The crux of the matter was not discrimination based on racial prejudice, but discrimination based on rational calculation of interests. As Lloyd Fisher has put it:

> Agricultural employers . . . are not without racial prejudice; but with the saving prudence of sound business men, the prejudice is shrewdly calculated, reversing the conventional order of discrimination. Agricultural employers are on the whole somewhat more likely to prefer Oriental, Filipino, and Mexican labor to native white. [Fisher, 1953, p. 14]

The fact that Chicanos were colonized in mining, agriculture, and ranching—all areas in which they were traditionally knowledgeable—demonstrates that these labor patterns were not a result of lack of skills on the part of the colonized workers.

Employers had several interests at stake in the creation of this type of labor system; the most obvious was in keeping labor costs to a minimum. If a group of workers could be identified as a low-wage labor pool, the effect would be to lower the employer's expenditures for labor. Other interests, however, were probably as important. A racially segmented labor force allowed the employers greater control of the labor supply. A reserve labor force, for example, gave greater elasticity to the supply of labor. In addition, the system gave employers greater control of their workers in other ways. The reserve labor force was used as leverage to weaken the bargaining power of all workers. The use of minority workers as buffers served to pacify the non-minority workers in periods of excess labor. Perhaps most importantly, the fact of a segmented labor force created built-in divisions among the workers, and helped prevent the emergence of class consciousness among them. Conflicts and antagonisms tended to be directed against other workers, rather than against employers. At the heart of the system, then, lay the interests of employers as a class.

Anglo workers in the Southwest were not interested in the development of a colonial labor force. They saw it as being in their interests to *exclude* the minority workers, rather than to see them subordinated. Here again, the dominant motive does not seem to have been racial prejudice, but rational calculation of interests. Lingenfelter describes the situation in mining:

> Many of the mining superintendents purposely hired men from as wide a range of nationalities as possible in the hope that cultural and linguistic differences would make union organization more difficult. But despite national rivalries the hardrock miners generally worked side by side with remarkable harmony—so long as Chinese, Mexicans, and Blacks were excluded. [Lingenfelter, 1974, p. 7]

While this author is correct in his depiction of the miners' attitude, he leaves out an important consideration: the minority workers were not hired on an equal basis with the others. As long as the mine operators persisted in trying to hire minorities at a lower wage, thereby either displacing the Anglo miners or exerting downward pressure on their wages, the Anglo miners saw it in their interest to agitate for barring the minorities. The attitudes and actions of the workers, then, were conditioned by the actions of employers in creating a colonial labor system.

The attitudes of small farmers tended to coincide with those of the Anglo workers. Since they did not employ labor, they had no stake in trying to create a colonial labor force. Instead, they found themselves competing with larger farmers who were able to undercut them by using cheap minority labor. When the California State Horticultural Society adopted a public resolution in the 1880s in favor of "Chinese cheap labor," the smaller farmers openly criticized it. As Lamar Jones notes, "opinion concerning Chinese labor had assumed a class character" (Jones, 1970, p. 25).

It is logical to assume, however, that the antagonisms that were created by these employer practices contributed to the spread of racist attitudes among the Anglo workers, so that in time racial attitudes took on a life of their own, independent of the circumstances that fostered them. It may also be the case that preexisting racial attitudes conditioned the response of the Anglo workers to the employers' practices, and led them to try to exclude the minorities rather than establish a common base with them. In this connection, it would be well to examine a couple of specific cases that lend themselves to various interpretations.

One of these cases has to do with events in the northern California gold fields in the late 1840s and early 1850s, when these fields were not worked as large hard-rock mines but as small panning and surface digging operations. Soon after these operations began, a wave of "anti-foreign" agitation spread among the Anglo miners. This took the form of mass meetings and intimidation, as well as passage of a "Foreign Miners' Tax." However, the tax was applied only to "foreigners" who were members of racial minorities, including Mexicans, other Latinos, and the Chinese, and it was these groups who were harassed to the point of being driven out of the mine fields. Other foreign miners, such as the French and Germans, were allowed to stay and were not taxed (Pitt, 1970, p. 64). At first glance, then, this would seem to be a case where antiminority attitudes and activities by the majority were not motivated by a response to employers' colonizing practices, but by feelings of White ethnic solidarity and racism.

Closer examination of the case reveals complicating factors, however, that make it considerably less clear-cut. In the case of Mexicans, it appears that already by 1849 there were persons (in this case Mexican entrepreneurs) who were attempting to establish mining operations in these fields on the basis of peonage. According to Pitt,

> When the Mexicans set to work as peons in the employ of their patrons, they did make themselves the target of the prospectors. Miners who began muttering against the Mexicans and plotting violence felt keenly conscious that the Spanish Americans were cheapening the value of labor. [Pitt, 1970, p. 57]

Once the anti-Mexican sentiment was set in motion, it was easily generalized to all Spanish-speaking miners, given the Anglo tendency to lump Chicanos, Mexicans, and Latin Americans together. Another factor in this situation is that the Mexican miners were at this stage the most expert miners, and tended to establish the most successful diggings (Morefield, 1971, p. 6).

Anti-Chinese feelings in the mine fields developed in 1852, and here the class factor appears to be even clearer than in the case of the Mexicans. According to Morefield,

> in the spring of 1852 feeling grew so quickly against them that it resulted in the passage of the second Foreign Miners Tax. The reasons for this sudden emergence of feeling can be found partly in the vast numbers of them that came suddenly in 1852, but primarily in the fact that they were being hired in China on contracts that gave them from $3 to $4 a month and board. . . .
>
> The miner realized the allies that the Chinese had, for in a resolution passed in Columbia on May 8, 1852, they condemned the ship owners, capitalists and merchants who wanted to flood the state with cheap labor in order to sell more goods. [Morefield, 1971, pp. 11–12]

Another case that might be considered to involve antiminority activities by Anglo workers not motivated by reaction to colonial labor practices is the "Cart War" in Texas in 1857. In this series of incidents, Anglo freight carriers attacked their Chicano counterparts who were hauling freight at cheaper prices in south Texas (Meier and Rivera, 1972, pp. 89–90; McWilliams, 1968, p. 106). However, it would be stretching the term to consider the Anglo teamsters "workers" in this case. What appears to have been at stake is simply competition between Anglo and Chicano businessmen, in which the Anglos took the competition out of the marketplace and the law into their own hands.

THE CHICANA WORKER

It is difficult to make generalizations about the role of Chicanas as workers in the nineteenth century, given the lack of mention of them in the historical materials. The general picture, however, appears to be that during and prior to the 1870s the work activities of Chicanas and Mexicanas were largely confined to the home. The division of roles corresponded closely to what some analysts now refer to as the "sexual division of production," in which the production of goods takes place primarily outside the household by men, whereas women are entrusted with the care of the home and the raising of children. If there were exceptions to this pattern, they must have been in the rural areas, where women tended gardens or looked after domestic animals.

In at least some areas, however, this rigid division started to break down in the late 1870s and in the 1880s. Griswold del Castillo makes mention of women being employed as laundresses by 1880 in Los Angeles (Griswold del Castillo, 1975, p. 155). In a more extended discussion, Camarillo described the situation in the Santa Barbara area. According to him, the entry of women into the labor market was stimulated in part by the dire economic straits that many Chicano families found themselves in during that period. It was after 1880 that Chicanas are first found working as domestics. It was also in the 1880s that Chicanas were incorporated into the agricultural labor market, as entire families entered the pattern of seasonal and migratory field work. Chicano women also found employment, starting about this time, in such agriculturally related enterprises as fruit canneries (Camarillo, 1975b, pp. 169–74). Thus patterns emerged which were to be consolidated and expanded in the twentieth century.

THE FOUR ECONOMIC SECTORS

Most Chicanos during the nineteenth century were in the subordinate segment of the labor force that has been referred to here as the colonial labor force, which of course encompassed other racial minorities as well. Still, it is not possible to claim that all Chicanos were in that segment. Broadly speaking, it appears that there were four general economic situations in which Chicanos found themselves, and I have referred to these broad categories as "sectors." These four sectors I have called peripheral, colonized, marginal, and integrated (see figure 2).

The *peripheral sector* consisted of Chicanos who found themselves on the periphery of the new economic order being established in the Southwest. They lived in rural areas which had not as yet been tightly incorporated into American commodity or labor markets. These areas, such as parts of south Texas, northern New Mexico, and southern Colorado, had been largely bypassed for the time being by the main lines of development of the new capitalist economy in the Southwest. In these areas the traditional, essentially precapitalist mode of organization of the economy remained in existence, although constantly vulnerable to penetration. These areas were by no means completely outside the new economic order, but they were on the periphery.

In the peripheral sector the process of displacement from the land took place at a slower pace, generally lasting throughout the nineteenth and even into the twentieth century. In some of these areas a Chicano peasantry continued to exist, producing in a subsistence mode or for a largely local market. In other areas what has been called the patrón–peon pattern remained dominant. Actually, this was not a homogeneous pattern, since considerable va-

FIGURE 2

FOUR CHICANO ECONOMIC SECTORS

	NONPERIPHERAL (Strongly affected by or incorporated into the American economy)		PERIPHERAL
	Urban	*Rural*	*Rural*
Colonized	Laborers (e.g. construction) Domestics Laundry workers	Laborers: mines, railroads, agriculture, and ranching Weak debt peonage (transitional)	Patron–peon pattern (sharecropping, *partido* system) Subsistence farming
Marginal	Displaced artisans, skilled workers	Displaced farmers and pastoralists (often move to urban areas)	
Integrated	A few skilled workers or proprietors (?) (e.g. carpenters, blacksmiths, bakers)		

riety existed in the relationship between patrón and peon. Generally, in this kind of situation, the patrón was a landlord and the peon some kind of tenant. Tenantry could be based on agriculture, with the tenant making payments in kind to the patrón. It could also be a kind of pastoral tenantry, such as in the *partido* system that dominated New Mexico and Colorado sheep ranching during this period. In the partido system, the landlord provided the tenant with a herd and with access to grazing lands, and the tenant was usually obligated to repay the patrón with a certain payment in sheep at regular intervals (Charles, 1940). The patrón–peon relationship could be very tight, as when a situation of virtual debt peonage existed. It could also be somewhat loose. In all cases, however, the peon was dependent on the patrón in a number of ways, and the relationship always included social and political obligations as well as economic ties. To the extent that links with the outside economy existed, they were mediated by the patrón.

Taylor and West provide us with a detailed look at one such situation: southern Colorado during the second half of the nineteenth century (Taylor and West, 1975). They describe the multifaceted nature of the patrón–peon relationship and the various ways in which the peons were dependent on the patrones. They also go into the breakdown of the traditional system as the area was penetrated by the American economic system.

> By 1900 pressures from outside were beginning to threaten the isolation and self-sufficiency of the plaza settlements and the independent power of the patrón. Mines, railroads, and the timber industry produced new landowners, new jobs, and a steady flow of non-Mexican immigrants into southern Colorado. In 1900 the Rocky Mountain Timber Company . . . acquired from the Maxwell Land Grant Company a wide strip along the southern border of Colorado . . . Mexican-Americans who, through their patrones, had leased these lands from the Maxwell Company were forced to renegotiate their leases. The timber firm insisted that the land be leased only on shares, thus forcing families off the land or severing the direct lines of fealty between patrón and peasant.
>
> Wage labor reduced the personal economic ties between the patrón and peasant. Landless families . . . came to expect cash wages rather than a portion of the crops for their labor. [Taylor and West, 1975, pp. 79–80]

By the turn of the century, this [traditional] way of life was under seige. As elsewhere, the coming of the railroad altered the foundations of the region's social structure. The bond of the railroad gradually integrated the isolated communities into a larger, Anglo-dominated world. On the Denver and Rio Grande came Anglo farmers, ranchers, and merchants who controlled an increasing share of the land and business of southern Colorado. . . .

As rural patrones lost their special claims on wealth and status, these

isolated societies were gradually compressed into a single class of subsistence farmers, herders, and laborers. [Ibid., pp. 94, 95]

Taylor and West have also provided an interesting description of a truly
transitional case (ibid., pp. 81–86). In 1867 John Lawrence moved into the
area to begin a career of farming and ranching. Within a short time he had
developed the trappings of a patrón, with his own Chicano sharecroppers and
partidarios and with the whole range of social and political obligations. Although his orientation was essentially capitalistic, Lawrence found that in
moving into a peripheral area it was in his interest to adapt to the prevailing
modes of economy and social organization. In harnessing this precapitalist
pattern of labor organization to capitalist ends of accumulation and growth,
however, he and others like him helped set the stage for the eventual under-
mining of the traditional patterns.

The *colonized sector* consists of Chicanos who are incorporated into the
new capitalist economy of the Southwest, but on a subordinate basis. In the
rural areas they could be found as nominally free wage labor on the railroads
and ranches and in the mines, or in some cases in a kind of weak debt-peonage
arrangement. In the cities they worked as laborers in various fields such as
construction, and Chicanas were employed as domestics and laundry workers.
This sector has been described in detail above.

The *marginal sector* refers to Chicanos who were strongly affected by
the new economic order, but who were unable to find a place in that order.
(The concept of marginality that I am using follows that of Nun [1969].)
Briefly, a marginal group is superfluous to a given system of production in
that it does not play a role within the system. Potential workers who are
unemployed and have no prospects of finding work within a given system are
thus defined as marginal. Chicanos in the peripheral sector were in areas
where the economy had not yet been thoroughly transformed by American
capitalism, but they were generally employed. Chicanos in the marginal sector were in areas where the economy had been transformed, but where their
labor was not yet needed by the new order.

Camarillo has provided an account of one such marginal sector. Speaking of Santa Barbara Chicanos around 1870, he notes that

> their destiny was inextricably tied to the developing tourist-agricultural
> economic system of Santa Barbara. Since most Chicanos prior to 1880
> were pastoralists, the tourist economy of the city and the agricultural
> development in the hinterlands placed the Spanish-surnamed worker in
> a precarious position outside any meaningful function in the burgeoning
> economy. [Camarillo, 1975a, pp. 9–11]

Apparently, a substantial number of Chicanos in the area found themselves in a marginal position in the 1870s, although this was not true of all

Chicanos who were displaced from their traditional economic pursuits. The Chicano unemployment rate during this period was phenomenally high. The same must have been true in other areas of the Southwest, although evidence is scanty.

The type of marginality found among the nineteenth-century Chicanos was transitory, however. The transitional period occurred after the disruption of the old order but before the new order had developed to the point of being able to incorporate all of the available labor power. With further development, the marginal Chicano was incorporated, usually into the colonized sector.

The *integrated sector* was at least theoretically possible, although few data can be cited to support its existence. This sector would consist of Chicanos who were incorporated into the Anglo capitalist economy on an equal or nonsubordinate basis—in other words, Chicanos who were integrated into the regular capitalist class structure. A Chicano worker who found himself in the noncolonized segment of the labor force would be in this sector. So would a small Chicano urban proprietor who was able to conduct his business on an equal basis with his Anglo competitors, or a Chicano rancher in similar circumstances. If such a sector existed in the nineteenth century, it was probably in the urban areas, where greater economic heterogeneity made a tight system of control more difficult to maintain. In the urban areas, also, there were more likely to be employers who did not depend heavily on minority labor and whose stake in creating and perpetuating a colonial labor force could be expected to be correspondingly weaker.

What little evidence there is for the urban areas, however, certainly does not indicate the existence of such a sector. The studies by Camarillo and Griswold del Castillo for two California urban areas show a marked degree of occupational stratification. The same is true for Barr's figures on San Antonio. In all these cities there was a small number of Chicano skilled workers, professionals, and proprietors, but there is no information on the conditions of their work. Griswold del Castillo reports on a case (in 1883) of Chicano workers who refused to work because they were paid $2 a day while Irish workmen on the same job got $2.50. He also notes that such wage discrimination seemed to be widespread (Griswold del Castillo, 1974, p. 82).

On the basis of such fragmentary evidence, it might be postulated that economic colonization of the Chicano was found everywhere, but on a somewhat weaker basis in the urban areas. Still, this must remain speculative until further evidence can be uncovered.

CHAPTER 4

From the Turn of the Century to the Great Depression

DURING THE COURSE of the twentieth century, important modifications have been made in the social and economic structure that was devised for Chicanos in the preceding century. The major factors that have shaped the Chicano reality during the modern era are migration, urbanization, and industrialization.

The interplay of these major factors can be conveniently traced by examining their development in each of three historical phases during the century. The first of these is the period 1900 to 1930, characterized by extensive immigration from Mexico and by a major expansion of the colonial labor force in the Southwest. In the following decade of economic depression, efforts were made to return many Mexicanos and Chicanos to Mexico as a means of alleviating the surplus of labor. During the contemporary period, from World War II to the present, there has been a resumption of immigration from Mexico and an acceleration of such trends as the urbanization of Chicanos and the movement into industrial occupations.

Each of these periods will be examined in turn, to show the changes in the structure of internal colonialism. This chapter deals with the first three decades of the century.

THE AMERICAN ECONOMY

In many ways, developments in the American economy during this period represented extensions of trends that had originated in the latter part of the nineteenth century. Industrialization continued to be the major driving force in the economy, and the tendencies toward big business and economic concentration remained strong. By 1920, 79 percent of net corporate income went to 5 percent of the corporations (Fite and Reese, 1973, p. 476). Some industries first became significant during this time, such as the automobile industry. Automobile registrations, a mere 8,000 in 1900, surpassed 8 million by 1920. In spite of this development, railroads continued to be the mainstay of commodity transportation. In communications the Bell System, owned by

American Telephone and Telegraph, attained a virtual monopoly over telephones in the first two decades of the century.

The period from 1900 through World War I was one of prosperity for the agricultural sector of the economy. As industry grew and the American population expanded, the demand for agricultural products remained strong. Prices for agricultural commodities were high, as farm acreage increased slowly after 1900 and yet there were no large surpluses of farm products (Fite and Reese, 1973, p. 491). In the 1920s, however, agriculture was generally depressed. With mechanization on the farm and increasing agricultural productivity, surpluses appeared in such staple crops as grain and cotton. Prices for these products dropped. One related development during the 1920s was the growth of farm tenancy, as opposed to ownership. Another trend of the times was a move to more specialized farming, particularly in fruits and vegetables (ibid., p. 494). In 1910, a long-term trend toward the deterioration of farm workers' wages in relation to factory workers' wages set in (Schwartz, 1945, p. 13).

The volume of America's foreign trade continued to climb, with agricultural products such as cotton and grain remaining in the forefront of exports until around 1910. American economic influence in foreign countries grew during the period, particularly in Latin America and the Caribbean area, including Mexico. As the American western frontier disappeared, the search for overseas outlets for investment and marketing intensified.

The structure of the labor force also underwent changes during this period. The proportion of workers engaged in farm work began to drop, a trend that has continued throughout the century. Whereas in 1900 farm workers constituted 17.7 percent of the total work force, by 1920 this had dropped to 11.7 percent. At the same time, the proportion of workers involved in blue-collar (manual) and in white-collar (clerical and sales) occupations increased (Szymanski, 1972, p. 107).

Migration into the United States from other countries continued to be an important factor in the growth of the American population. From the turn of the century to World War I, migration from southern and eastern Europe was particularly important. This particular stream of migration was greatly reduced by the war, and by the restrictive legislation that was passed in the 1920s. Increased migration from non-European countries, including Mexico, helped fill the gap (Divine, 1957, p. 192).

The trend toward the urbanization of America also continued strongly during this period. By 1920, for the first time in American history, the urban population of the United States exceeded the rural population.

The Economy of the Southwest

While the Southwest shared in a general way in the trends affecting the United States as a whole, it is also true that it continued to be a distinct economic subregion during the first three decades of the century. The pattern of regional specialization in agriculture and mineral extraction that had developed in the nineteenth century continued to characterize the area, with a definite lag in the development of industry when compared to the rest of the country. Since the Southwest exports agricultural and mineral products to the rest of the country, and imports manufactured goods, some writers have referred to the economic pattern as "regional colonialism." This usage is distinct from the concept of internal colonialism used here, since it refers to a regional rather than an ethnic or racial phenomenon.

Agriculture continued to expand dynamically throughout the Southwest in this period. Intensive agriculture was still on the upswing, continuing a late nineteenth-century trend. Taylor and Vasey, writing in the mid-1930s, noted that "during the past 40 years, the significant feature of California agriculture has been not expansion of the area under cultivation, but intensification of the use of areas already cultivated" (Taylor and Vasey, 1936, p. 283). According to their figures, intensive crops in California increased from 6.6 percent of all crops in 1869 to 78.4 percent in 1929 (ibid., p. 285).

The growth of intensive crops was closely tied to the development of irrigation systems. During this thirty-year period such major agricultural areas as the Imperial Valley in California, the Salt River Valley in Arizona, and the Rio Grande Valley and Winter Garden area of Texas were brought under irrigation. These developments were made possible in large part through the Reclamation Act of 1902, which made federal funds available for large-scale irrigation and reclamation projects (McWilliams, 1968, p. 175; Pendleton, 1950, p. 1188). This was part of a broader, continuing trend toward specialized large-scale farms using seasonal labor (Pendleton, 1950, p. 106).

Of these labor-intensive crops, cotton was the most important and figures significantly in the economies of California, Texas, Arizona, and New Mexico. According to Ricardo Romo, the cotton crop in California increased in value from less than $12,000 in 1909 to over $9 million in 1919, and that of Arizona from $730 to over $20 million in the same period (Romo, 1975a, p. 60). During this period cotton moved into central and western Texas, and into Arizona's Salt River Valley (Pendleton, 1950, pp. 25, 72ff.; Wyllys, 1950, p. 263). The increased demand for cotton during World War I was partly responsible for this increase.

Sugar beets were another labor-intensive crop that saw dramatic growth at this time. This crop was particularly important in California and Colorado, where it came to depend heavily upon Mexican labor. The production of sugar beets was stimulated by the passing of the Dingley Tariff in 1897, which afforded a measure of protection from foreign competition (McWilliams, 1968, p. 180).

Such areas as the Rio Grande Valley, the Salt River Valley, and the

Imperial and San Joaquin valleys of California also grew a wide variety of fruits and vegetables, including citrus, lettuce, spinach, beans, carrots, dates, canteloupes, and nuts. By 1929 the Southwest produced 40 percent of the United States supply of these crops (McWilliams, 1968, p. 185). All were labor intensive.

Aside from agriculture, the two other traditional Southwestern economic activities, railroads and mining, were important components of the area's economic growth. The railways generally continued to expand their mileage during this period. In California, total trackage reached approximately 8,000 miles by World War I, after which it leveled out (Caughey, 1970, p. 367). Texas tracks totaled some 10,000 miles in 1900 and 16,000 miles in 1920, reaching a peak in 1932 and then declining (Richardson, 1958, p. 351). Arizona railroads expanded to 2,524 miles in 1930 (Wyllys, 1950, p. 278).

Mining continued to expand output, although many areas suffered declines as particular deposits ran out. Copper production expanded in Arizona and New Mexico. The most dramatic development in mineral extraction, however, had to do with the emergence of petroleum production as a major economic activity in Texas and California. Oil was especially important in Texas, since it was closely tied to the subsequent industrial development of the state. Most of the dramatic discoveries of oil fields in Texas were made between 1900 and 1930. Starting from virtually nothing in 1900, Texas oil production reached 100 million barrels annually in 1920 and over 250 million barrels in 1928 (Richardson, 1958, p. 345). Petroleum production also assumed major proportions in California, with the state's yearly output reaching 104 million barrels in 1914 and 264 million barrels in 1923 (Caughey, 1970, pp. 366, 439).

The industrial development in the Southwest from 1900 to 1930 was very closely related to the agricultural and mineral-extracting activities of the area. The production of cotton, for example, led to the development of textile mills. Fruit and vegetable production resulted in packing and canning establishments being set up. Sheep and cattle raising, which continued to be important economic activities in most Southwestern states, brought into being the meat packing industry, which developed primarily after the turn of the century. Together, the various food-processing industries were a major component of the Southwestern economy. In Texas, the food production industry ranked first among industries in 1929, exceeding petroleum refining by $95 million to $91 million of value added by manufacture (Caldwell, 1965, p. 409).

Lumber and mining provide further examples of the close relationship between the development of industry in this area and the exploitation of the region's natural resources. The lumber industry was important in Texas,

California, and Arizona, with the lumber-processing plants generally located close to the timber-cutting areas. In mining, there were attempts to establish more ore-processing plants in the Southwest and also to manufacture the machinery needed for the extraction of the ores. El Paso, for example, expanded its industrial capacities in smelting and the production of mining machinery during this period. By 1917, El Paso Smelter was the largest employer in the El Paso area (García, 1975b, p. 30).

The production of oil had even more widespread ramifications in terms of industrialization. It not only provided the materials for the petroleum-refining industry, but stimulated the development of a chemical industry, led to improvements in transportation systems such as the railroads and deep-water ports, and brought about machine shops which often expanded into general tool manufacturing. According to Caldwell, the production of oil and gas was the key to the subsequent industrialization of Texas (Caldwell, 1965, pp. 406–8). Still, in 1929 only 2.3 percent of the Texas population was engaged in manufacturing, compared to 7.2 percent for the United States as a whole (ibid., p. 410).

In general, then, the economic development of the Southwest from 1900 to 1930 was based on an expansion of the agricultural and mineral extracting activities that had characterized the region in the nineteenth century, and on industries which were tied to those activities. At the end of the period, the region still had not developed into a full-fledged industrial society, such as existed in the Northeastern and Midwestern United States. Still, it was moving in that direction, and these developments conditioned the kinds of occupational opportunities that were available to Chicanos.

The economy of the region was generally prosperous for most of this period, with relatively short but significant downturns, as in 1907–8 and 1921–22.

Changes in the economy were reflected in the balance between rural and urban residence in the Southwest. In Texas, for example, the percentage of the population residing in urban areas rose from approximately 17 to 41 percent between 1900 and 1930 (Connor, 1971, p. 348).

IMMIGRATION

The most dramatic development during the first three decades of the century was the transformation of the Chicano reality through the first large-scale immigration into the Southwest from Mexico. This immigration greatly expanded the Chicano presence in the region and had far-reaching consequences. Structurally, this development was reflected in a large numerical increase in the Chicano-Mexicano labor force. The major structural change brought about by immigration, then, was quantitative rather than qualitative.

The fact that the new Mexican immigrants were fitted into the existing colonial structure is best brought out in the frequent comments by observers and students of that period that little or no distinction was made by Anglos between the older Chicano settlers and the new arrivals. Paul Taylor noted this in his study of Colorado in the late 1920s: "Occupationally and socially the economic standing of Spanish Americans and Mexicans in northeastern Colorado is essentially the same. Indeed . . . most Americans refer to them all as 'Mexicans' quite indiscriminately" (Taylor, 1929, p. 212).

Of course, there had been immigration from Mexico prior to the twentieth century. A 1930 report gives the figures (table 1) for the Mexican-born population of the United States in the latter part of the nineteenth century, showing net increases in each decade. More systematic statistics on immigration are not available for that period.

In the early part of the twentieth century there was a fairly dramatic increase in the number of Mexicans immigrating to the United States. The official figures for the number of immigrant Mexican aliens admitted in each year of the first decade are given in table 2.

While these figures seem to indicate a sharp increase beginning around 1908, the impression is misleading. Before 1908, the United States Immigration Bureau counted only Mexican immigrants who arrived through seaports, and it was not until after that date that it began to count those entering by land (Reisler, 1973, p. 29). Thus while it is impossible to tell with precision the exact timing of the upsurge in immigration from Mexico, it seems clear from various accounts and from general census data (presented below) that it began sometime around the turn of the century.

The overall dimensions of the officially recorded Mexican immigration for the 1900–1930 period can be seen in the breakdown for five-year periods (table 3).

There are other limitations of these data which should be constantly kept in mind. Figures taken from different sources do not always match, as can be seen from comparing the 1900–1909 figures in table 3 with the yearly figures given in table 2. Also, Ricardo Romo has compared the American data for Mexican immigration from 1910 to 1930 with corresponding data from Mexican government sources and found that the Mexican figures are generally significantly higher (Romo, 1975b, p. 178). In addition, these data cover only those Mexicans legally admitted for residence in the United States. While it is generally felt that the more irregular or undocumented type of immigration was not particularly significant in the nineteenth century, it seems reasonable to assume that by the 1920s it had attained considerable importance (Grebler, 1966, p. 24; Reisler, 1973, pp. 94–96). Adding to the problem is the fact that Mexican workers who were admitted into the United States for a limited period often wound up staying. Between 1917 and 1921 over 72,000 Mexican

TABLE 1

MEXICAN–BORN POPULATION OF THE
UNITED STATES, 1870–1900

1870	42,435
1880	68,399
1890	77,853
1900	103,393

Source: *Mexicans in California* (1930), p. 29.

TABLE 2

IMMIGRANT MEXICANS ADMITTED
TO UNITED STATES, 1900–1910

1900	237
1901	347
1902	709
1903	528
1904	1,009
1905	2,637
1906	1,997
1907	1,406
1908	6,067
1909	16,251
1910	17,760

Source: Samora, *Los Mojados* (1971), p. 68.

TABLE 3

MEXICAN IMMIGRATION TO THE
UNITED STATES, 1900–1929

1900–1904	2,259
1905–1909	21,732
1910–1914	82,588
1915–1919	91,075
1920–1924	249,248
1925–1929	238,527

Source: Grebler, *Mexican Immigration to the United States* (1966), p. 8.

workers were admitted to the United States temporarily, because of a claimed labor shortage on the part of Southwestern employers. It appears that about half of these workers did not return to Mexico at the end of the period for which they had been admitted (Kiser, 1972, pp. 130–31).

Taken altogether, then, the total Mexican migration to the United States in the first three decades of the twentieth century was of considerable magnitude. The effects were striking, whether looked at from the point of view of the American Southwest or Mexico. It has been estimated that by 1928 more than one-tenth of Mexico's population had moved to the United States (Corwin, 1973b, p. 11).

The great majority of these immigrants settled in the Southwest. Table 4 shows the number and proportion of persons of Mexican birth living in the Southwestern states from 1900 to 1930. As can be seen from that table, Texas, California, and Arizona accounted for the bulk of the Mexican immigration during this thirty-year period. While Texas continued to be the main attraction for Mexican immigrants, the trend toward California is clear. As we will see later, this was also true for the Chicano population as a whole.

Data are also available on the intended state of residence of immigrants from Mexico. Some of these figures are summarized in table 5.

The fact that the numbers intending to reside in Texas remain higher than the proportion of immigrants actually living there is a result of the tendency for Mexicans to enter the United States via Texas and then move on to other states, such as California (Romo, 1975a, p. 49). A small but significant number also began to seek work and to settle in such states as Kansas and Illinois during this period. In such cities as Chicago, Chicanos began to appear in the labor force around the time of the First World War (see appendix).

TABLE 4

NUMBER AND PROPORTION
OF PERSONS OF MEXICAN BIRTH
LIVING IN THE UNITED STATES, 1900–1930

	1900		1910		1920		1930	
	Number	*% of Total*	*Number*	*% of Total*	*Number*	*% of Total*	*Number*	*% of Total*
Texas	71,062	68.7	125,016	56.3	251,827	51.8		41.6
California	8,086	7.8	33,694	15.2	88,771	18.2		31.2
Arizona	14,172	13.7	29,987	13.5	61,580	12.7		7.6
New Mexico	6,649	6.4	11,918	5.4	20,272	4.2		2.6
Colorado	274	.3	2,602	1.2	11,037	2.3		2.1
Southwest	100,243	96.9	203,217	91.6	433,487	89.1		85.1
Other U.S.	3,150	3.0	18,698	8.4	52,931	10.9		14.9
Total	103,393		221,915		486,418		639,017	

Sources: The figures for 1900, 1910, and 1920 are from *Mexicans in California*, Report of Governor C. C. Young's Mexican Fact-finding Committee, October 1930, table 9, p. 31. The figures for 1930 are from Grebler, *Mexican Immigration to the United States* (1966), pp. 54, 102. Percentages do not equal 100 percent because of rounding. The Grebler study does not provide a numerical state-by-state breakdown for 1930.

TABLE 5

INTENDED STATE OF RESIDENCE

OF MEXICAN IMMIGRANTS, 1910–29

(PERCENTAGE DISTRIBUTION)

	1910–14	*1915–19*	*1920–24*	*1925–29*
Texas	77.8	65.6	67.1	63.3
California	5.1	8.4	14.4	18.3
Arizona	11.9	13.5	12.3	7.7
New Mexico	0.6	2.7	1.3	0.9
Colorado	0.2	0.4	0.4	0.5
Other states	4.4	9.4	4.5	9.3

Source: Grebler, *Mexican Immigration to the United States,* table 23, p. 104, from Annual Reports of the Immigration and Naturalization Service.

The background of the immigrants prior to migrating is a little-explored topic. The impression most writers have is that the immigrants during this period were largely agricultural workers in Mexico, notwithstanding the fact that the Mexican Revolution of 1910–20 also caused people of higher occupational categories to migrate. Still, there are indications that the immigrants were not necessarily representative of the largely rural, agricultural population in Mexico at that time. Data on occupational background have been tabulated by Leo Grebler from government forms filled out by Mexican immigrants for the 1910–29 period. According to these data, most of the immigrants designated occupations which fall under the heading "Laborers except Farm and Mine." Over 70 percent of the immigrants fell under that heading. For most of the period between 1910 and 1929, less than 5 percent of the immigrants listed themselves as farm laborers or foremen (Grebler, 1966, p. 48). Of course, it may be that many immigrants with varied work experience preferred to list non-farm occupations because of the low status assigned to farm labor. On the basis of 1930 data, another writer has suggested that Chicanos engaged part-time in agricultural work and part-time in other kinds of work prefer to designate their nonagricultural work as their occupation for census purposes (Fuller, 1940, p. 19859). However, a 1944 survey in San Bernardino, California, of men who had come to the United States from Mexico in the early part of the century indicated that only about a third of them had been engaged in hacienda work in Mexico. Almost another third were employed as *arrieros* (teamsters or freighters). The remaining group reported a wide range of occupations, including woodcutters, stonemasons, shoemakers, miners, and so on. According to this study, "occupations which involved a degree of travel, at least from one town to another, predominated" (Tuck, 1946, p. 69). The factor of mobility, then, may have been important in selecting those most likely to immigrate.

It also appears that Mexican immigrants as a whole have been similar to other immigrant groups in terms of occupational background. According to Grebler, "the share of laborers and service workers . . . among Mexican immigrants in recent periods resembles quite closely the share of these occupations among all immigrants in 1910–1919. Without belaboring the point statistically, there is evidence that the earlier immigrants from European countries included a large percentage of persons in low-grade occupations; this was true even for British immigrants" (Grebler, 1966, p. 49). This would tend to undermine the idea that Chicanos' economic deprivation is the result of Mexican immigrants' occupational backgrounds, rather than a product of the colonial labor system in the United States.

What factors led to the first large-scale migration from Mexico to the United States at this time? Since there were important forces at work on both sides of the border, it is possible to look at this question from the standpoint of "push" and "pull" factors.

On the "push" side, considerable emphasis is usually placed on the political upheaval associated with the Mexican Revolution of 1910–20. While this was undoubtedly a compelling reason for some Mexicans, particularly those who happened to be on the losing side at a given moment, it should be kept in mind that the upward trend in immigration began in the previous decade. In addition, immigration to the United States was much heavier in the 1920s than during the 1910s. Both of these considerations point to economic and social factors as the most important.

Another important pressure within Mexico was the demographic increase in the latter part of the century. From 1875 to 1910 Mexico's population increased by some 50 percent, and a disproportionate part of this increase was in the central area (Cardoso, 1974, pp. 22–23).

The improvements that were made in the late nineteenth century in the Mexican transportation system also should be taken into account, although this was more a facilitating factor than a direct cause of migration. Development of the Mexican railroads entered the picture in two ways. The establishment of good railway links between central Mexico and the northern border at this time made it easier and cheaper for those inclined to move to do so. At the same time, the building and maintenance of the railroads brought into being a mobile work force in Mexico that often went on to work for American railroads in the Southwest (Romo, 1975a, pp. 29–30; Clark, 1908, p. 470).

More generally, economic conditions during the Porfirian regime in

Mexico (1876–1910) were highly unfavorable for a substantial part of the population. Although considerable development of the economic infrastructure took place during this period, real wages paid to workers declined (Katz, 1974, p. 24). Inflation, a problem for some time, became even worse after the outbreak of the revolution, and remained severe during the 1920s (Cardoso, 1974, p. 25; Romo, 1975a, p. 39).

In addition, a large number of agricultural workers were displaced from the land as the process of modernization was ruthlessly pursued. "The number of laborers available to central Mexican haciendas greatly increased from 1876 to 1910, as the massive expropriations of that period created a new landless proletariat, which the limited industry in most parts of central Mexico could not absorb" (Katz, 1974, p. 28). The involvement of foreign, particularly American, capital in this process should not be minimized. Parkes describes the situation in Porfirian Mexico in these terms:

> American interests—the Hearsts, the Guggenheims, United States Steel, the Anaconda Corporation, Standard Oil, McCormick, Doheny—owned three quarters of the mines and more than half the oil fields; they owned sugar plantations, coffee *fincas,* cotton, rubber, orchilla, and maguey plantations, and—along the American border—enormous cattle ranches. The American investment in Mexico, which by 1910 had grown to more than a billion dollars, exceeded the total capital owned by the Mexicans themselves. [Parkes, 1970, p. 309]

While the capital provided by foreigners was used to modernize Mexico economically, the development that resulted was unbalanced.

> As a whole, Latin America became part of the world economy. The products of its mines and plantations provided the base of numerous manufacturing industries and fed millions of people in North America and Europe. Much of this growth was the product of European and American capital concentrating on export industries—particularly mining and tropical foods—public utilities, and transportation.... These enterprises yielded surer incomes by preparing commodities for sale in world markets or collecting tariffs on the use of public services. Little was done to satisfy internal markets or develop viable national economies. [Bernstein, 1966, p. 9]

The development, then, was a dependent development that precluded the emergence of a full-scale industrial economy that would have been able to absorb the displaced rural population. By participating in a system that relegated most Third World countries, including Mexico, to a neocolonial status, American capitalism was significantly involved in the "push" side of Mexican immigration, and not simply on the "pull" side. (The literature on Latin American economic dependence is extensive. For an introduction to this literature, see Bonilla and Girling, 1973; Emmanuel, 1972; Fann and Hodges, 1971; Frank, 1967; Rhodes, 1970; Stein and Stein, 1970; Dos Santos, 1970; Chilcote and Edelstein, 1974; Cockcroft, Frank, and Johnson, 1972; and the Spring 1974 edition of *Latin American Perspectives*.)

While these various "push" factors are important in understanding the sources of Mexican immigration, in themselves they provide a very partial explanation of the scope and timing of that mass movement. It is certainly a misplaced emphasis to argue, as Corwin does, that "primitive rural conditions were the principal cause of a campesino exodus that spilled into Mexican towns and cities and eventually over the United States border" (Corwin, 1973a, p. 558). The process of rural displacement had been going on for some time before 1900, and a labor surplus had also existed earlier, particularly in central Mexico (Katz, 1974, pp. 23, 28; Womack, 1968, pp. 45ff.). These considerations point to the "pull" factors as decisive.

There can be no doubt that the overwhelming "pull" was the desire of Southwestern employers for cheap labor and for labor which could be manipulated in ways beneficial to the interests of the employers. During most of the period under consideration, the demand was not for labor as such but for low-wage labor. The argument of employers that Anglo labor could not be found boiled down to the fact that Anglo labor could not be found at the wages these employers were prepared to pay. In many cases the low-wage structure of Southwestern industries which habitually used colonial labor had become built into the economy. As Fuller points out with respect to California agriculture, land values had become capitalized upon the basis of past cheap labor (Fuller, 1940, p. 19865; see also McWilliams, 1968, p. 177). If these employers were now forced to pay regular wages, the higher costs of production would have been reflected in a deflation of land values and a consequent loss in the value of their property.

The general demand for labor was of course closely tied to the developments in the Southwestern economy that have been described earlier. The increased use of irrigation and the spread of intensive agriculture in such areas as California's Imperial Valley, Arizona's Salt River Valley, the Rio Grande Valley of Texas, and the Colorado sugar beet fields kept the need for agricultural labor high. Taylor and Vasey note that "intensive agriculture, founded upon irrigation, has subordinated the typical farm hand. Requiring large numbers of hand laborers, it has built up in California a semi-industrialized rural proletariat" (Taylor and Vasey, 1936, p. 283).

The labor shortage associated with World War I helped to speed along these processes. According to Paul Taylor, it was during the war that Mexican labor first became dominant in Imperial Valley agriculture (Taylor, 1928, p. 8). The demand for labor remained high during most of the 1920s, with the exception of the economic downturn immediately after the war.

The particular impact of these developments upon Mexican labor and Mexican immigration was conditioned by the relative nonavailability of other sources of cheap labor during this period. Chinese labor had been restricted by legislation passed in the nineteenth century, and Japanese labor was restricted by the Gentlemen's Agreement of 1907 and then by the immigration laws passed in 1921 and 1924 (see below). Filipino labor was introduced but apparently was not available in the desired quantity. Mexican labor was the only other practical source of cheap labor from a Third World country (Fisher, 1953, p. 30; Taylor, 1928, p. 16). European immigrant labor had never been extensively used as colonial labor in the Southwest, although there were situations where certain European groups had been so used. German Russians, for example, had been employed in the Colorado beet fields prior to the First World War (Taylor, 1929, p. 103). In any case, the war and then the immigration restrictions of the 1920s effectively dried up this potential labor pool.

The "pull" that was exerted from the Southwest was visibly represented by the labor contractors who traveled far and wide to spread the word to potential employees.

> Southwestern employers interested in inexpensive common labor continued to send labor agents to Mexico, where every year the agents encountered success. "Each week five or six trains are run from Laredo," the Los Angeles *Times* stated in 1916, "carrying Mexicans who have been employed by labor agents, and similar shipments are being made from other border points." [Romo, 1975a, p. 56]

Speaking of the Mexicans in San Bernardino, Ruth Tuck states that "in every immigrant story, the labor contractor appears, directly or indirectly. There was a strong pull of labor-soliciting from the United States" (Tuck, 1946, p. 59). Mario García has described graphically the activities of various types of labor contractors in El Paso during this period, recruiting Mexicans for work in agriculture, railroads, and mining companies (García, 1975b, pp. 89ff.). According to him, at times "the competition became so aggressive that the agencies stationed their Mexican employees at the Santa Fe Bridge where they literally pounced on the immigrants as they crossed the border" (ibid., p. 95).

Prohibitions against foreign contract laborers during much of this period were ignored. From El Paso, a major distribution point, Mexican workers spread out to the Southwest and Midwest. In his study of the Colorado sugar beet fields, Taylor reports the arrival of the first trainloads of Mexican workers from El Paso in 1918 (Taylor, 1929, p. 105). Another writer notes: "There is no doubt that much of the Mexican immigration in the years before the 1930 depression was the result of the active recruiting by the labor representatives of the large sugar firms'' (Elac, 1972, p. 57). In Arizona, cotton growers banded together to recruit labor. Recruiters were sent to Mexico, and whole families were moved in special trains with their fares paid by the growers (Pendleton, 1950, p. 109).

The ''pull,'' then, that was exerted by the American economy was very much an active and aggressive force, one that sought out Mexican workers in a systematic manner. It was these efforts, and the eagerness of Southwestern employers for easily exploitable workers, that set the pattern for the waves of Mexican immigration that have continued to the present day. The interests of these employers have been reflected in the setting and implementation of American immigration policy, which, however, is the product of various and often contradictory forces.

Immigration Policies

The first federal laws regulating immigration were passed in 1882. The Chinese Exclusion Act, which was passed in that year, barred immigration from China. Originally a temporary measure, it was made permanent in 1904 (Divine, 1957, p. 20). In that same year restrictions were placed on the types of persons that would be allowed to immigrate. Convicts, paupers, and others were declared inadmissible, and other categories have been added over the years. These acts were the result of a number of factors, including the desire of organized labor to limit the importation of low-wage workers, and a general nativist and racist reaction to the growth of immigration from areas other than northern and western Europe.

In 1885 an Alien Contract Labor Law was passed, which prohibited the recruiting and importation of contract labor from foreign countries. In 1907 an executive agreement was made between the governments of Japan and the United States, referred to as the Gentlemen's Agreement. Under the terms of this understanding, the government of Japan pledged to cooperate in efforts to limit the immigration of Japanese to the United States. In 1917 the Immigration and Nationality Act set up new restrictions. It established a literacy test, provided for a ''head tax'' of $8, and excluded persons deemed ''likely to become a public charge'' (Divine, 1957, p. 5; Romo, 1975a, p. 56). This law was largely aimed at reducing the volume of ''new immigrants'' from southern and eastern Europe.

In 1921 a temporary Quota Law was passed by Congress which established quotas for immigration, based on the nationality of immigrants already in the United States as of 1910, and set an upper limit on total immigration from Europe. In 1924 a permanent Immigration Act set new quotas, based on the proportion of the various nationalities in the United States as of 1890 and reducing the upper limit for European immigration to 150,000 per year. Further changes were made in 1927 (Divine, 1957, p. 17). While these laws were aimed primarily at reducing immigration from southern and eastern Europe, the 1924 law included a provision to bar all aliens ineligible for citizenship, a stipulation intended to more effectively close the door on Japanese immigrants. The year 1924 also saw the establishment of the Border Patrol.

These various acts and agreements affected Mexican immigration in different ways. The restrictions on Asian immigration increased the demand for Mexican labor, particularly in California, where Asians had been most relied upon for menial work. The Alien Contract Labor Law and the provisions of the 1917 Immigration and Nationality Act pertaining to the literacy test, the head tax, and those "likely to become a public charge" made it more difficult to recruit labor from Mexico, as from other foreign countries. However, these barriers were by no means insuperable for persistent employers. In some cases these provisions were simply ignored. During the First World War, Congress bowed to employer pressure and allowed the secretary of labor to exempt Mexicans from the head tax, the literacy tax, and the contract labor provision. Under this exemption, a considerable number of Mexican workers were brought in between 1917 and 1921 (Cárdenas, 1975, p. 68; Romo, 1975a, p. 58; Kiser, 1972, pp. 127–31; Reisler, 1973, pp. 47ff.).

The nationality quota laws that were passed in the 1920s were primarily aimed at European immigration, and so they were not applied to the Western Hemisphere. By thus reducing immigration from southern and eastern Europe and leaving Canada and Latin America unrestricted, these acts served to heighten the demand for immigrant labor from Mexico. This does not mean that immigration from Mexico was unnoticed by those who favored restriction. During the 1920s several efforts were made to restrict Mexican immigration by organized labor and nativist interest groups, but the interests of Southwestern employers prevailed. (Cárdenas, 1975, pp. 69–72; Divine, 1957, pp. 54ff.). Still, restrictionists kept up the pressure and in 1929 won a partial victory. In that year the State Department moved to cut back Mexican immigration by tightening administrative procedures. American consuls in Mexico were ordered to apply strictly the existing regulations concerning contract labor, the literacy test, and those "likely to become a public charge." This measure was effective in cutting back the flow of Mexican immigrants (Divine, 1957, pp. 62–63).

During this period, immigration legislation was a battleground for forces favoring and opposing restriction. The restrictionist forces included Anglo workers, who perceived that employer exploitation of ethnic and racial minorities adversely affected their interests. The exclusionary sentiments of the workers were a continuation of attitudes formed in earlier periods, which were still very much alive in the Southwest. Allied with these workers were a number of nativist groups who feared the consequences for the United States of the continued importation of "inferior" and culturally different foreigners. On the opposing side were employers' interest groups. Southwestern employers were particularly active on issues which affected Asian and Mexican labor. Referring to the 1917–29 immigration exemptions for Mexicans, Kiser notes:

> Powerful, western economic groups with substantial political power were major supporters of the Mexican labor program, and without their demands for the program it would never have come into being. Among the most important of these groups were the railroads, coal mines, sugar-beet growers, and cotton and fruit farmers. Congressmen such as Rep. Carl Hayden and other governmental officials represented them well at the highest levels of government. While the major groups and spokesmen supporting the Mexican labor program were from the West, southern interests sometimes offered strong support. [Kiser, 1972, p. 129]

Fuller has described the efforts of Southwestern employers to exempt Mexicans from the quota restrictions that were set up in the 1920s, and pointed out their "cheap labor" motivation (Fuller, 1940, pp. 19863ff.). Divine has pointed to the same pattern:

> In contrast to the restrictionist emphasis on racial arguments, the opponents of Western Hemisphere quotas stressed economic factors. The economy of the Southwest, they asserted, depended upon farming, livestock, and transportation industries which required a large number of hand workers. Since many of these jobs were both difficult and unpleasant, native American workers refused to perform them. . . . Witness after witness reiterated this theme, asserting that rather than competing with American workers, the Mexicans did the menial labor which was vital to the agriculture and industry of the Southwest. . . . The Mexican laborers, by accepting these undesirable tasks, enabled agriculture and industry to flourish, thereby creating attractive opportunities for American workers in the higher job levels. . . .
> In the course of the testimony on this aspect of Mexican immigration, the representatives of economic interests showed the basic reason for their support of Mexican immigration . . . despite their repeated denials the employers of the Southwest favored unlimited Mexican immigration because it provided them with a source of cheap labor which would be exploited to the fullest possible extent. [Divine, 1957, pp. 57–58, 59]

Establishment of the Border Patrol in 1924 caused initial discomfort to employers, particularly when raids were staged on undocumented immigrant workers, as in California's Imperial Valley in 1925. The response of the growers to this threat is indicative of a more general and long-standing pattern. They organized themselves, and with the assistance of local chambers of commerce were able to pressure the Department of Labor into working out an understanding. Through this understanding, the Immigration Bureau established a procedure for regularizing the presence of undocumented Mexicans working in Imperial Valley fields (Reisler, 1973, pp. 114ff.).

The relationships between Mexican immigration and Southwestern economic interests in colonial labor have thus been very close, and immigration patterns and policies cannot be understood without close attention to this factor.

Overall Chicano Population Distribution

The new immigrants combined with the Chicano population in the Southwest to determine the overall distribution of Spanish-speaking people in this region. Unfortunately, only estimates are available for the overall size of this population during this period. Oscar Martínez has estimated that the combined Chicano/Mexicano population in the Southwest in 1900 was between 375,000 and 552,000 (Martínez, 1975, p. 56). No good estimates seem to exist for 1910. Fuller estimates the 1920 combined Chicano/Mexicano population in the Southwest (Texas, California, Arizona, New Mexico) at about 630,000 (Fuller, 1940, p. 19852). The 1930 U.S. Census counts 1,225,207 "Mexicans" for the same four-state region, but this figure apparently excludes many Chicanos of the third and later generations. In addition, it is flawed in that it depended on census enumerators to classify respondents as belonging to the Mexican "race" (see below), and thus is undoubtedly a low estimate. A Chicano researcher has estimated the 1900–1930 Chicano/Mexicano population of Texas as: 1900 = 165,000; 1910 = 279,000; 1920 = 510,000; 1930 = 695,000 (Roberto Villarreal, cited in Nelson Cisneros, 1975, p. 240).

The geographic distribution of Chicanos from 1900 to 1930 paralleled that of Mexican immigrants, with a shift in concentration from Texas to California (Grebler, 1966, p. 54). Texas, however, continued to be the state with the largest number of Chicanos. During this period there was a tendency for Chicanos to move outside the Southwest, particularly to the Midwest, although the overwhelming majority remained in the Southwest.

It also seems clear that Chicanos were becoming more of an urban people during this thirty-year period, although it is difficult to document the extent of this change. An indication of the shift, however, can be derived from census figures that show Chicanos of Mexican or mixed parentage living in urban areas to have increased from 39.9 to 51.5 percent from 1920 to 1930. During the same period, Mexican immigrants residing in urban areas rose from 47.4 to 57.5 percent (Hutchinson, 1956, p. 26). The census classifies as urban any community with more than 2,500 residents. By the 1920s,

Chicanos were strongly represented in most of the Southwest's cities. Two independent estimates place the Chicano population of Los Angeles in the late 1920s at 190,000 and 250,000. The total population of the city was slightly over 1,200,000 in 1930 (Romo, 1975a, pp. 7–8). Chicanos were estimated to be approximately 43 percent of the population of San Antonio in 1920 and 48 percent in 1930 (Nelson Cisneros, 1975, p. 250). A special 1916 census showed "Mexicans" to represent 32,724 of the total El Paso population of 61,892 (García, 1975c, p. 197). Camarillo estimates Chicanos to have been between 13.1 and 15.3 percent of the population of Santa Barbara in 1930 (Camarillo, 1975b, p. 307). According to Romo, the percentage of the "Mexican" population classified as urban by the 1930 census was as follows for four states in the Southwest: New Mexico 18.6 percent; Arizona, 36.0; Texas 46.6; California 66.3 (1977, p. 194).

The urbanization of the Chicano population, of course, was closely related to the kinds of occupational opportunities that were becoming available. The remainder of this chapter is devoted to an examination of the Chicano's role in the economy of the Southwest during this time.

THE CHICANO'S ROLE IN THE ECONOMY

Changes in the economic situation of Chicanos in the first three decades of the century can be described in terms of the four economic "sectors" that were identified in the preceding chapter.

The peripheral sector, which was on its way out by the end of the nineteenth century, was eliminated in the twentieth. As American capitalism penetrated the Southwest more thoroughly, the older Hispanic class system was reduced to a vestige.

The marginal sector does not appear to have been significant during this time. The period was one of economic expansion in the Southwest, and expansion was accompanied by a strong demand for cheap labor. The economy absorbed Chicanos who had occupied peripheral or marginal positions earlier, and reached aggressively into Mexico for more workers.

The major development lay in the absolute and relative growth of the colonial sector of the labor force. As Mexican immigrants flowed into the Southwest and were incorporated into the segmented labor market, the colonial work force underwent a major quantitative expansion. At the same time, there was still no clear evidence of a distinct integrated sector of Chicano workers at this time. Because of the increasing scope and complexity of the economy, it is well to look at this situation in some detail. The role of the Chicano and Mexicano in the economy can be reviewed under the headings of agriculture and ranching, mining, the railroads, and urban/industrial occupations.

Agriculture and Ranching

It was during this period that Chicano and Mexicano workers became the dominant agricultural work force in the Southwest. A 1922 report estimated that this group accounted for half of the cotton pickers and three-quarters of the fruit and vegetable workers in the area (Reisler, 1974, p. 106). Another estimate placed the number of Chicano sugar beet workers at 30,000 out of a total work force for that crop of 58,000 in 1927 (McWilliams, 1968, p. 181). In Colorado, "Mexican" workers (a term used to designate both Chicanos and Mexicanos) increased their representation from 9 to 59 percent of the hand workers in the sugar beet fields from 1909 to 1927 (Taylor, 1929, p. 107). A 1929 survey found that Chicanos accounted for more than 80 percent of the farm-labor work force in Santa Barbara and other southern California counties (Camarillo, 1975b, p. 225). All accounts agree on the significance of the Chicano presence in the agricultural work force of the Southwest.

The first characteristic of colonial labor (discussed earlier) is that of labor repression. The most extreme form of labor repression in the Southwest was that of debt peonage, which had been prohibited by federal statute in 1867, but which continued in modified form into the twentieth century in some sectors of the economy. According to Paul Taylor's account, Texas farmers and lawmen were well aware of the law and of the possible penalties for its violation (Taylor, 1971, pp. 147ff.). Still, the practice of making wage advances to Chicano workers and attempting to hold them through debt was by no means unknown. Now, however, it relied more on psychological pressure and intimidation than on direct and overt compulsion. Of course, if the agents of the law could be involved in some way or other in persuading the workers to stay and "work off their debt," all the better.

David Montejano, in his detailed study of labor repression in south Texas agriculture in the 1920s, provides us with a description on one variation on this theme.

> In 1927 court testimony at the Raymondville Peonage Cases uncovered a fascinating "compact" between local cotton farmers, the county justice of the peace, the county attorney, and the county sheriff and his deputies in Willacy County. During times when labor was needed, local farmers would recruit contract laborers, who discovered, upon arrival, that the terms they had agreed to were misrepresentations. Anyone who then refused to work was picked up by the local deputies, found guilty of vagrancy, and fined double the amount owed the farmer for transportation or food. The convicted were then given the option of "working off" the fines by picking cotton for the farmer who had recruited them. Any laborers passing through the county during the picking season also experienced the same fate: convicted of vagrancy, they were informed

that the fines "should" be worked off in the cotton fields. Naturally, such "convict labor" were routinely guarded by armed deputies while working cotton. To complement this method of recruiting labor, a pass system was instituted to prevent unauthorized pickers from leaving the county. Laborers leaving the area had to have passes signed by one of the local farmers involved in the compact. [Montejano, 1977, p. 28]

The conviction of several farmers and lawmen in the Raymondville peonage cases helped curtail this practice.

Texas farmers also tried to restrict labor mobility at the statewide level in order to protect "their" Mexican workers from being seduced to the Midwest by sugar beet and industrial employers. However, state laws which imposed exorbitant fees on "outside" recruiters were invalidated by federal courts (ibid., pp. 32–36). In this case, it is clear that the failure of Texas employers to crystallize a systematic set of labor restrictive measures was due to competition from other capitalist employers.

The second aspect of colonial labor, dual wages, continued to be a prominent practice in Southwestern agriculture. Victor Clark, in his 1908 survey, makes extensive reference to the "Mexican wage" in agriculture. He notes that in 1907 Mexican farmhands in west Texas were paid $1 to $1.25 a day, whereas White farm labor commanded $1.75 to $2 a day (Clark, 1908, p. 483). Paul Taylor also documents the practice in widely separated locations in the late 1920s. Writing of the Colorado beet fields, he states: "Mexicans in general farm work may receive the same as other classes of labor, but they frequently receive lower wages. These differentials in wages are sometimes differences in the cash rate paid, and sometimes a failure to receive board, in cases where other laborers would" (Taylor, 1929, p. 144). For the Imperial Valley, Taylor found that white ranch labor was commonly paid 50¢ to $1 per day more than Mexican labor (Taylor, 1928, p. 37). In Dimmit County, Texas, at about the same time, Mexican field labor was paid $1.50 to $2 per day, and Anglo workers $2.50. In this area Chicano workers were now being employed to drive tractors, but were still paid a substantially lower wage than Anglo tractor drivers. In summarizing the situation there, Taylor states that "Mexican labor in Dimmit County is 'cheap' both in the sense of 'low-wage labor' and in that it frequently receives less than Americans receive for the same type and amount of work" (Taylor, 1930, p. 337). Taylor also found that, in south Texas, even lower wages were received by undocumented workers from Mexico than by native Chicanos or documented workers (ibid., p. 138n.).

In areas where no wage differential was in evidence, it appears to be because Mexicans and Chicano labor dominated the agricultural labor force to such an extent that growers felt no need to attract Anglo labor with a higher wage. In this way the dual wage system was often replaced by a low-wage occupationally stratified system, which is the third aspect of colonial labor. Again, some of the best evidence for this comes from Paul Taylor's works for the late 1920s. In Dimmit County, for example, a situation existed where almost all field labor was done by Chicanos and Mexicanos (Taylor, 1930, p. 325). As one grower from that area stated: "We need more Mexicans; otherwise prices of labor will go up" (p. 333). Dimmit County ranches continued the pattern of having Anglos as the "boss cowboys," with Chicanos confined to the regular cowboy positions (p. 321). In Nueces County, Taylor estimated that for the 1929 harvest 97 percent of the local cotton pickers were "Mexican" and 3 percent Negro. "Outside" seasonal labor was estimated to consist of 65 percent Mexicans, 20 percent Negroes, and 15 percent Anglos (Taylor, 1971, p. 103). Most agricultural foremen in that area continued to be Anglo (p. 131). There was also a racial differentiation in the tenant farmer pattern. Most of the tenants who supplied only their own labor and paid the landowner half the crop were Chicanos. The majority of tenants who supplied their own implements and supplies and only paid the landlord one-third or one-fourth of the crop were Anglo. Taylor makes it clear that the landowners preferred it this way, because they felt they could exercise greater control over Chicanos on halves than over Anglos on halves. This factor did not enter into tenant arrangements on thirds and fourths since those tenants were pretty much on their own (pp. 131–32).

In the Colorado sugar beet area, Chicano labor was confined to hand labor in the fields, whereas machine labor was done by the farmers or their regular Anglo hired hands. In addition, the workers in the factories that processed the sugar beets were white (Taylor, 1929, pp. 119, 123). In the Imperial Valley of California there was also a clear pattern of reserving the more skilled, machine-operating agricultural jobs for Anglos. That this was due to the growers' habit of job typing is clear from Taylor's statement: "The consensus of opinion of ranchers large and small . . . is that only the small minority of Mexicans are fitted for these types of labor at the present time" (Taylor, 1928, p. 42). Yet in parts of Texas where the growers apparently had less choice, Chicanos drove tractors and performed related work satisfactorily.

In California as a whole, growers came to rely heavily on Chicano workers and Mexican immigrants for the lowest-status jobs in agriculture, many of them seasonal in nature. The situation is summarized in the following quote from Varden Fuller:

> Finally, by the twenties the concept of abnormality associated with employment of itinerant and casual workers had largely passed away. California agriculture was declared *by nature* to be such as to demand a permanent supply of itinerant laborers. Since white people refused to perform such "menial" tasks, such a labor supply by its very nature had to be "un-American." In demanding that immigration restriction upon

Mexico should not prevent continued augmentation of the farm labor supply, employer spokesmen talked of the "practical versus Utopian" aspects of the farm labor problem—with the explicit interpretation that the status quo was "practical"—all else being "Utopian." [Fuller, 1940, p. 19882]

The division of the agricultural work force by race and ethnicity made it much more difficult to form strong worker organizations, and this acted in the interests of growers. "The dichotomy . . . which the growers had developed between field labor and factory or shed labor, with the foreign groups being assigned to the former and the white workers to the latter, created a barrier which made unionization extremely difficult" (McWilliams, 1971, p. 102). That this was a deliberate policy is shown in many ways, not least by the use of segregation to support the system. "To keep Mexicans earmarked for exclusive employment in a few large-scale industries in the lowest brackets of employment, their employers have set them apart from other employees in separate camps, in company towns, and in segregated *colonias*" (McWilliams, 1968, p. 215). Occupational stratification, then, continued to play a major role in the system of colonial labor, and was a policy deliberately instituted by employers because they saw it as being in their interests to do so.

The fourth aspect of colonial labor is the use of minority workers as a reserve. This function took on considerably greater significance in the early part of the twentieth century than before. At least four types of reserves of Chicano and Mexicano workers can be identified.

1. *International.* The discussion of immigration has already documented the demand for workers from Mexico during this period. The other side of the coin consisted of the assumption that Mexican workers were not to remain in the United States as citizens but would return or be returned to Mexico when their services were no longer needed. The literature of the period is full of references to the homing instinct of the Mexican immigrant worker, and employer representatives routinely used this argument before congressional committees in support of laws allowing continued Mexican immigration. The economic crunch of 1920–21 allowed this assumption to be put into practice. As unemployment mounted, so did resentment against the Mexican worker, usually also unemployed. "During the depression of 1921–1922, rather than provide Mexicans with relief, localities initiated, on a limited basis, a policy of transporting workers and their families back to Mexico, often under duress. This solution was to be widely adopted in the early 1930's by many municipal welfare officials who wanted to rid their communities of an even greater number of unemployed Mexicans" (Reisler, 1976, p. 54). The attempts to deport Mexicans from the Salt River Valley area have been described in detail by Pendleton (1950, pp. 133ff.).

2. *Regional*. Chicano workers who lived in one part of the Southwest were often drawn upon as a labor reserve by other areas that needed seasonal labor. The Colorado beet industry, for example, drew Chicano workers from their marginal dry farms in New Mexico in the spring of each year (Taylor, 1929, p. 123). The Rio Grande Valley of Texas has also served as a kind of regional labor reserve for many areas.

3. *Local*. Local communities also served as labor pools for surrounding agricultural areas. Paul Taylor describes one situation as follows:

> Probably well over half the Mexicans of Dimmit County live in towns. This urban concentration is stimulated by the character of the labor demand, which not only fluctuates seasonally but shifts every few days from field to field. The towns, therefore, serve as fluid reservoirs of agricultural laborers who ride out in the morning on trucks in whatever direction their work may lie on that day. [Taylor, 1930, p. 304]

In the northeastern Colorado sugar beet areas, the monopolistic sugar company that owned the beet processing factories was responsible for recruiting outside labor. Since significant costs were involved in this recruiting and transportation, the company tried to get Chicano and Mexicano workers to settle in the local communities in order to build up a local labor reserve. But because of the limited employment opportunities, Chicanos who chose to settle in the area often found themselves unemployed as much as half of the year (Taylor, 1929, pp. 123, 136).

4. *Particular*. In some areas, growers preferred to have their own individual labor reserves. This was done by making an arrangement with Chicano Workers that would keep them in the area during slack times. In Nueces County, "the primary purpose of maintaining Mexican share-croppers on halves is to immobilize them so that ample labor will be on hand through the year and a large nucleus to start the picking season.... Thus farmers, in the manner of many industrial employers, maintain individual labor reserves" (Taylor, 1971, p. 121; see also Martínez, 1972, p. 37).

By making full use of the various types of reserves and the other colonial mechanisms, growers were able to take full advantage of the ethnic and racial diversity of the Southwest. A spokesman for the Arizona Cotton Growers' Association spoke of the 1919–20 season as follows:

> Thus in the face of the greatest demand for labor the world has ever seen, with the country at the highest point of prosperity it has ever known, the cotton growers of the Salt River Valley maintained as perfectly an elastic supply of labor as the world has ever seen and maintained an even low level of prices for wages throughout its territory. Outsiders looked, studied, and went away amazed at the accomplishment of such an organization. [Pendleton, 1950, p. 109]

Drawing upon Mexico as a labor reserve was justified by the growers on the grounds of a shortage of agricultural laborers in the Southwest. But the consensus of writers on that period is that no true shortage of labor existed during the first three decades of the century, except for limited periods, as during World War I (Reisler, 1976 pp. 81ff.; Taylor, 1930, pp. 333–34; Pendleton, 1950, pp. 107, 123). As Reisler put it, "in the minds of California growers, a labor shortage existed whenever they were unable to hire sufficient workers to harvest crops at the utmost speed and at the most efficacious moment for the lowest possible wage" (Reisler, 1976, p. 82).

The fifth aspect of colonial labor, the use of minority workers as a buffer to cushion the effects of economic downturns on other workers, is hardly mentioned in the writings on early twentieth-century labor. In one of the rare references to this practice, Reisler comments:

> In California . . . the plight of Mexican workers approached desperation in 1921. Unemployment became so acute in that state that some Americans were willing to accept the low-paying, back-breaking agricultural jobs which had traditionally been the lot of foreign laborers. California growers' organizations recommended, therefore, that for the duration of the depression white Americans rather than Mexicans or Orientals be hired for farm work. [Reisler, 1976, p. 50]

There should be no doubt that the perpetuation of a colonial labor system was primarily the result of the hiring practices of large agribusiness concerns. In the Imperial Valley, for example, the average size of farms was under 100 acres in 1927. Yet the melon and lettuce farms, the heaviest users of Chicano labor, averaged 667 and 336 acres respectively. These farms were largely owned by large companies, not individual farmers (Taylor, 1928, pp. 31–32). In Colorado, the beet industry was dominated by one large corporation, Great Western Sugar Company. This company owned all the sugar beet factories in the area, financed the growers, purchased the entire crop of beets, and recruited all the outside hand labor for the fields (Taylor, 1929, pp. 115–16). According to Taylor, "this permeation of the financial, agricultural, and labor aspects of beet growing by the factory side of the industry is characteristic not only of Colorado, but of all the major areas of beet production in the United States" (ibid., p. 116). In Dimmit County as well, the recruitment of outside labor was carried out by the big farmers (Taylor, 1930, p. 434).

In California as a whole, agriculture was dominated by the large agricultural units. In 1930, some 37 percent of all the large-scale farms in the country were located in that state. The largest 10 percent of farms controlled 80 percent of the farm land and produced more than 50 percent of the total value of output (Fuller, 1940, p. 19780). It was these large growers who were the primary employers of minority labor. According to a 1928 survey, over 90 percent of farms of more than 640 acres hired Mexican or Filipino labor, compared to 38 percent of farms under 20 acres (ibid., p. 19872). In addition, 83 percent of the larger growers (over 80 acres) preferred Mexican and other minority labor to White labor, while 59 percent of the smaller farms (under 20 acres) preferred White labor (*Mexicans in California,* 1930, p. 165).

Mining

Chicano labor continued to be a major factor in Southwestern mining during this period. Carey McWilliams estimates that Chicanos constituted approximately 60 percent of the common labor in the mines from 1900 to 1940, although he does not give the source of his estimate (McWilliams, 1968, p. 186). A 1911 study indicated that 60 percent of Arizona's smelter workers were "Mexican" (Park, 1961, p. 265). About 43 percent of Arizona's copper miners were said to be Chicano in 1927 (Reisler, 1976, p. 97). According to the 1930 census, roughly 20 percent of Arizona's and 16 percent of New Mexico's population was engaged in mining (Hernández-Alvarez, 1966, p. 489).

Of the five aspects of colonial labor, the practice of labor repression seems to have declined by this time, and little evidence exists of the use of minority workers as buffers. There is also little evidence on occupational stratification, although Clark makes reference to the practice of using Chicano labor in the more marginal types of mining enterprises. According to him, "the Mexican supplements . . . other kinds of labor. He will be found mining copper and silver . . . in some new mine opened up in a new district, to the entire exclusion of white labor, yet later, if the property proves valuable, he may be supplanted wholly by skilled American miners. In a district where white labor is chiefly used a few Mexicans will sometimes be found in smaller and less profitable workings" (Clark, 1908, p. 486).

With respect to wage differentials, Clark indicates in 1908 that Chicanos in mining received $2 per day, compared to $3 to $5 for Anglos. He also felt that wage differentials were smaller farther from the border (ibid., pp. 486, 492). Joseph Park agrees with the $2 figure for Chicano workers for 1907, noting that the wages of Anglo workers had recently been set at $4 per day. In 1917, one mining company was recorded as paying Mexican laborers $3.65 to $4.15 per day, with Anglo laborers receiving $4.65 to $5.15. According to Park, the large numbers of alien Mexican workers in the southern Arizona mining district tended to eliminate the wage differential for laborers, with all laborers being paid at the lower wage. In that area, the wage for more highly skilled miners was also pulled down. In the Globe-Miami area, farther north in the state, the number of Mexican workers was less in spite of some influx during the war years. There the dual wage system remained strong and the wages of the skilled miner classifications were higher (Park, 1961, p. 261). This is a specific illustration of the process mentioned earlier, whereby the dual wage system tended to be weakened or replaced by an occupationally stratified low-wage system where there was an abundance of Chicano and Mexicano labor. Park also took note of the effects of unionism on the dual wage system. Up to 1910, the Western Federation of Miners had been strongly anti-Mexican, and had worked to have anti-alien provisions written into the Arizona state constitution that was being drawn up at the time. With the defeat of these efforts, the union was forced to include Mexican workers in order to present a stronger front against management. As Mexican and Chicano workers began to be identified more closely with the previously Anglo miners' union, the wages of the minority workers began to rise in union districts, "holding a promise of an early end to the two-wage system that discriminated between Mexican and Anglo-American laborers throughout the territorial period" (ibid., p. 279).

The use of Chicanos as reserve labor for the mines was also a feature of this period. As one mine superintendent put it, "Mexicans make good reserve labor, for emergencies and odd jobs" (Clark, 1908, p. 488). The use of Chicanos as strikebreakers was noted in Clark's 1908 labor survey, as in the 1903–4 Colorado coal strike. Describing the effects of using Chicanos in this manner, a company representative was quoted as saying: "The shock of the strike is greatly lessened and its pressure upon the operators postponed until the latter may in some degree forearm themselves and the strength of the strikers is somewhat exhausted. Thus the native Mexican acts as a buffer to the blows of the strikers" (ibid., p. 492). Clark goes on to note that the hostility of the Anglo miners to the Mexican workers was caused by their use in this manner and as cheap labor (ibid.). Speaking of the first decade of the century, Park pointed out that "strike action had proven generally impotent in areas where aliens were employed in large numbers because of the reluctance of non-alien employees to risk a walkout against employers who were not only ready to replace them with Mexican nationals, but had demonstrated that strikes would be met with armed troops and the threat of imprisonment" (Park, 1961, p. 263).

Railroads

Railroad companies continued to be major employers of Chicano labor through 1930. A 1922 survey estimated that Chicano workers comprised 85 percent of the Southwest's railroad track workers. In 1928, the six major Western railroads were cited as employing between 33,000 and 48,000 Chicano track workers, depending upon the season. This represented about 75 percent of the railroads' work force (*Mexicans in California*, 1930, p. 71). The six major lines were the Southern Pacific, the Union Pacific, the Western

Pacific, the Atchison, Topeka and Santa Fe, the Colorado and Southern, and the Denver and Rio Grande Western. Chicano workers in the late 1920s made up 67 percent of the section crews, which were assigned to maintain a particular section of track, and 90 percent of the extra crews, which also maintained the track but moved about as needed (Hufford, 1971, p. 51). In some areas, such as El Paso, substantial numbers of Chicanos also worked in the railroads' shops in the cities. The El Paso directory listed 29 Spanish-surname employees of the railroads in 1900, but 211, or 15 percent of the work force, in 1910. The 1920 directory listed 1,010 Spanish-surname railroad workers out of a total of 2,753, or 37 percent (García, 1975b, pp. 110–12).

With respect to conditions of work, the situation appeared to have changed somewhat from the nineteenth century, although more in some aspects than in others. Little mention is found of wage differentials, although Clark's 1908 survey noted that the Southern Pacific line in California was supposed to be paying Greek laborers $1.60 per day, Japanese $1.45, and "Mexicans" $1.25. "Foremen said that the Mexicans did as much work as men of either of the other nationalities, and that the discrimination in wages was due to arbitrary orders issued from headquarters" (Clark, 1908, p. 479). Railroad officials claimed before a congressional committee in 1928 that there were no wage differentials in force at that time (Hufford, 1971, pp. 51–52). If this claim was true, it may have been because Chicanos were so heavily represented in the railroads' work force that they tended to establish a uniformly low rate for laborers.

One writer comments on the situation of the Pacific Electric line in 1903 as follows:

> Labor on all lines which employed Mexicans was ethnically stratified. Only Anglos served as carmen (engineers, motormen, conductors, and so forth), while Mexicans were employed almost exclusively on track work (construction crews building new lines or "extra" and "section" gangs maintaining existing lines). Thus, when the Pacific Electric strike broke out in 1903, Mexican track workers and Anglo carmen were in separate unions, reflecting the ethnic and occupational separation that existed on the P.E. [Wollenberg, 1975, p. 102]

Occupational stratification was also noted by Victor Clark. He described Chicano and Mexicano workers as confined to track maintenance and construction, with some Chicano section bosses but generally Anglo foremen (Clark, 1908, p. 477). In Nueces County in 1929, Paul Taylor found that almost all the track laborers were Chicano, but that some Chicanos were now employed as foremen (Taylor, 1971, pp. 158–59). In the El Paso railway shops, most of the Chicanos were laborers, although by 1920 a number were to be found among the skilled workers, in such occupations as machinist, bolt maker, and blacksmith. "A small number held clerical and foreman positions presumably over other Mexicans. Few Mexicans, however, held engineering or managerial jobs as these occupations remained in American hands" (García, 1975b, p. 111).

Since railroads did not experience the same wide fluctuations in labor demand as agricultural employers, Chicanos did not have the same significance for them as a labor reserve. It is certainly true, however, that the railroads used Mexico as a low-wage labor pool as their need for laborers expanded. At times, railways outside the Southwest also made use of Chicanos and Mexicanos as a reserve force of strikebreakers (ibid., p. 99).

Chicanos in Urban Areas: Blue-Collar and Service Workers

As has been shown, Chicanos in the first three decades of the century became increasingly urbanized, as did the Southwest as a whole. The economic situation of the Chicanos in the cities requires careful examination, since the occupational structure here was more complex than in the non-urban settings associated with agriculture, mining, and to a large degree railroads. To the extent that the colonial structure was being modified, one would expect it to happen more rapidly in the urban areas, with their greater complexity and dynamism and their more fluid social structure. If there was a truly integrated sector, it should be found here. In order to deal with this topic in an orderly manner, the discussion below deals first with manual and service work and then with white-collar and "middle class" occupations.

The situation in the cities was different from that in non-urban areas in that urban employers for the most part did not feel the same pressing need for low-wage Mexican and Chicano labor as did employers in agriculture, mining, and railroads. Generally, the latter carried the burden of convincing governmental bodies to continue to allow them to use Mexico as a labor reserve. Still, even in the absence of the direct recruitment of the non-urban employers, Chicanos and Mexicanos filtered into the cities in search of better employment opportunities. There, for the most part, they were to find a variation of the colonial economy that existed in the countryside.

In most of the urban areas, Chicanos found ready entrance to jobs in construction and road work. Victor Clark noticed their presence in Los Angeles construction projects, and noted that "in southern California and in Texas Mexicans do most of the excavating and road building, and are otherwise employed on public works" (Clark, 1908, p. 495). Paul Taylor also found Chicanos working in construction, although the cities in the areas he studied were not large and were closely tied to the agricultural economy (Taylor, 1930, pp. 356, 371; 1928, pp. 60–61). A Texas official estimated in 1928 that Chicanos performed up to 75 percent of all construction labor in that state (Reisler, 1976, p. 98). A survey of 159 California building and construction firms in 1928 found that 62 percent employed Mexican labor, and that

16.4 percent of the employees in the 159 firms were "Mexican" (*Mexicans in California*, 1930, pp. 89–90).

Chicanos were by no means confined to the construction industry, however. In 1928 California Governor C. C. Young's Mexican Fact-finding Committee conducted a mail survey of manufacturing industries in the state to find out the extent of Mexican and Chicano representation in employment. Of the 695 industrial firms replying, 312, or 45 percent, employed "Mexicans," a term which clearly included Chicanos. The breakdown by industry is given in table 6. As can be seen from the table, representation of Chicano employees varied considerably from industry to industry. "Stone, clay and glass products" (which included cement plants), had the highest percentage, whereas the chemical industry had the lowest.

The committee also found that the 312 plants reporting Mexican workers employed 12,113 "Mexicans," which constituted 17.1 percent of their total employees (*Mexicans in California*, 1930, p. 81). On the basis of its data, the committee estimated that California industrial establishments employed approximately 28,000 Chicanos (ibid., p. 87). It is clear from the data that most of the Chicanos were employed by large firms. The 11 firms that had 200 or more workers employed 33 percent of the Chicano employees, and the 33 firms with over 100 workers employed almost 56 percent. Chicano industrial workers were also concentrated geographically. Over half of the reported Chicano employees were in the county of Los Angeles (p. 84).

A 1929 survey found Chicano workers broadly represented in a wide variety of enterprises in San Antonio. The Alamo Iron Works employed 75 "Mexican" and 336 "White" workers; McKenzie Construction employed 50 Mexicans and 142 Whites; San Antonio Portland Cement Company employed 129 Mexicans and 42 Whites; Buerler Candy Company had 450 Mexicans and 350 Whites; Joseph Love Infant Wear Company had 800 Mexicans and 100 Whites; and so on. Altogether, the survey reported 4,139 Mexicans and 1,894 Whites in San Antonio factories. "Mexicans" also represented 79 percent of the laundry workers, 21 percent of employees of mercantile establishments, and 57 percent of workers hired by the city and public service corporations (Hufford, 1971, pp. 55–57). Even higher percentages were found in El Paso, where only 1 of 23 firms surveyed in 1928 showed less than 55 percent Chicano employment, and several clothing companies had over 98 percent (ibid., p. 54). The largest employer in that city, El Paso Smelter, consistently employed over 80 percent Chicanos from 1900 to 1928 (García, 1975b, p. 109; Hufford, 1971, p. 54).

The colonial labor system that had been created in the urban areas of the Southwest in the nineteenth century persisted into the twentieth, with some modifications. As in the earlier period, there is no evidence that Chicanos were subjected to systematic labor repression in the cities. With respect to a

TABLE 6

"MEXICAN" EMPLOYEES IN 695 INDUSTRIAL ESTABLISHMENTS
IN CALIFORNIA, 1928 (GROUPS OF INDUSTRIES)

| Groups of Industries | Total | Firms Reporting Employing Mexicans | | Total Employees of All Reporting Firms as of May 15, 1928 | Total Mexicans Employed as of May 15, 1928 | Percent Mexicans of Total Employees |
		Number	Percent of Total			
All Industries	695	312	45.0	111,736	12,113	10.8
Stone, clay, glass products	47	38	80.9	7,172	2,657	38.4
Metals, machinery, con- veyances	166	76	45.8	24,143	2,652	11.0
Wood manufactures	120	56	46.7	24,487	2,147	8.8
Leather and rubber goods	18	7	38.9	2,341	122	5.2
Chemicals, oils, paints	30	17	56.7	13,843	520	3.8
Printing and paper goods	94	19	20.2	9,056	373	4.1
Textiles	19	11	57.9	2,488	393	15.8
Clothing, millinery, laundering	61	26	42.6	8,061	831	10.3
Foods, beverages, tobacco	123	53	43.1	15,596	1,629	10.4
Water, light, power	3	3	100.0	3,410	681	20.0
Miscellaneous	14	6	42.9	1,139	108	9.5

Source: *Mexicans in California*, Report of Governor C. C. Young's Mexican Fact-finding Committee, table 24, p. 81.

dual wage structure, the references are somewhat mixed. Victor Clark reported in 1908 that Chicano urban laborers in San Francisco earned the same as Anglo workers, and that there was no dual wage structure on government irrigation projects in the Southwest. However, he also states that Chicano laborers in Los Angeles received less than their Anglo counterparts (Clark, 1908, pp. 494–95). Paul Taylor found in 1928 that the Imperial Valley Irrigation District paid Chicano workers 25 cents an hour and Anglo workers 40 cents an hour (Taylor, 1928, pp. 59–60). Camarillo points out that in pre–World War I Santa Barbara, Anglo teamsters were paid $4 to $4.50 per day, while Chicano teamsters earned only $2 to $2.50. Chicano construction workers were paid from $1.25 to $1.50 per day, regardless of job function or skill (Camarillo, 1975b, pp. 248, 219). García notes the existence of a dual wage structure in El Paso industries in the first two decades of the century, affecting the few skilled Chicano workers as well as the many unskilled and semiskilled (García, 1975b, pp. 114, 137, 210).

Occupational stratification remained an even more marked characteristic of the urban labor system in the first three decades of the century, as data for several major cities make clear. In Los Angeles, over 93 percent of Chicanos were concentrated in blue-collar occupations in 1918, compared to 53 percent for Anglos. Some 70 percent of Chicanos were found in the unskilled blue-collar category, compared to only 6 percent for Anglos (Romo, 1975a, p. 140). Moreover, during the 1920s there appeared to be virtually no upward mobility for Chicanos in Los Angeles, at least as measured by movement from manual to non-manual occupations. Yet a study based on the previous decade has shown considerable mobility for the general population of that city (ibid., p. 149).

A 1927 survey in San Antonio included 1,282 male Chicanos in the labor force. Of these, 618 were classified by the researcher as "common laborers," earning an average of $13.68 a week, which, as he noted, "would not permit of a healthy, well-clothed, well-fed family, to say nothing of the lack of social or educational opportunities" (Knox, 1971, p. 16). Two hundred eighty were classified as skilled workers, but generally of a non-union, "helper" type (ibid., p. 18). Some 87 were small businessmen, 41 were professionals, and 270 were put in a miscellaneous category, "regular jobs," that included clerks and government employees as well as truck drivers and others (ibid., pp. 16–19).

In El Paso a small degree of occupational mobility was apparent from 1900 to 1920. If we combine the categories of laborer, service worker, and operative (semiskilled), we find 72 percent of Chicanos represented in 1900 and 68 percent in 1920. During this period the non-Spanish-surname population of El Paso in this combined category remained fairly stable at around 21 percent. Chicanos also increased their representation slightly in the skilled worker and clerical categories, although Anglos showed much greater gains in the latter area (García, 1975c, p. 199). Chicanos employed at El Paso Smelter appeared to be almost entirely manual laborers (García, 1975b, p. 109).

In Santa Barbara, Camarillo found through a study of city directories that the occupational structure in the first three decades of the century remained relatively fixed. Of the Chicanos whose occupation could be determined, approximately 49 percent were in unskilled jobs in 1897. In 1930 the figure was still around 49 percent. Semiskilled Chicano workers had increased from 13 to 22 percent, but the proportion of skilled workers had dropped from 17 to about 12 percent. The combined total of Chicanos in white-collar, professional, and proprietorial occupations declined from 9 to 4 percent in the same period. While the non-Chicano occupational structure also did not change much, the proportional distribution was quite different. In 1930, only some 11 percent of this group was in the unskilled category, and about 23 percent were in professional or proprietorial jobs (Camarillo, 1975b, pp. 184, 256, 267, 270). By looking at Chicano workers who remained in Santa Barbara at least one decade, Camarillo found a number of unskilled workers who moved to semiskilled occupations.

> The move from the unskilled to semiskilled status, although possessing certain features of upward mobility (e.g., opportunity for more full-time jobs and less menial work), did not constitute true upward mobility. First . . . the monetary level between the two was roughly equivalent throughout the period studied. Secondly, both occupational levels were also subject to employment instability. Most significantly, those that may have attained semiskilled status in an earlier directory period were commonly found in the unskilled laborer status in a later period. . . .
>
> Many Chicano workers during the first three decades of the century demonstrated this quality which characterized them as a floating unskilled-semiskilled manual labor working class. [Ibid., pp. 257, 260]

Camarillo leaves no doubt that the basic reason for the persistence of this pattern lay in the fact that employment opportunities for Chicanos and Mexicanos were severely restricted by the practices of employers (ibid., p. 217).

> The number of Mexicano workers in the construction-building industry and in agricultural-related industries was roughly equivalent. In both areas, the type of employment open to Spanish-speaking peoples had been determined prior to the arrival of the majority of Mexicanos—they continued the occupational patterns initiated by the native-Chicanos of the late nineteenth century. [Ibid., pp. 220–21]

The remaining aspects of colonial labor have to do with the use of minorities as a reserve or as buffers. There are few references to these practices for the urban areas, although it seems clear that Chicanos and Mexicanos were drawn upon in the urban areas, as in the rural areas, when the labor supply was tight. It was during this period that Chicanos began to appear in significant numbers in such Midwestern cities as Chicago, as the labor shortages associated with World War I and the 1920s made themselves felt. According to Paul Taylor, a pool of Chicano workers was desired by Midwestern employers as a kind of "strike insurance." He quoted two informants as follows:

> The Mexicans come in and go out. The factories and mills want to have as many around as possible to prevent strikes; if there are a couple of thousand waiting for a job, those who are working won't strike.
>
> Most of the large employers employ a few Mexicans; they usually employ a few of the newest, lowest class of laborers to help keep down wages and avoid strikes. [Taylor, 1932, p. 94]

In San Antonio, a Chicano labor reserve served to undercut union organizing efforts (Knox, 1971, p. 18).

Paul Taylor also documents the use of Chicanos as buffers, as when disproportionately large numbers were fired in the recession of 1921 (Taylor, 1932, p. 94). It seems reasonable to believe that similar practices were in effect in urban areas of the Southwest, and that the consistently high unemployment rates for Chicano workers reported on by various writers were one result of this policy (Connell, 1971, p. 41; Camarillo, 1975b, p. 226; Romo, 1975a, p. 155).

The existence of a colonized sector in the cities, thus, is not in doubt. The more interesting question is whether there was an integrated sector at the level of manual and service workers. On the whole, the evidence would seem to indicate that there was not. Even the Chicanos who were classified as skilled workers do not seem to have occupied the same status as Anglo skilled workers. In San Antonio, for example, Chicano skilled workers generally did not belong to unions, and most of them formed a kind of "floating helper" pool who worked irregularly or were used by non-union contractors (Knox, 1971, p. 18). Another writer noted that skilled workers moving to the United States from Mexico usually did not belong to unions, and either dropped down to unskilled labor or were able to practice their skills only among the Chicano rather than the general population (Hufford, 1971, p. 50). Hufford also notes that "Mexican skilled labor is usually employed as 'helpers' and receives, in such cases, a lower wage rate than the skilled white worker" (ibid., p. 53).

Chicanos in Urban Areas:
White-Collar Workers and the "Middle Class"

In the literature of this period there is considerable reference to Chicano white-collar workers in the cities, especially clerks. It is also clear that there was a small but significant Chicano middle class, which had several components. These included small businessmen and managers, and professionals such as teachers. Whether these are seen as one class or several, they were "middle" in the sense of occupying a middle position in the economy between blue-collar and service workers on the one hand and the larger capitalists (mostly Anglo) on the other. They were also "middle" in the sense of serving as middlemen between the Chicano population and the dominant institutions of the society. It remains to be seen whether these people were themselves in the colonized sector of the economy or whether they could be said to be fully integrated into the dominant class system.

Paul Taylor in his investigations was sensitive to the existence of this class of Chicanos. He noted that in Dimmit County in Texas there were a number of Chicano clerks, labor contractors, truckers, teachers, and some Chicano-run shoe repair shops, garages, and movie theaters. However, it is apparent from his account that these Chicanos were not integrated into the Anglo middle class, but were confined to a kind of Chicano subeconomy. The clerks were hired by Anglo stores not to serve the general public, but to bring in Chicano trade. They were paid considerably less than Anglo clerks. The labor contractors provided Anglo employers with Chicano and Mexicano workers. The Chicano teachers were hired only by private Chicano schools or to work in the segregated public schools with Chicano students. The Chicano-run businesses were described as "little stores in the front room of their houses just to keep from going to the fields to labor," and were not comparable to Anglo-owned businesses. They were apparently completely dependent on a Chicano clientele (Taylor, 1930, pp. 370–71). As Taylor puts it: "The opportunities to rise by these routes, particularly as clerks and businessmen, depend principally upon the volume of patronage in the Mexican colony, and therefore are largely limited by what the colony can support" (ibid., p. 371).

In Nueces County as well, and particularly in Corpus Christi and Robstown, there were a number of Chicano clerks, the majority women. Their status was similar to that of the clerks in Dimmit County, although the wage differential was apparently not as uniform (Taylor, 1971, p. 177). Among Chicano-owned businesses were restaurants, groceries, bakeries, markets, filling stations, dry goods, tailor, and barber shops. Taylor estimates there may have been some forty or fifty Chicano businesses in Corpus Christi in 1929. There were also some Chicano public employees, and a Chicano newspaper. Most of the businesses, as in Dimmit County, relied on Chicano patronage (ibid., pp. 177–78).

Knox, in his 1927 sample of 1,282 male Chicanos in the San Antonio labor force, classified about 3 percent as "professionals and semi-professionals." This category included 19 printers and newspapermen, 11 musicians, 5 contractors, 2 typists, 3 bookkeepers, 1 druggist, 1 jeweler, and 1 preacher. "This group serves its own people, excepting the musicians who play in the American theatres. The newspapers printed in Spanish keep a Mexican force only, and the wage drawn indicates that they do not belong to the regular American printer's union" (Knox, 1971, p. 19). The contractors were small businessmen who served the Mexican market only. Knox lists separately 74 Chicano storekeepers and 13 butchers. These men earned an average of about $21 per week, which marks them as small businessmen (ibid., p. 17). Knox's sample was drawn only from the Chicano residential section of San Antonio, and he states that a few other, more successful Chicanos lived outside the *barrio* (ibid., p. 19). However, he presents no data for this group.

El Paso during this period also had a significant representation of white-collar and middle-class Chicanos. City directories for 1920 indicate that about 15 percent of employed Chicanos were in clerical occupations, 2 percent were managers, and a little over 3 percent were professionals (García, 1975c, p. 199). Chicanos earned their living as independent garbagemen and taxi drivers, minor public officials, and small businessmen. There were even a few doctors, dentists, real estate agents, and attorneys (García, 1975b, pp. 119, 125, 139, 145, 146). In 1920 El Paso had 57 barber shops, 56 shoe-making shops, and 446 groceries operated by Chicanos (ibid., p. 145). Here, as elsewhere, Chicano professionals and businessmen were largely confined to a Chicano clientele. "Limited in capital, the 'comerciantes' existed apart from the Anglo business community and remained dependent on the Mexican population" (ibid., p. 151).

In California, it appears that the Chicano white-collar and professional-proprietorial groups remained even smaller than in Texas. In Los Angeles, figures for 1918 indicate that only slightly over 6 percent of Chicanos were involved in non-manual occupations (Romo, 1975a, p. 140). In Santa Barbara, Chicano-owned businesses remained small and restricted to the barrio (Camarillo, 1975b, p. 205).

In general, then, the Chicano "middle classes" constituted a subordinate segment at their particular class level, as the white- and blue-collar workers did at theirs. There was little if any true integration of Chicanos into the class structure on an equal basis, at any level. Thus virtually the entire Chicano population could be said to fall into the colonized sector in the period 1900 to 1930.

THE SITUATION IN 1930

The U.S. census which was published for 1930 is the first to provide an approximation of the Chicano population in the Southwest. Earlier censuses provided information only about foreign birth or parentage. Enumerators for the 1930 census were asked to classify as Mexican "all persons born in Mexico, or having parents born in Mexico, who are not definitely white, Negro, Indian or Japanese." While this measure theoretically would apply only to the first and second generation, enumerators included a substantial number of third- and later-generation Chicanos (Longmore and Hitt, 1943, p. 139). If there is a bias in the occupational statistics, it is probably in undercounting Chicanos in higher occupational categories. Chicanos in New Mexico would probably be the most undercounted in total numbers because of the long-term residence of Chicanos in that area and because more of them may have been counted as "white."

The 1930 census listed for the entire United States 431,677 "Mexican" males and 67,088 "Mexican" females who were "gainful workers 10 years old and over." Approximately 86 percent of the males and 94 percent of the females were employed in the five states of the Southwest. The figures by state are given in table 7.

Census data for 1930 can also be broken down by the type of industry in which Chicanos were employed. These data are presented in table 8 for the Southwest. The classifications used by the Census Bureau in 1930 for industrial distribution are not strictly comparable to the classifications that were used in later years.

In table 9, some figures from the 1930 census summarize the information on the occupational level of Chicanos. This table presents data on occupational level, broken down by state and sex.

In addition to the bias cited above, it is probable that the figures understate the proportion of Chicanos in agricultural occupations. As mentioned earlier, Varden Fuller, on the basis of estimates of Chicano labor in California agriculture, feels that many Chicanos who worked seasonally in agriculture and pursued some other line of work the rest of the time may have been more inclined to report the nonagricultural work as their occupation (Fuller, 1940, p. 19859).

As can be seen from these various tabulations, the largest number of Chicano workers resided in Texas, with a second large concentration in California. Male Chicano workers in the officially counted labor force outnumbered female workers by a ratio of approximately six to one. Agriculture continued to be the greatest area of employment, although by 1930 a substantial number of Chicanos were concentrated in manufacturing. Chicanos were strikingly underrepresented in all of the more prestigious and better-paid occupations in the society.

The Chicana Worker

During this period large proportions of the Chicana work force were employed in two types of situations. In the first, entire families were em-

TABLE 7

TOTAL EMPLOYED "MEXICAN" WORKERS

IN 1930, BY STATE AND SEX

FOR THE SOUTHWEST

	Males	Females
Texas	196,980	39,221
New Mexico	15,714	1,542
Colorado	15,920	1,640
Arizona	31,202	4,786
California	112,119	15,973
	371,935	63,162

Source: *Fifteenth Census of the United States: 1930. Volume 5: General Report on Occupations*, table 4.

TABLE 8

INDUSTRIAL DISTRIBUTION OF CHICANOS, 1930,

BY SEX, FOR THE SOUTHWEST (PERCENTAGES)

	Males	Females	Total
Agriculture	44.9	20.7	41.4
Forestry & fishing	0.5	—	0.4
Mining	3.9	—	3.3
Manufacturing	23.9	19.3	23.2
Transportation & communication	13.2	0.4	11.3
Trade	6.2	9.3	6.7
Public service	1.0	0.1	0.8
Professional service	1.2	2.9	1.5
Domestic & personal service	4.4	44.8	10.2
Clerical	0.9	2.5	1.1
Total	100.1	100.0	99.9

Source: *Fifteenth Census of the United States: 1930. Volume 5: General Report on Occupations*, table 4.

TABLE 9

OCCUPATIONAL DISTRIBUTION OF CHICANOS, 1930, BY STATES OF THE SOUTHWEST AND SEX (PERCENTAGES)

Occupational Level	Texas		New Mexico		Colorado		Arizona		California		Southwest	
	M	F	M	F	M	F	M	F	M	F	M	F
Professional & technical	0.8	2.9	0.5	3.6	0.3	1.0	0.6	3.4	1.0	3.0	0.9	2.9
Managers, proprietors, & officials	3.4	2.6	1.3	2.8	0.4	0.4	2.9	3.3	1.9	1.8	2.8	2.4
Clerical	1.1	4.3	0.5	3.6	0.3	2.1	1.4	8.2	1.0	9.5	1.0	5.8
Sales	2.6	4.4	1.3	2.5	0.6	1.4	2.7	6.6	2.2	4.1	2.4	4.3
Craftsmen & foremen (skilled)	7.3	0.4	4.6	0.3	2.2	0.3	7.9	0.5	7.0	1.4	6.8	0.6

Occupational Level	Texas		New Mexico		Colorado		Arizona		California		Southwest	
	M	F	M	F	M	F	M	F	M	F	M	F
Operatives (semiskilled)	6.1	16.4	19.2	9.0	14.7	6.3	26.1	13.1	8.1	40.8	9.1	21.9
Laborers (unskilled)	23.6	2.3	20.7	1.6	25.3	3.4	26.5	1.5	37.6	4.7	28.2	2.8
Service	4.2	39.7	3.0	67.2	1.7	41.6	3.0	55.0	4.2	27.5	4.0	38.4
Farm laborers	35.0	25.9	35.1	5.2	48.8	41.5	26.4	7.9	35.7	7.1	35.1	19.7
Farmers & farm managers	15.9	1.2	13.9	4.2	5.7	2.1	2.5	0.6	1.3	0.1	9.8	1.0

Sources: Data for Southwest males from Briggs et al., *The Chicano Worker*, p. 76. Other data computed from *Fifteenth Census of the United States: 1930. Population. Volume 5: General Report on Occupations*, Table 4. The census classification was for "Mexican" gainful workers 10 years old and over. The data have been reclassified under major occupational categories used by the Bureau of the Census after 1930, on the basis of a table in E. P. Hutchinson, *Immigrants and Their Children* (New York: Wiley, 1966), appendix D.

ployed at piece-work rates. This was to be found in many aspects of South-western agriculture. Paul Taylor reports that in Colorado the practice prior to the First World War had been to import primarily male agricultural workers. During the 1920s, however, the practice changed to employing entire families. Apparently the companies felt that the families provided a more stable work force than single males, and could be relied on more to return year after year (Taylor, 1929, p. 134). Thus the 1930 census shows a fifth of Chicana workers employed as farm laborers. The proportion of women employed in agriculture was especially high in Colorado and Texas.

In the second situation, Chicanas were employed in jobs which were typed as particularly suitable for female labor. These included low-paid service jobs (domestics, waitresses) and jobs in laundries, garment factories, and food-processing plants. Most of these occupations can be seen as extensions of the kind of work women have traditionally done in the home.

Manuel Gamio, in his collection of biographical materials on Mexican immigrants published in 1931, describes the experiences of Dolores Sánchez after moving from Mexico to Los Angeles. She first goes to work cleaning an apartment building, but finds the work too tiring and low-paid. After some difficulty, she learns to operate an electric sewing machine and goes to work in a garment factory that employs only Chicanas and Mexicanas. There she earns $3 a day—$18 a week at piece-work rates. Anglo seamstresses in other factories are paid a minimum of $4 a day. By combining her wages with that of her husband, she is able to survive (Gamio, 1971a, p. 250).

The experience of Dolores Sánchez was common for Chicanas in the labor force. El Paso city directories indicate that Chicanas constituted over 75 percent of domestics and over 90 percent of laundresses in that city in 1920 (García, 1975b, p. 129). In Santa Barbara agriculture, Chicano males were relegated to the fields and the women to the packing houses (Camarillo, 1975b, p. 222). The 1930 census shows the greatest concentration of Chicanas in farm labor, as operatives (semiskilled workers) in the clothing, food, and laundry industries, and as domestics. The classification of many of these clothing, food, and laundry workers as operatives accounts for the fact that a higher proportion of Chicanas than Chicanos is listed as semiskilled workers in the census figures.

Alberto Camarillo, in his study of the Santa Barbara area, provides a comparison of the Chicano and Chicana occupational structure (table 10).

Knox, in his study of 1,550 Chicano families in San Antonio, found 16 percent of Chicanas working in the same types of jobs reported elsewhere: as domestics, in laundries, and in garment factories. A few were employed in stores, in a cigar factory, and as pecan shellers (Knox, 1971, pp. 23–24).

Chicana workers were, of course, affected by the same system of occupational stratification and dual wages that applied to all Chicanos. A hearing

TABLE 10

COMPARISON OF CHICANO AND CHICANA
OCCUPATIONAL STRUCTURE IN SANTA BARBARA,
1909-10 AND 1930 (PERCENTAGES)

	1909–1910		*1930*	
	M	F	M	F
Rancher/farmer	3.3	—	0.8	—
Professional	1.2	—	0.4	2.1
Proprietorial	1.7	—	2.9	2.1
Skilled	16.1	16.6	11.6	11.6
Semiskilled	25.2	16.6	21.8	28.7
Unskilled (incl. domestic)	40.7	66.7	49.2	55.5
Unknown	11.8	—	13.3	—

Source: Alberto Camarillo, "The Making of a Chicano Community" (1975), pp. 256, 259, 270, 271.

before the Texas Industrial Welfare Commission, held in El Paso in 1919, showed how the system applied to Chicanas. A laundry owner testified that Chicana and Mexicana workers were given the less desirable jobs in the plant, while more valued positions such as markers, sorters, checkers, and supervisors went to Anglo women. The Anglo employees received an average of $16.55 a week, while Chicanas were paid an average $6 a week. A department store owner verified that Anglo saleswomen were paid $37.50 to $40 a week, while Chicanas received $10 to $20 a week. This situation was apparently general throughout El Paso, and presumably in other Southwestern cities as well (García, 1975c, pp. 202-3).

At the same time, Chicanas as well as Anglo women were adversely affected by the practice of paying women less than men for the same kind of work. Data for individual plants in San Antonio and Dallas in the late 1920s clearly bring this out. The San Antonio Drug Company is listed as paying males $23.90 and females $13.30 per week for the same type of work. The San Antonio Steam Laundry paid men $35 and women $10.31. The corresponding wages at Sanger Brothers department store in Dallas were $34 and $22, and so on (Hufford, 1971, pp. 58-59). Racial and sexual subordination combined to place Chicana and Mexicana at the bottom of the occupational hierarchy.

A THEORETICAL REFORMULATION

A greater range of data is available for the first part of the twentieth century than for the nineteenth. On the basis of these data it is possible to extend and better interrelate some theoretical concepts that were introduced in chapter 3 for the purpose of reflecting the structural position of Chicanos in the political economy of the Southwest. The ultimate purpose is to base a theory of racial inequality on these concepts.

The concept of *class* has been used here in line with the general Marxist definition. Stated most simply, a class is a group of people who share a common position in the economy with respect to the means and the process of production (Dahrendorf, 1959, chap. 1). This is just an approximation of the Marxist concept of class, but it should serve to differentiate it from the more common American social science usage which defines classes as strata based on levels of income. (A more thorough discussion of class is presented in chapter 7.)

For purposes of the present analysis, the class structure of the United States in the early part of the century can be represented by a simplified diagram (see figure 3).

The most heterogeneous category in this diagram is the "middle" classes. For the sake of avoiding unnecessary complications, I will not subdivide it at this point, but a more extensive breakdown and discussion can be found in chapter 7. Most Chicanos, of course, were not in this category but in the various branches of the working class.

A second theoretical concept (introduced earlier) is the *economic "sector,"* which indicates the degree and nature of integration into the dominant economic system. The four sectors which were outlined are the peripheral, which is essentially outside the dominant system of economic relations in the

FIGURE 3

UNITED STATES CLASS STRUCTURE

Capitalists *(Employers of Labor)*	*"Middle" Classes*	*Working Class*
Industrial and agricultural	Small business	White collar
	Managers and supervisors	Blue collar
	Professionals and technicians	Agricultural
	Small farmers	Service

society; the marginal, which is incorporated into the dominant system but is largely superfluous to the economic needs of that system; the colonial, which is incorporated into the dominant system but on a subordinate basis; and the integrated, which refers to full integration into the economic system and its class structure on the basis of equality. The marginal sector can be seen as a kind of "underclass" in the society.

A third concept, which I would like to introduce at this point, is that of the *class segment*. The concept of the segment is borrowed from the literature on segmented labor markets, which posits that the modern capitalist labor market is segmented along several dimensions, among which are race and sex. Some reference was made to this in chapter 3, and an elaboration is contained in chapter 7. The argument I am making here is that segmented labor markets are in part a reflection of a broader social pattern, that of a segmented class system. The definition of a class segment can be put this way:

A class segment is a portion of a class which is set off from the rest of the class by some readily identifiable and relatively stable criterion, such as race, ethnicity, or sex, and whose status in relation to the means and process of production is affected by that demarcation.

A subordinate class segment in which the segmentation is based on race and/or ethnicity can be called a *colonized class segment*. Existence of a colonial labor force in the Southwest in the twentieth century is a reflection of the fact that Chicano (and other racial minority) workers have constituted such a colonized class segment. The five aspects of colonial labor (described earlier) represent the ways in which Chicano workers have been set off from the rest of the class by altering their relationship to the means and process of production.

The existence of class segmentation is reflected in other ways as well and not simply in a colonial labor system. Such related phenomena as political and educational subordination can be analyzed in this manner, and will be discussed later.

It should be made clear that class segmentation is not restricted to the working class. The concept can be applied equally well to the middle classes and to employers—assuming that racial minorities are represented at those levels and are set off from the rest of the class. In fact, the evidence is clear that racial class segmentation existed at the middle-class level. While there is little evidence at the employer level, there has obviously continued to be representation of Chicanos here as well, as in the case of the reduced *rico* group in New Mexico. Since they too occupied a subordinate position in the class system, colonial class segmentation could be said to occur across the entire class system.

This is not to say that all Chicanos should be classified as occupying a colonized class segment position. It is entirely possible for some members of a

FIGURE 4

CLASS, CLASS SEGMENT, AND COLONY

Capitalist Class	"Middle" Classes	Working Class
Chicano colonized class segment	Chicano colonized class segment	Chicano colonized class segment

Subordinate Chicano class segments together constitute an internal colony.

FIGURE 5

CLASS, RACIAL CLASS SEGMENT,
AND SEXUAL CLASS SEGMENT

	Capitalist Class	"Middle" Classes	Working Class
Chicano class segment	Chicano class segment	Chicano class segment
	Class segment based on sex	Class segment based on sex	Class segment based on sex

Class position of Chicanas

racial minority to constitute a class segment while others are integrated into the regular class structure or occupy marginal or peripheral positions. The existence of colonized class segments is always an empirical matter, and can only be determined through empirical investigation. Furthermore, the situation is a dynamic one, subject to changes with the passing of time. No group is frozen into a colonial class segment structure, and struggles against such a condition can make a considerable difference. Many other factors, of course, also enter in.

The discussion up to this point has been based on looking at the position of Chicanos within each class. However, there is another dimension to the Chicano social structure. The various Chicano colonized class segments do not live completely separate from each other, although class divisions are very real. The different class segments can be considered *together* to constitute an *internal colony,* a dimension of reality that cuts across class lines. This is viewing the same reality from a different perspective, one that takes into account the interrelationships and the commonalities among Chicanos in the various class segments. These would include economic relationships, such as exist where a Chicano merchant is restricted to selling to other Chicanos. They also include occupation of the same geographical space, the sharing of a common experience of discrimination, a shared language and other aspects of culture, and a sense of a common historical origin and destiny (the concept of "La Raza," etc.).

Neither of these ways of viewing the Chicano reality is more true than the other—the colony has a certain integral nature, but class divisions are also found within it. This accounts for seemingly contradictory behaviors in different circumstances, as when the same Chicanos who stand together on certain political and social issues (e.g., voting rights, bilingual education) divide along class lines on others (e.g., certain struggles for "community control"). The concept of the internal colony will be further developed in chapter 7. For the time being, the two dimensions of reality outlined above can be diagrammed as in figure 4.

Another dimension of subordination that can be related to those above is sex. Chicanas in the labor force generally find themselves in not one but two subordinate class segments, one based on race and another on sex. Their place in the occupational structure can be seen as representing a kind of intersection or overlap of the two kinds of class segments. In figure 5 this area of overlap is indicated by shading.

In figure 5 the placing of the Chicano class segments above those of class segments based on sex is not intended to indicate that one is less subordinate than the other. Both types of class segments are subordinate in nature, and their interaction serves to place the Chicana in an even more disadvantaged position than is held by persons who fall into one but not both kinds of segments.

CHAPTER 5

The Contemporary Period

THE CONTEMPORARY PERIOD of Chicano economic history may be said to start with the Great Depression, which marked the end of a period of economic expansion and large-scale immigration from Mexico. At the same time, it set in motion certain forces in the American political economy that have resulted, in the post-Depression years, in important changes in the economic status of Chicanos, particularly in terms of a greater integration into the class structure. At this point it is still not clear whether the decade of the 1970s represents a possible reversal of these trends or simply a slowing down in the rate of change.

This chapter begins with the Depression decade, continues with an examination of the period 1940 to 1970, and concludes with a tentative analysis of the seventies.

THE DEPRESSION

The major economic dislocations of the Depression are well known: a substantial drop in the level of economic activity, dramatic declines in wage rates in industry and agriculture, and a decline in the length of the average workweek. These conditions lasted throughout the decade, appearing to improve in the mid-1930s and worsening again with the recession of 1937, although not all the way to the previous lows. There were other economic trends as well which had a substantial impact on industries in which Chicanos were concentrated. In agriculture, the concentration of the land into larger and larger units continued and the ties between agriculture and other business sectors continued to draw closer (McWilliams, 1942, p. 25). A parallel process of concentration occurred in the mining industry. In copper, for example, three firms—Anaconda, Kennecott and Phelps-Dodge—controlled 80 percent of the national output by 1940, compared to 40 percent ten years earlier (Nash, 1973, p. 167). Federal policies during the period did nothing to halt this trend toward concentration. In California during the 1930s, some 44 percent of federal benefit payments made to agricultural concerns went to less than 2 percent of the largest farms (ibid., p. 161).

The mechanization of agriculture (another trend predating the Depression) continued to displace agricultural labor. By the late 1930s machines were used extensively in cultivating produce, and were becoming significant in cotton and sugar beets as well (McWilliams, 1968, p. 187, and 1971, p. 274).

The Southwest during this period continued to differ from the rest of the nation in its concentration of economic activities in agriculture and the extractive industries, with manufacturing still lagging behind.

While the Great Depression affected everyone, it had a specific impact on Chicanos and others who found themselves in a subordinate position in the economy. Some of the effects of the Depression were felt immediately, while others took time to work themselves out through indirect routes. The immediate effects consisted of a worsening of the position of Chicano/Mexicano workers, particularly through two aspects of subordinate segmentation that have been described earlier: the reserve role and the buffer role that racial minorities have been called upon to play. Both aspects were related to the high levels of unemployment that existed during the 1930s.

In this case, the reserve role manifested itself in a campaign to ship Mexicano workers back to Mexico as a way of decreasing unemployment and lightening relief rolls. As Kiser puts it,

> The Depression led American employers of Mexicans to re-evaluate their position. The employers who had long exerted successful pressure to keep cheap Mexican labor no longer felt the need for it because the domestic pool of surplus labor willing to work for low wages reached enormous size. [Kiser, 1972, p. 134]

As Abraham Hoffman pointed out in his carefully detailed study, the idea that the Depression could be cured by getting rid of alien workers and giving their jobs to Anglos was current during that decade, although it had little basis in fact (Hoffman, 1974, p. 40). During the 1970s, we have witnessed strikingly similar proposals being offered as remedies for the persistently high rate of unemployment.

The movement to return Mexicanos to the reserve took two forms, deportation and repatriation. During the early 1930s the federal government carried on a highly publicized drive to apprehend and deport aliens who could not produce documents to demonstrate that they were in the country legally. In southern California, the drive centered on Los Angeles (Hoffman, 1974, p. 41). From 1931 on, the main efforts were directed toward locally sponsored "repatriation" drives in which people were provided transportation and encouraged to leave the county, but without legal compulsion as under deportation proceedings. The most intensive of these campaigns was in Los Angeles County, although there were similar drives in many other areas of the Southwest and Midwest. Hoffman estimates that from 1929 to 1935 the federal government removed by deportation or voluntary departure (under threat of deportation) over 80,000 Mexicanos. The repatriation drives removed many more, for an estimated total of some half-million persons of Mexican origin during that seven-year period (ibid., p. 126).

How many who left were actually American citizens is difficult to determine, although it is clear that many of the children had been born in the United States and thus were citizens. While it is true that the bulk of these left "voluntarily," Hoffman notes that "the pressure on the Mexican community from the deportation campaign contributed significantly to the huge repatriation from Los Angeles that followed the antialien drive" (ibid., p. 65). The ironic injustice of the situation is perhaps best summed up in Grebler's statement: "Only a few years earlier, many of those now ejected had been actively recruited by American enterprises" (Grebler, 1966, p. 29). In Texas, the Mexican-born population dropped nearly 40 percent from 1930 to 1940 (Connor, 1971, p. 350).

The drives to return Mexicanos to their homeland was accompanied by restrictions on new immigration to the United States. These restrictions were put into practice primarily through federal administrative regulations rather than new legislation (Divine, 1957, pp. 77–84).

Those Chicanos and Mexicanos who remained continued to be used as regional and local labor reserves throughout the Southwest. The Colorado sugar beet industry continued to recruit seasonal workers from New Mexico and Arizona to maintain a labor surplus, although apparently at a reduced rate (McWilliams, 1942, p. 114). The growers in that area could also continue to rely on local Chicano residents for their seasonal labor requirements. The complicity of the state bureaucracy in perpetuating and regulating this pattern is indicated in the following quote.

> As with other crops, growers exerted pressure on the relief authorities to make sure that their workers would be forced off relief in time for them to thin beets. In 1938, for instance, the director of the Colorado WPA asserted that it was customary for his organization to lay off men with Spanish and Mexican names each spring on the assumption that they were beet laborers and should be out in the fields. [Schwartz, 1945, p. 117]

Writing of the same period for the southern Texas Winter Garden area, Selden Menefee notes that

> both growers and contractors desire to see the Mexican colony in Crystal City maintained at its present size, in spite of increasing slackness of employment during the spinach season, as insurance against a possible future labor shortage. [Menefee, 1941, p. 18]

The use of Chicanos and Mexicanos as a buffer in the economy was also highlighted during the Depression. In Southwestern agriculture, Chicanos

A mining crew in Metcalf, Arizona.

Workers at the extracting furnace of the Waldron, Texas, mercury mine in 1916.

*A train carrying families being repatriated to Mexico pulls out of
Los Angeles in 1931.*

A portion of a panoramic photograph of Mexican workers in San Antonio Texas, taken in 1924. The original caption reads, "The C. Campa labor agency & W.J. Lewis, of Alamo City Employment Agency, distributing bread three times a day to Mexicans who are in distress waiting to be sent to a job."

Shelling pecans by hand in San Antonio, Texas, in the 1930s.

Field worker in Coachella Valley of California, 1935.

In 1935, Dorothea Lange took this portrait of a Mexican laborer in the Imperial Valley. Her notes comment, "He helped drive the French out of Mexico, fought against Maximilian, and has helped by serving the crops for many years, building up the valley."

(Courtesy of the Dorothea Lange Collection, Oakland Museum, Oakland, Ca.)

Mexican labor off to the melon fields in California's Imperial Valley, 1935.

(Courtesy of the Library of Congress)

Agricultural laborers arriving from Mexico to help in harvesting beets during the Second World War (Stockton, California, 1943).

(Courtesy of the Library of Congress)

San Bernardino, California, 1943. Chicana "suppliers" for incoming trains.

(Courtesy of the Library of Congress)

were displaced from their traditional low-paid jobs by newly destitute local Anglos and the new wave of Dust Bowl migrants who were such a prominent part of the labor scene in the 1930s. Mark Reisler estimates that in the second half of the decade over 350,000 adults entered California from other parts of the country, seeking employment, many of them from the Dust Bowl states of Oklahoma, Kansas, Texas, Arkansas, and Missouri.

> By the mid-1930's Mexicans were no longer the backbone of California's agricultural labor force. In 1936 an estimated 85% to 90% of the state's migratory labor supply consisted of white Americans, as compared to less than 20% prior to the depression. [Reisler, 1976, p. 247]

The same trend appeared in Colorado agriculture, where in one region Chicano fruit pickers were replaced by migrants from the Dust Bowl (McWilliams, 1942, p. 115). The same was true with Arizona cotton, where the trend began even earlier (Brown and Cassmore, 1939, p. 66).

James Officer, in his historical account of Tucson, notes that the local Chicano population was acutely aware that during the Depression the tendency to make the Chicano "the last one hired and the first one fired" was strongly accentuated (Officer, 1960, p. 15).

In California, Arizona, and Texas, laws were passed during the Depression stipulating that American citizens were to be hired for construction and public works jobs. "Although these measures applied to all aliens, in the Southwest they were designed to bar Mexicans from the unskilled construction jobs which they had held for well over a decade. As a result of this discriminatory legislation, contractors often refused to hire Mexicans for private construction jobs as well as public projects" (Reisler, 1976, p. 228).

Closely connected to both of these labor segmentation phenomena was a curious role reversal that took place in some parts of the Southwest for a short period. As the Depression spurred organizing efforts among Chicano and Mexicano agricultural laborers, the desperate Dust Bowl migrants were at times used as strikebreakers against them by the employers (McWilliams, 1942, p. 40).

Chicanos and Mexicanos who managed to stay in the Southwest and to hold on to jobs found themselves in the unenviable position of remaining at the bottom of an economy in crisis. The situation in agriculture remained one of rigid occupational stratification, or as Carey McWilliams stated succinctly, "after years of residence in Colorado, Mexican sugar-beet workers remain Mexican sugar-beet workers" (McWilliams, 1942, p. 119). In Texas, a 1937 survey showed that approximately 85 percent of the migratory agricultural workers were Chicano and Mexicano (Menefee and Cassmore, 1940, p. 26). A similar situation could be found in the urban areas. In her account of the Los Angeles textile factory scene in the '30s, labor organizer Rose Pesotta noted that about 75 percent of textile employees were Chicanas, who were preferred by employers because they could be more easily exploited (Pesotta, 1944, p. 21). The Los Angeles factories were flagrant violators of New Deal legislation aimed at providing some protection for the workers (ibid., p. 40).

The pecan shelling industry of San Antonio provides an interesting case study for this period. The industry, which had been partly mechanized at one time, reverted to hand work during the Depression, "when the presence of a large amount of cheap Mexican labor caused wages to be driven so low as to make handwork profitable once more" (Menefee and Cassmore, 1940, p. x). This was the leading industry in employment in the city, with some 8,000 Chicano men, women, and children working for 5¢ an hour in 1938. As the authors of one study noted, "The better paid jobs in San Antonio are held for the most part by white Americans of European stock" (ibid., p. 30). The passing of the Fair Labor Standards Act in 1938, with its minimum-wage and other provisions, led to widespread attempts at evasion, and then to the remechanization of the industry (ibid., p. 19). Many of the city's Chicanos were forced on relief or public works programs. As of 1939, over half the workers in the San Antonio area Works Progress Administration programs were Chicano, although Chicanos were at most 40 percent of the population (ibid., p. 40).

The plight of Chicanos was particularly acute in rural and nonindustrialized areas such as northern New Mexico, where there were few sources of employment. Here one can see in microcosm forces that were at work throughout the Southwest, as well as the continuation of earlier trends, as a number of studies of Hispano village life in the 1930s indicate. Apparently, as the job situation tightened, a number of villagers who had gravitated to employment outside the village found themselves out of work and attempted to return to the land. The economic base of the villages had been so undercut by agricultural capitalist interests in league with federal reclamation projects that they for the most part were no longer viable (Leonard and Loomis, 1941, pp. 6–7; Walter, 1939, p. 154). A great number of the villagers were forced to survive on a combination of garden plots and government relief programs. According to one estimate, 60 percent of the villagers were forced into some type of relief program (Walter, 1939, p. 152). The federal WPA jobs that many were compelled to rely on provided survival, but at an even lower standard of living than the "outside" jobs that many had secured in the 1920s. Many attempted to escape from that situation by leaving the villages, with mixed results.

> The combination of threats to the old village life has brought thousands of refugees to the suburban villages surrounding the growing urban centers of the state, especially Albuquerque, Santa Fe, and Las Vegas. Here they attempt to readjust by entering the prevailing American wage economy, but so far the effort has met with a discouraging incidence of

failure. New Mexico is not an industrial state, and only in relatively "boom" times, such as in the 1920's is there an expanding labor demand. For what little wage work these urban communities offer, the competition is great. In this competition, the Spanish-speaking worker invariably is maneuvered into a marginal position. He is the last to be employed, the first to be laid off, and his work, is always that which commands the least pay. [Ibid., p. 156].

While there are few references to dual wage systems in the literature dealing with Chicano workers in the '30s and we may presume that the practice was weakening, it continued in force in at least some areas. Thus a study of women in Texas industries in 1931 and 1932 states:

The survey disclosed that Mexican women were receiving very much lower wages than white women, even when working side by side in the same occupation and establishment. [Sullivan and Blair, 1936, p. 5]

Over half of the Spanish-speaking women surveyed were employed in clothing establishments and laundry plants. A computation for factories, stores, and laundries found the median earning of Anglo women to be $8.75 per week, Chicanas $5.85, and black women $5.95 (ibid., p. 14). The authors provided a number of individual cases to illustrate the conditions of these workers. A 19-year-old Chicana woman, quoted as saying "Can't live on what I make; the prices are lower each time I get a bundle [of sewing]. What can I do?" was living with a tubercular mother and unemployed sister. Her earnings were the family's only income, and she was paid at the rate of not quite 3¢ an hour, or $1.25 a week (ibid., p. 76).

Labor Struggles

The economic position of Chicanos and Mexicanos was primarily determined by the structure of the Southwestern political economy and by the practices pursued by the large employers and their governmental allies. This, however, does not mean that these workers were passive in the face of their obvious subordination. A number of classic accounts (Taylor, 1928; McWilliams, 1971; Jamieson, 1945) have described the efforts made by Chicano and Mexicano workers to organize and carry out labor struggles in this period, and a new generation of labor historians is now attempting to chronicle these events in a more systematic manner.

While the 1930s was a period of intense labor activity, labor conflicts and union organizing had begun much earlier. Around the turn of the century, Chicano workers had combined with Japanese workers to form a labor association in the Oxnard, California, area and to carry out a strike (in 1903) against the practices of the Western Agricultural Contracting Company (Gómez-Quiñones, 1972, pp. 24–25). In the same year, Chicano trackmen in Los

Angeles organized the Mexican Federal Union and engaged in a strike against the Pacific Electric Railway and the Los Angeles Railway (ibid., pp. 26-27).

Around the same time, the Federal Labor Union was formed in the Laredo, Texas, area as an umbrella union for Chicano railway workers. This union, formed on socialist trade union principles, carried out a successful strike in 1906 in which the differential treatment of Chicano and Anglo workers was a central theme (Zamora, 1975, pp. 223-24). In 1915 a massive strike occurred in Arizona against the Clifton, Morenci, and Metcalf mines, where Chicanos and Mexicanos represented over 70 percent of the labor force and were instrumental in organizing the strike (Gómez-Quiñones, 1972, p. 31). A key demand of that struggle was the elimination of the dual wage system.

In the late 1920s a new surge of Chicano labor activity began which was to carry over strongly into the 1930s. The first permanent Chicano/Mexicano union in the Imperial Valley of California was formed in 1928, and participated in a number of strike actions in the early years of the Depression (Weber, 1972, p. 313). In her article surveying these activities, Weber has shown the central influence of Mexican/Chicano ideologies and patterns of organizing for the period 1928 to 1934 (ibid., pp. 310ff.). Nelson Cisneros has surveyed Chicano working-class activities in Texas from 1920 to 1940, indicating the upsurge of unionism and militant strike activity in agriculture during the 1930s (Nelson Cisneros, 1975, p. 243). Labor unrest in the countryside reached its peak in 1933, as the position of agricultural workers continued to deteriorate. It was during the 1930s that the Catholic Workers Union was formed in Crystal City, Texas, as well as the Laredo-based Agricultural Worker's Union (ibid., pp. 247-48). In 1937 the Chicano/Mexicano Texas Agricultural Worker's Organizing Committee was absorbed into the CIO's United Cannery, Agricultural, Packing and Allied Workers of America (UCAPAWA) Union. This organization carried out a number of strikes but did not survive beyond the Depression decade (ibid., pp. 249-50).

One of the most dramatic agricultural labor struggles of the decade took place in the El Monte, California, berry fields in 1933, under the leadership of the Confederación de Uniones de Campesionos y Obreros (CUCOM). Most of the workers involved were Chicanos, Mexicanos, and Filipinos (López, 1970, pp. 102, 109). The strike spread to nearby areas and eventually enlisted an estimated 5,000 workers. The strike resulted in limited wage gains.

One of the significant effects of the wave of agricultural unrest that peaked in 1933 was to call into being a counteroffensive by the growers and their allies. The repressive activities of the newly formed Associated Farmers of California after 1934 has been outlined by Carey McWilliams in some detail (McWilliams, 1971, pp. 230ff.) and was one of the factors that accounted for the decline in militant union activity in the fields in the latter part of the decade.

Valuable as these activities were for continuing the tradition of struggle that has existed among Chicanos since the Mexican American War, the overall impact on their immediate economic situation was limited. The conclusion of Nelson Cisneros with respect to Texas could be applied to other parts of the Southwest as well:

> The . . . description of the social and economic conditions of Chicanos in Texas during the period 1920–1940 indicates that trade unionism was one potential mechanism to alleviate their exploitation. In the instances that unions were formed, Chicanos sometimes gained immediately from this activity, but on the whole, these gains were limited and did not attack the basic causes of the problem: namely, the relegation of the Chicano to the lowest paid positions and the most dehumanizing forms of labor in a capitalist system. [Nelson Cisneros, 1975, p. 259]

Laying the Basis for Change

On the surface, the 1930s marked (if anything) a step backward for Chicanos and a strengthening of the segmentation boundary that relegated them to the bottom of the class system. However, important changes were taking place in the structure of the American political economy that were to have an important although largely indirect impact on the status of Chicanos and other minorities.

The most important of these trends was the much greater integration of government and economy that took place in that decade. This process, of course, had been going on for some time. James Weinstein and Gabriel Kolko have documented the way in which the most progressive sector of big business took the lead in encouraging a strong government role in the economy during the first two decades of the century, as a means of gaining stability and heading off radical challenges (Weinstein, 1968; Kolko, 1967). The development of the Federal Trade Commission, created in 1914, was a response by these business leaders and their political representatives to the insecurity and uncertainty produced by antitrust litigation (Weinstein, 1968, chap. 3). Nevertheless, the crisis of capitalism that was created by the Great Depression accelerated these trends, as did the external crisis produced subsequently by the Second World War.

As the government assumed greater responsibility for regulating and stimulating the economy, management of the relationship between capital and labor came increasingly into its orbit. Large American business enterprises had been fighting a tenacious battle against unionization for decades, and they had been largely successful through the 1920s by using a wide variety of tactics which included repression, paternalistic "welfare work," and company unions. David Brody has argued that the paternalistic welfare capitalism of the 1920s was strong, and that the open shop might have remained a permanent feature of American capitalism if the Great Depression had not come along (Brody, 1972, p. 243). As the New Deal administration under Roosevelt sought to carry out its mandate to preserve American capitalism through reform, the regularization of labor relations through the recognition of labor unions was put on the political agenda. While individual employers in many cases continued to resist unionization, the resistance was generally short-lived and the longer-range view of what was good for the system came to prevail.

The first major effort under the New Deal was embodied in the National Industrial Recovery Act of 1933, whose Section 7(a) encouraged workers to form unions and bargain collectively. This section of the act was declared unconstitutional in 1935, but the National Labor Relations Act (Wagner Act), passed in the same year, guaranteed the right to organize and bargain collectively. It also strengthened the enforcement powers of the National Labor Relations Board, which had been established earlier and was now empowered to issue cease and desist orders against employers engaged in unfair labor practices (Perry and Perry, 1963, p. 314). This act was declared constitutional in 1937, and labor had gained a vital foothold in American industry. Its position was further strengthened by the necessity for labor peace imposed by World War II, and by the mid-1940s most large industrial employers had been unionized.

Adding to the significance of this development was the change that had taken place in the nature of unionism itself. Whereas in earlier periods the union movement had been dominated by conservative and narrowly based craft unions, the founding of the Congress of Industrial Organizations (CIO) in 1935 signaled the coming of broadly based industrial unions. Since there were few Chicanos in the skilled trades on which the craft unions were based, the emergence of the more inclusive labor organizations made the unionization movement far more significant in racial terms.

To the extent these developments were beneficial, however, the benefits were not immediately apparent. The short-term impact of government regulations of industry could be quite negative on Chicanos. As noted above, the minimum-wage provisions of the Fair Labor Standards Act caused many of San Antonio's pecan shellers to lose their jobs. Those who remained were much better off, but those who were laid off in favor of mechanization lost what was in many cases their only opportunity for employment, miserable as that was.

The other major trend that provided a basis for change was the continued move to the urban areas. While it is difficult to make any statements about the magnitude of this shift because the 1940 census provided no method of identifying Chicanos, it seems clear that such a movement was taking place. In California, the displacement of Chicanos from agricultural labor left them little recourse but to move to the cities. In New Mexico, the erosion of village life produced a shift of the Hispano population to urban areas, as is borne out by the quotes above. According to Paul Walter, many Hispanos occupied an in-between or transitional position in that they continued to maintain their residence in the villages but worked in the cities. A number of these workers occupied skilled positions and earned union wages, indicating that they were in the process of being absorbed into the regular class structure, although the process was by no means complete (Walter, 1938, pp. 222, 225).

THE 1940s, '50s, AND '60s

A typology of four economic "sectors" was presented in chapter 3, consisting of the peripheral, colonized, marginal, and integrated. This categorization can be used to describe and analyze the changes that have been taking place in the economic situation of Chicanos. The *peripheral* sector is an essentially meaningless category for the contemporary period, as all parts of the Southwest have been effectively integrated into the United States economy. In my view, the developments in recent decades can be summarized as a diminution of the *colonial* sector, the growth of an *integrated* sector, and a reemergence of a significant *marginal* sector. Seen in terms of the class segmentation model outlined in chapter 4, these developments represent a weakening of the racial segmentation barrier combined with the appearance of a group which can only be described as largely outside the class structure.

The Colonial Sector

It should be clear that the existence of economic subordination is not an absolute matter. Degrees of subordination exist, so that it is possible not simply to classify a worker as in the colonized sector but to describe to what extent he or she is subjected to economic inequality based on race. With respect to the working class, for example, five aspects of economic subordination were identified earlier: captive labor, dual wages, occupational stratification, the reserve role, and the buffer role. In the twentieth century, some of these aspects have significantly diminished or been eliminated, while others continue to play an important role. Thus we may still want to describe some Chicanos as in the colonized sector, while recognizing that the degree of colonization has lessened over time.

It may be that the existence of a colonized sector during the contemporary period is still easier to see in the rural than in the urban economy. For various reasons, the greater integration of the economy with the state that has occurred in recent times has not produced equal protection for rural and urban workers, and thus rural employers have been able to continue manipulating racial and other divisions among their workers with relative ease. The fact that agricultural workers are still excluded from coverage under the National Labor Relations Act and thus do not have the right to bargain collectively has meant that, for the most part, agricultural employers have not had to contend with recognized unions. This means that their hiring and promotion practices have not had to accommodate themselves to union seniority policies and the like. In addition, the circumstance that many of the large agricultural employers have continued to have a high proportion of their labor force made up of minority workers has given them a relatively high stake in maintaining a system of racial subordination. As Padfield and Martin maintain with respect to Arizona:

> Although Arizona agriculture has never depended upon monopolistic institutions such as slavery, sharecropping, or peonage, it has historically relied upon noncompetitive labor either in the form of labor surplus, or highly mobile, unsophisticated immigrant populations. The whole cost structure of Southwestern agriculture in general is based upon this structure. [Padfield and Martin, 1965, p. 253]

Over the years, reliance on racial minorities for agricultural labor has been a major factor in allowing employers to retain a structure of very low wages. Even while an overt dual wage system has tended to die out, the effect of this wage depression on all agricultural workers continues to make itself felt. The median earning of White male farm laborers in the five Southwestern states in 1970 was only $3,333, and that of males characterized by the Census Bureau as "Spanish American" was $3,123 (Ryscavage and Mellor, 1973, p. 6). While the difference between the two groups is not large, the important point to keep in mind is that the presence of large numbers of racial minorities in agriculture (e.g., 42 percent of California farm workers are Chicano [Briggs, 1973, p. 23]) has been an important factor in allowing employers to keep wages down for all workers. Since minority workers are a disproportionate part of the agricultural labor force, they suffer disproportionately from this situation.

During this period, occupational stratification has continued to be a prominent aspect of the agricultural labor structure. Ozzie Simmons describes the situation in Texas' Lower Rio Grande Valley in the early 1950s:

> Field and shed labor have been supplied by the Mexicans since the beginning of the Valley's development so that the present division of labor is regarded as partaking of the nature of things. The stigma attached to labor role functions by the Anglo is indicated by the statement of an Anglo packer who said that he could not employ Anglos as shed workers because "these guys are ashamed to work in a packing shed."

That unskilled labor is Mexican labor is borne out by the fact that Anglo Americans are always placed in positions which require even slight skill and responsibility. All the checkers and counters of incoming harvest loads and of piece production in the packing sheds and canneries . . . are Anglo Americans, as are the semi-supervisory personnel in these places. [Simmons, 1952, p. 205]

A more recent and sophisticated study of farm labor in Arizona shows an interesting evolution in this situation. This 1962 sample of farm workers consisted of 30 percent Mexican Americans, 10 percent Mexican immigrants, 35 percent Anglos, and smaller percentages of Blacks, Native Americans, and Filipinos (Padfield and Martin, 1965, p. 147). The authors identify various farm labor "subcultures," of which the most significant are the following. The *Anglo-Aggregate* farm group consisted of Anglo workers who lived in some sort of family group. "Its participants occupy the top supervisory positions. They operate the most expensive and complicated machinery. They are the most highly paid of all farm workers. For all intents and purposes they are industrial workers" (ibid., p. 180).

The *Mexican-American* farm group are "those farm workers of Mexican descent who are American citizens or who have immigration papers to become citizens (green carders). They comprise the largest single subculture in Arizona agriculture" (ibid., p. 181).

The *Anglo-Isolate* farm group were social isolates in that they did not live in families. Generally they were older and middle-aged men who were social and vocational rejects and who occupied low occupational positions on the farm. This was a larger group than the Anglo-Aggregate.

The Anglo workers thus were divided into two major groups, one of which was heavily represented in the higher farm occupational positions and one of which was almost exclusively confined to the lowest (ibid., pp. 177–279). The Mexican-American group was described in the following terms:

Mexican-Americans are an integral part of the Arizona farm technological system. The technological role of the Mexican-American group is that of workhorse of the Arizona farm technological system. They are the backbone of the farm labor supply at all occupational levels. [Ibid., p. 277]

This group was an important component at all occupational levels, including the supervisory.

While the situation in the various Arizona crops varied considerably, that in cotton seems to be the most typical and the best indicator of prevailing trends in Southwestern agriculture. Here the original situation was one of heavy reliance on stoop labor performed largely by Chicanos and other minorities. As mechanization gradually took place, a new class of machine operators came into being, composed primarily of Anglos.

In cotton the groups gradually being displaced by machines—Indians, Negroes, and Mexican-Americans—began moving up in the occupational class systems to eventually take over machine operators' jobs. To be sure, many thousands of individual seasonal workers have been put out of work in cotton altogether. But the sociologically important point is that today it is common to see non-Anglo machine operators. In the late forties, when picking machines were introduced, this sight was rare. [Ibid., pp. 285–86]

Thus while the system of occupational stratification could still be seen in operation in Arizona agriculture in the 1960s, it was clearly somewhat weakened in comparison with earlier periods.

Another aspect of the colonized sector from 1940 to the present had to do with the *reserve role,* and it could be argued that this has been the most significant aspect during this period. There are several dimensions to this aspect, including the *bracero* program, the border commuter worker, the undocumented worker from Mexico, and the migratory labor pattern. The impact of these factors is by no means confined to the rural economy, but the impact there is certainly concentrated. As pointed out repeatedly in the literature, Southwestern farmers have consciously sought to maintain a labor surplus. Padfield and Martin in their discussion of Arizona agriculture describe a "labor-obsessed industry which, in the midst of labor surpluses created by automation in other industries, fears a shortage of labor amenable to the peculiar controls upon which their present economics are based" (ibid., p. 254). In the discussion of the 1930s (above), the efforts of growers in the Texas Winter Garden area to maintain a Chicano labor surplus were cited. In a study based on the 1970s experience of Crystal City, which is in that area, another writer noted indications that employer groups in that city were interested not in attracting industry generally, but only those types of industries which were dependent on cheap and non-union labor, so as not to compete unfairly for their surplus labor supply (Shockley, 1974, p. 179).

A highly significant chapter in this story of reserve labor began in the early 1940s with the demands on labor supply created by World War II. As many of their workers moved into better-paying industrial jobs, agricultural employers in the Southwest began agitating for the importation of Mexican workers, and this resulted in the initiation of the bracero program in 1942, under which large numbers of Mexicans were brought in on temporary contracts supervised by the American government. Harry Schwartz notes that "for the latter . . . this represented an ironical 360-degree turn of the wheel: importation in the 1920's; repatriation or deportation in the 1930's; importation once again in the 1940's" (Schwartz, 1945, p. 63).

The program was started as a wartime expedient under an executive agreement between the United States and Mexican governments. However, it was extended after the war, and formalized in 1951 as Public Law 78 under the pressure of a labor shortage created by yet another war, this time in Korea. Conceived as a temporary measure, it was again extended until its demise in 1964 (see table 11). The impact of this program on the United States was substantial. In 1945, 58,000 braceros were to be found in American agriculture, with another 62,000 working on the railroads (Galarza, 1964, p. 53). The use of braceros in railroads was terminated in 1946, largely because of the political pressure generated by the major railway workers union (Lawrence, 1977).

In agriculture, however, the use of braceros continued to increase after the war. The year 1959 saw the bracero program at its peak, with almost 450,000 imported in that year (ibid., p. 79). Braceros tended to be concentrated in California, Texas, Arizona, and New Mexico, with significant amounts also in Arkansas and Colorado. Nevertheless, one student of the program estimates that in the late 1950s no less than 10 percent of the annual man-days of farm wage work in the United States was performed by braceros (Elac, 1972, p. 73). In 1960 they comprised 26 percent of the seasonal hired labor force in U.S. agriculture (Galarza 1964, p. 94).

TABLE 11

NUMBERS OF BRACEROS IMPORTED INTO
THE UNITED STATES, 1942-64

Year	Total	Year	Total
1942	4,203	1954	310,476
1943	52,098	1955	390,846
1944	62,170	1956	444,581
1945	49,454	1957	450,422
1946	32,043	1958	418,885
1947	19,632	1959	447,535
1948	33,288	1960	427,240
1949	143,455	1961	294,149
1950	76,519	1962	282,556
1951	211,098	1963	195,450
1952	187,894	1964	181,738
1953	198,424		

Source: Samora, "Mexican Immigration," in Gus Tyler, ed., *Mexican-Americans Tomorrow* (1975), p. 72.

Galarza, in his classic study of the bracero, notes that various advantages accrued to the growers. The bracero program represented a planned and orderly process of labor recruitment. Public funds were spent in initiating and implementing the program, and the workers thus recruited were under contractual obligation to stay on the farm rather than migrate to urban employment, as other workers often did. At the end of the contractual period, they would be sent back to Mexico. The program also provided for a complicated wage-setting mechanism that worked to the advantage of the growers (Galarza, 1964, pp. 44-45, 135ff.; President's Commission on Migratory Labor, 1951, pp. 59-60). Whereas, technically, growers were not supposed to be eligible for braceros unless they were suffering from a labor shortage, in practice they were able to set wages low enough to discourage domestic workers from applying and thus create a labor shortage which allowed them to be certified under the provisions of the program (Craig, 1971, p. 67). In addition, and perhaps most importantly, the bracero program represented a use of the Mexican labor reserve to undercut attempts at farm unionization, especially by the National Farm Labor Union and its successor, the National Agricultural Workers Union, which were active in California during this time (Galarza, 1977, p. 204).

The benefits from the bracero program were disproportionately appropriated by the large growers, since they were the ones to hire the bulk of this labor. In the late 1950s, over 94 percent of the braceros went to some 50,000 growers in five states, and over 98 percent of the nation's commercial farmers received no braceros (Hawley, 1966, p. 157). The various adverse effects— which were not supposed to happen but did—were borne by others. Domestic workers were displaced from jobs; farm wages in California showed a downward trend; housing for workers on the farms deteriorated; and unions experienced even greater difficulties in organizing in the countryside (Galarza, 1964, pp. 204-17).

In spite of the fact that only a limited number of growers benefited from the program, they were remarkably successful in extending it far beyond the period envisioned in the beginning. The employers, through astute coalition building and symbolic manipulation, were able to apply sufficient pressure at key political points to keep the program alive time and again (Hawley, 1966, pp. 157ff.). Its eventual expiration was the product of a number of factors. One was the effort made by the Department of Labor in the late 1950s to curb some of the worst abuses associated with the bracero program. Another was the coming to power in 1960 of a national administration more attuned to the needs and demands of domestic labor, which had become increasingly mobilized against the program (Craig, 1971, pp. 153, 157). But added to these factors was the important fact that alternatives were available to the growers. Cotton growers, who had long employed the largest number of braceros, were able to mechanize their operations, which they accomplished at a rapid rate in the late 1950s and early 1960s—to the point where 70 percent of all U.S. cotton was mechanically harvested in 1962 (ibid., p. 180). In addition, undocumented workers from Mexico, variously referred to by several unsavory terms such as "wetbacks" and "illegal aliens," had been in use all along and had even been used by growers as political leverage. In this connection, Galarza notes:

> The labor policy of commercial farmers and their associations consisted, on the one hand, of keeping the bracero machinery in working order and constantly striving to bring it more in line with their views; and on the other, of maintaining a substantial demand for wetbacks as a counterweight until such time as unresponsive or ignorant federal officials might come to reason. [Galarza, 1964, p. 57]

While the braceros and the undocumented workers have been the most important elements in the use of Mexican labor in the Southwest in recent decades, they do not exhaust the possibilities for the inventive spirit of the agricultural employers and their governmental allies. During the late 1940s and early 1950s for example, it was common practice for "wetbacks" to be "dried out" by the Immigration Service and returned to their employers as braceros. From 1947 to 1949, 74,000 braceros were contracted directly from Mexico while 142,000 "wetbacks" were "dehydrated" (Craig, 1971, p. 67). This practice was later limited by Public Law 78.

Another practice, which has only recently received attention, is the hiring by Southwestern employers of persons who live in Mexico and commute to work. Some of these commuters are American citizens and some are Mexican citizens who hold "white cards," allowing visits of no longer than 72 hours. These latter are not technically eligible for work in the United States. The greatest number of these commuters, however, are the so-called "green-carders," who are classified by the American government as resident immigrants even though they may actually live in Mexico. The classification of such persons as resident immigrants is a convenient fiction, intended to suit the interests of Southwestern employers.

David North, in the most comprehensive recent study of these commuters, feels that an estimate of 100,000 persons' crossing the Mexican border to work in the United States is a conservative figure (North, 1970, p. 30). Most of these border crossers are green-card holders. He makes reference to this group as "this generation's bracero," although that may be overstating the situation to some extent, and underplaying the role of the undocumented worker. Another writer cites a Labor Department survey of 1961 that found 15 percent of Laredo's workers to be commuters from Mexico, and this is considered an underestimate because many commuters adopt a fictional local address (Jones, 1965, p. 47).

The Laredo study found that commuters were employed in a wide range of occupations, "with concentrations in garment, hotel, restaurant, retail, wholesale, and service activities" (ibid.). A substantial number were employed in office and clerical jobs at very low wages (ibid., p. 65). A private 1969 survey of 400 green-card commuters also found a considerable range of employment, with 39 percent employed as unskilled labor in agriculture, 16 percent in nondomestic service jobs, 5 percent as semiskilled garment operators, 8 percent in clerical, managerial, and sales positions, and so on (North, 1970, p. 111).

The benefits to the border employers from using commuter labor are in line with those deriving more generally from a reserve labor force. Commuter labor tends to drive down wages along most of the border area, as Lamar Jones documents for Laredo (Jones, 1965, p. 49). There has also been extensive use of commuter workers as strikebreakers. David North provides several examples, ranging from an El Paso packing plant in 1960 to a San Diego laundry and a number of agricultural strikes in south Texas from 1965 to 1967 (North, 1970, pp. 55, 65, 169). Regulations intended to limit the practice, such as a requirement that commuters cannot be hired as strikebreakers after a strike is officially certified, have proved ineffective (ibid., pp. 54, 87). More generally, it seems that one incentive for using commuters is to create a climate within the firm that makes it difficult to unionize. Commuters, because of their noncitizen status, are often reluctant to join unions, and their potential use as strikebreakers also acts to inhibit the growth of strong and militant unions. Such factors appear to enter significantly into the calculations of firms in considering their locations. Lamar Jones quotes from a 1962 Laredo Chamber of Commerce document to the effect that

> Both large supply and good attitude of industrial labor are related to the fact that Laredo has a permanent surplus of labor. . . . While seven labor unions, in addition to the complex of railroad organizations, are found in Laredo the labor history has been remarkably good. Union leaders do not have member support for militant demands, again a point related to the surplus labor situation. . . . Because of the pressure of surplus labor highly qualified workers can be secured for low wages. [Jones, 1965, p. 70]

The total impact of commuter workers is difficult to gauge, as information is based on spot checks, partial surveys, and "guesstimates." As one writer aptly put it in 1966: "The over-all data . . . leave the question of how many border-crossers commute to work unanswered. . . . U.S. authorities have never produced any continuous, reliable data. . . . So long as this condition persists, one is impelled to conjecture that obscurity is a functional state of affairs" (Grebler, 1966, p. 62). The situation has not changed since then.

Of all the aspects of reserve labor, however, it is the phenomenon of the undocumented worker which best illustrates the links between the structure of colonial domination of racial minorities within the Southwest and the neocolonial relationship which has long existed between the United States and Mexico. It is also arguably the area in which are found the most misconceptions and misleading assumptions, a number of which are indicated in the discussion below.

All during the twentieth century there have been present in the Southwest large numbers of persons from Mexico who did not have the documents to certify that they were in the country legally. The fact that a person does not have such documents does not in itself prove that he or she is in the country illegally, since legal status is a complex matter, subject in many cases to complicated litigation. Prior to the 1930s, as noted earlier, no "big deal" was made of the existence of undocumented Mexicans in the Southwest, and the Border Patrol was not created until 1924. Little distinction was made in the popular mind or in the minds of employers concerning legal status, as long as the region's labor needs were being met. Since then, however, a number of factors have intervened to draw the line more sharply between persons of Mexican origin who could demonstrate their legal status in the country (through citizenship, resident alien status, or whatever) and those who could not. The deportation/repatriation drives of the Depression period were clearly the first of these demarcating factors, and the cycles of labor shortage and surplus that have occurred since then have reinforced the pattern. The bracero program, by establishing a type of worker who was clearly set off as a Mexican national only temporarily in the United States, probably helped to make the distinction clearer. More recently, concern for the political implications of a continued influx of immigrants from Mexico has surfaced, of which more will be said later. It is perhaps also true that the growth of a distinct Chicano culture in the Southwest, drawing upon but also diverging from Mexican culture, has served to reinforce the distinction, although clearly there is no one-to-one relationship between cultural identification and legal standing.

By the very nature of the phenomenon, it is impossible to make accurate estimates of the number of undocumented workers from Mexico in the Southwest at any time. Virtually the only indicator of their number is the yearly statistics from the Immigration Service as to the number of persons apprehended and returned to Mexico. Such statistics are highly imperfect indicators for several reasons. One is that the enforcement efforts of the Border Patrol vary considerably from time to time for political reasons. Another is that returned workers may cross the border several times in one year. Despite these cautions, such statistics are almost universally used by researchers for lack of any others, but only to indicate broad trends and not specific totals. It seems fairly clear that the influx of undocumented immigrants from Mexico resumed with the Second World War and the consequent labor shortage. Ernesto Galarza feels that "even though bracero recruitment rose rapidly between 1942 and 1945, the hiring of illegals increased apace as the growers sought to make the most out of both types of labor" (Galarza, 1964, p. 58; see also Galarza, 1977, p. 240). The number of apprehensions by the Border Patrol rose particularly rapidly after 1944, reaching a peak with the so-called Operation Wetback, when over 1 million undocumented workers returned to Mexico in 1954 (ibid., p. 59). Nelson and Meyers, in their 1950 study of the Lower Rio Grande Valley, noted that much of its agricultural labor was done by undocumented workers (Nelson and Meyers, 1950, p. 22). During the following decade, if we can judge by Immigration Service figures, the number of undocumented workers in the Southwest remained at a relatively low level (see table 12). Starting around 1965, the apprehension statistics again started to rise, reaching over 680,000 in 1974 and over 660,000 in 1975 ("Illegal Alien Arrests Drop in Southwest," Los Angeles *Times*, Aug. 12, 1975). An unpublished study for the Immigration and Naturalization Service by Lesko Associates estimates that over 8 million undocumented persons were in the United States in 1975, with slightly over 5 million of Mexican origin ("Panel Plans New Effort against Illegal Aliens," San Diego *Union*, Nov. 6, 1975). Other researchers have generally felt that this figure was too high.

The most obvious influence on the rate of immigration from Mexico has been the condition of the United States labor market. The first wave in the post-Depression period was stimulated by the labor demands of World War II, which also brought the bracero program into being. The major enforcement effort by the Border Patrol in the early 1950s appears to have been designed to get employers to rely primarily on braceros for their cheap labor, and the policy seems to have been partly successful for a time. When subsequent administrations attempted to offset the "adverse effects" of the bracero program (described above), the undocumented worker alternative again became more attractive to employers. With the termination of the bracero program in 1964, the latest round of immigration began and continued into the 1970s.

While the bracero program thus served for a time as a partial substitute for the migration of undocumented labor, most students of the subject are agreed that the program was itself a major stimulus for that migration (Samora, 1971, p. 44). Corwin argues that "the bracero program, more so than the revolutionary violence in Mexico . . . or the special exemptions of 1917–1921, became a great catalyst for Mexican migration, legal and illegal" (Corwin, 1973a, p. 627). The bracero program acted as a magnet, drawing Mexican workers into the northern part of Mexico. When many were not accepted as braceros, they crossed the border anyway. The procedure of "drying out" the "wetbacks" also played a part, since it conferred official

TABLE 12

UNDOCUMENTED PERSONS FROM MEXICO
APPREHENDED BY THE BORDER PATROL, 1943–73

Year	Total	Year	Total
1943	8,189	1959	30,196
1944	26,689	1960	29,651
1945	63,602	1961	29,817
1946	91,456	1962	30,272
1947	182,986	1963	39,124
1948	179,385	1964	43,844
1949	278,538	1965	55,349
1950	458,215	1966	89,751
1951	500,000	1967	108,327
1952	543,538	1968	151,000
1953	865,318	1969	201,000
1954	1,075,168	1970	277,377
1955	242,608	1971	348,178
1956	72,442	1972	430,213
1957	44,451	1973	577,000
1958	37,242		

Source: Samora, "Mexican Immigration," p. 70.

status on workers who did not have it at the time, and in effect sanctioned irregular immigration (President's Commission on Migratory Labor, 1951, p. 74; Coalson, 1977, p. 83).

In addition, it can plausibly be argued that a stage has now been reached where the process becomes at least in part self-sustaining. The large Mexicano and Chicano communities in the Southwest provide informational contacts and resources for potential immigrant workers, and there is an extensive network of persons who make a living from providing transportation and making other arrangements for such irregular immigration (Corwin, 1973a, p. 582). The point is that the process has probably attained a sufficiently broad base and is institutionalized to the point that it generates its own momentum to a considerable degree.

In understanding the dynamics of the situation as it has developed historically, however, the role of employers and employer preferences must be seen as central. It is important to dispel what I see as one of the key misconceptions surrounding this subject, which can be referred to as "the myth of employer naivete." According to this assumption, employers are largely unaware of the documented or undocumented status of their workers and do not have preferences one way or the other. On the contrary, there is a wealth of direct and indirect evidence that employers are well aware of their workers' status, and that many have a strong preference for the undocumented worker. On the first point, most of the undocumented workers surveyed in one study felt that their employers knew of their status (North and Houstoun, 1976, p. 132). In addition, stories abound of unscrupulous employers turning their undocumented workers over to the Border Patrol at the end of the harvest season in order not to have to pay them their wages, and this practice presupposes knowledge of the employees' status.

The employers' preference for undocumented workers is also well documented, and again presupposes ability to distinguish that status. Saunders and Leonard note the preference of packing and canning shed operators in the Lower Rio Grande Valley for this type of labor (Saunders and Leonard, 1951, p. 57). Corwin agrees that employers favor such workers because they are more readily exploitable and can be turned over to immigration authorities if they cause trouble (Corwin, 1973a, p. 582). Perhaps the strongest evidence comes from a recent attempt in California to displace undocumented workers from jobs in the Los Angeles area and turn the jobs over to citizens.

> Nearly 99% of the employers contacted by the state have refused to accept help in hiring U.S. workers to replace illegal aliens apprehended by the federal government, often in the garment, hotel or restaurant fields.
>
> Both federal and state officials maintain that employers who use the illegal aliens want workers who can be exploited, and it is easier to take advantage of illegals who work for less money than most American citizens are willing to accept.
>
> Fred Brenner, head of the California Employment Development Department here, said "Almost all employers who have lost illegals to the immigration authorities say they don't want to use our services, or give us substandard job orders to which we cannot refer American citizens because they pay less than the minimum wage laws allow or pay less than the wage rates prevailing in their industries."
>
> The state officials say that the efforts required to call the employers who have lost illegal alien workers is so unproductive that referrals from the federal agency are often not even followed.
>
> "The cost-effectiveness of such referrals is almost zero," Brenner said. ["Bid to Give Illegal Aliens' Jobs to Americans Failing," Los Angeles Times, July 3, 1975]

In another newspaper account, a California avocado grower echoed many of the traditional themes sounded by Southwestern employers:

A Fallbrook avocado grower says food prices would soar and strawberries "would cost $1 apiece, not a box," if Congress approves the Rodino bill barring use of alien farm workers.

The grower, Allen Chaikin, said the Avocado Growers Bargaining Council is urging its members to oppose the bill. He is secretary to the council.

Chaikin, a member of the California Avocado Advisory Board for nine years . . . said he would favor legislation that would protect jobs for unemployed Americans from illegal aliens. "I'm all for it, if it protects a job an American would take, but it is different in farming."

"Nobody in this country will do stoop labor," Chaikin said. ["Alien Labor Bill Stirs Price Fears," San Diego *Union,* Jan. 4, 1976]

The preferences and perceptions of employers have apparently reached a point where they are able to discriminate against the commuter worker in favor of the undocumented worker. Reports appeared in the press in March 1976 to the effect that a number of green-card workers in the San Diego area were complaining to the Immigration and Naturalization Service because growers were laying them off and replacing them with undocumented workers. The stimulus for this development appears to have been implementation of the new California Agricultural Relations Act, which is supposed to guarantee farm workers the right to organize unions and bargain collectively. Apparently the growers felt that the undocumented workers would be less susceptible to unionization than the commuter worker ("Idled Green Card Workers Angered by Illegal Aliens," San Diego *Union,* Mar. 12, 1976). The ironic note in their complaint seems to have escaped the complaining workers.

The clear-cut preference by many employers for undocumented workers is an important part of the overall pattern, since it helps to explain why the pressures to cross the border have remained strong in the 1970s, at a time when the U.S. unemployment rate has stubbornly remained at a high level.

The types of jobs which undocumented workers have held is another indication of their changing circumstances. A 1953 occupational check of 31,000 apprehended Mexican workers showed that 5 percent worked in industry and other trades in such cities as El Paso, San Antonio, and Los Angeles (Tomasek, 1957, p. 195). Analysis of a small sample of similar workers in 1969 showed 72 percent working in agriculture (North, 1970, p. 111), but other studies for recent periods tend to put the figure closer to 60 percent, which includes workers in canneries and packing houses as well as in the fields ("Blocking of Jobs for Illegal Aliens Urged," Los Angeles *Times,* Feb. 5, 1975; Samora, 1971, p. 82). The actual figure is almost surely appreciably lower than 60 percent, since these data are all based on apprehensions, and it is generally agreed that these statistics are strongly biased toward the agricultural areas. The data, then, incomplete as they are, indicate a substantial shift in the occupational pattern of undocumented workers since the 1950s from rural to urban occupations. They tend to be concentrated in unskilled, semi-skilled, and low-level service occupations, although with some representation at the skilled worker level (North and Houstoun, 1976, p. 110).

The role of the Border Patrol is important in grasping the whole complex of understandings and arrangements that have come to characterize the situation of undocumented workers in the Southwest, and it is subject to frequent misinterpretation. The general assumption is that the Border Patrol is intended simply to keep these workers out and that it does the best job it can, given its limited resources. This is not only the attitude of the public at large but often finds expression in the writings of scholars. Thus Arthur Corwin in a long review essay on Mexican emigration asks the question: "Why did the Mexican border remain an unsolved problem in immigration-law enforcement, unabated in the mid-1970's?" He answers himself: "The most forthright explanation is that the United States Immigration and Naturalization Service (INS) has never been given enough support—personnel, facilities, legislative authority, and public cooperation—to stop border leaks and return illegal aliens from interior communities" (Corwin, 1973a, p. 585). He also lists as reasons a lack of legal authority, "public relations pressures" emanating from U.S.–Mexico relations, and the growth of ethnic militancy in the Southwest (ibid., pp. 585–87). In my opinion, this is a serious misreading of the situation, and there is considerable evidence to support the claim that things are as they are on the border because of the interplay of some very special interests.

One investigator, reporting on the border picture during the Second World War, noted that "in conversations with State Department officials, an immigration officer confessed that the service was deporting only those workers not engaged in harvesting perishable crops" (Scruggs, 1961, p. 153). George Coalson reports the following quotes from a 1950 discussion with the director of the El Paso Immigration District:

> Over the years, from the time I came on the job as District Director in March 1929, nearly every year at cotton-chopping or cotton-picking time, the farmers send a complaint to the Secretary of Labor . . . or to the Commissioner of Immigration, I am certain for no other purpose than to cause an investigation that would result in one of two things: Either I get word from some higher official to go easy until cotton-chopping time was over, or cotton-picking time was over, or the men who were doing the work would be so upset by the investigation that they would go easy on their own. [Coalson, 1977, p. 81]

The following quotes from a careful examination of undocumented workers in Texas in 1951 gave a remarkably similar picture, with more detail on the day-to-day workings of the Border Patrol:

The Patrol Inspector carries out his part of the ritual pleasantly enough knowing that if he chose to take the trouble, he could probably come back to the same place the next day and pick up the same alien again. The whole thing has many characteristics of a game in which the alien tries to escape capture as long as he can (but without suffering any real penalty if he is caught), the employer helps him to avoid the Patrol, and the Patrol Inspectors try to capture enough to run up a respectable daily score and keep up the reputation of their sector for apprehending and returning more aliens than any other. [Saunders and Leonard, 1951, p. 73]

No official word is given that the farmers are to be left alone, but the Inspectors soon learn that they are apt to be called up before some kind of investigating board if they are too zealous in doing their jobs. Actually very few such investigations are ever held, but the fear of "trouble" is real enough to have an adverse influence on work of Inspectors. . . .

Between the farmers and the Patrol Inspectors there exists a considerable amount of informal co-operation from which both benefit. [Ibid., pp. 79, 80]

A more recent survey of the same operations stresses the institutionalization of the practices noted above and summarizes the situation as follows:

The role of the Border Patrol in the U.S.–Mexico Borderlands is a delicate one, functionally characterized more as a peace-keeping operation than a strict law enforcement service. Inasmuch as the INS and its various agencies are sensitive and responsive to political, social and economic pressures which might cause them to lose congressional support during budgetary hearings, their legal operations are frequently curtailed to fit local expectations. For instance, the subtle effect of deploying personnel in those services least likely to interfere with local farm interests in border areas has been documented. . . . Although the linewatch activities resulted in the least productive rate of apprehension of illegal aliens, 35 percent of the total officer time was spent in that Border Patrol activity whereas only 9 percent of the officers' hours were used for Farm-Ranch checks, the most productive activity in discovering and apprehending [illegal Mexican aliens]. Either the linewatch is mainly a deterrent function . . . or else is the least disruptive but still visible use of control officers without becoming enmeshed in controversies with the politically and economically powerful agribusiness interests in the Borderlands. [Stoddard, 1976a, 174–75]

The one historical period in which the Border Patrol seems to have zealously performed its duty was during and after Operation Wetback in 1954, under rather special circumstances. This operation not only took place after the so-called "wetback strikes" of 1951 and 1952 but, more importantly, came into being at a time when the bracero program was operating to the general satisfaction of Southwestern agribusiness (Galarza, 1964, p. 70).

It thus appears that the Border Patrol does not "do its best" in terms of its official function in all circumstances, although it could be argued that it attempts to do its best at all times in pursuing its unofficial function, which is the regulation of the reserve labor supply from Mexico in the interest of Southwestern employers.

In addition to their economic function, and linked to it, undocumented workers perform an important political function in the United States. Several times they have been called upon to play the role of scapegoat in times of economic distress. The most notorious example was of course during the Great Depression, but the 1970s have again seen a flood of newspaper articles and television "documentaries" blatantly stating or subtly implying that if only the "problem" of the "illegal aliens" could be solved, unemployment rates and/or welfare rolls could be substantially reduced (see, e.g., "Saxbe Calls Illegal Aliens a U.S. Crisis," Los Angeles Times, Oct. 31, 1974; "The Flood of Illegal Aliens: What to Do?" Los Angeles Times, June 13, 1975). The current wave of near-hysteria represents the fourth turn of the cycle, the first coming after World War I, the second during the Depression, and the third after the Korean War.

It may be, however, that a new element has been added during the current decade, and that the cycle is not destined to keep on repeating itself forever. For the first time there is serious talk of penalizing employers for hiring undocumented workers. Ironic as this may sound, given the long history of employer-government collusion in manipulating the reserve labor force, it could be interpreted as a reflection of new circumstances. Two possibilities suggest themselves. One is the emergence of a substantial "underclass" of truly marginal persons in the society, whose labor is not actually needed by the productive apparatus of the economy. (This topic is discussed at greater length further on in this chapter.) The second possibility is that a combination of factors has given rise to genuine worries about the long-term political stability of the Southwest. In a long memo sent to Secretary of State Kissinger by Arthur Corwin in June 1975, these worries are laid out (Corwin, 1975). In it, Corwin argues that the combination of rapid population growth in Mexico, continued inflow of undocumented workers across the border, and rising nationalist and Third World sentiment among Chicanos and Mexicanos in the Southwest could lead to an "American Quebec" in that area and a "reconquest of Aztlan." Whether American officials would go that far in their speculations on the future is uncertain, but it may be that the magnitude of the phenomenon and the projections of Mexican population growth have raised the question of political stability in the Southwest in the minds of more than one person.

Up to this point the discussion of the reserve role has centered on the use of workers who live in Mexico or are in the United States but lack documents. There is another aspect of the reserve role that continues strongly to this day and involves a larger proportion of long-time residents in the Southwest: the migratory labor stream. This system had developed primarily around the 1920s, as the automobile came into more general use and roads were gradually improved (Coalson, 1977, p. 23). It involved families or groups of families who migrated from one part of the Southwest to another in search of seasonal agricultural employment. Sometimes the migrants stayed within one state, but many others traveled across state lines. The employment of New Mexico workers in Colorado was described earlier; south Texas constituted one reservoir from which such seasonal migrants originated, and there were others throughout the Southwest. While many families managed to remain employed throughout a substantial part of the year by following the crops, wages were low and virtually all families were unemployed at least part of the year, many for long periods. In Texas, the migrant farm-labor force in the mid-1960s was estimated to be about 95 percent Mexican American, although this figure presumably included Mexicanos as well as Chicanos (Jones, 1965, p. 103). These migrants were employed primarily by farms that used large quantities of labor (President's Commission on Migratory Labor, 1951, p. 7). Two recent influences on migratory labor patterns have been the bracero program and the mechanization of farm labor. Several observers have noted that the presence of braceros in areas of heavy Chicano population have forced more Chicano families into the migrant stream. Coalson depicts the relationship in this manner:

> Though theoretically braceros were paid the prevailing wage in the area in which they were employed and in no case less than fifty cents an hour, actually many farmers paid thirty-five to forty cents an hour. Therefore, with cheap foreign labor readily accessible to the Valley farmers, Texas-Mexicans living in the area were unable to make a satisfactory living and moved northward in search of employment. Some stayed within the boundaries of Texas, while others were attracted by higher wages in other states. [Coalson, 1977, p. 108]

As mechanization on the farm increasingly made itself felt, these migrants had to look farther and farther afield in order to make ends meet, with the result that the interstate pattern began to take precedence over the intrastate pattern (Jones, 1965, p. 162).

One of the most flagrant abuses of the entire pattern of farm labor, and seasonal migratory labor in particular, is the persisting use of child labor in the fields. This practice has been documented many times, as in the report of the National Child Labor Committee on Colorado Agriculture in the early

1950s. (Thomas and Taylor, 1951, p. 75). A study published in 1973 has documented the extent of this unscrupulous practice in the 1970s. (Taylor, 1973).

The Integrated Sector

The areas described in the previous section are those in which it is easiest to demonstrate the continued existence of a strong colonized sector. In other areas of the United States economy, particularly in the urban industrial area, the situation is less clear. While it is indisputable that the segmentation barrier has weakened since the Depression, it is difficult to say whether there are Chicanos who are completely integrated into the class structure on the basis of equality. It appears to be the case that there are such persons who are substantially integrated, and others who are integrated to a greater or lesser extent. One way to get an overall sense of the general trends is to examine U.S. Census statistics on Chicanos in the occupational structure. These are presented in tables 13 to 18.

Certain factors need to be taken into account in making use of these charts. They are based on U.S. Census data, and some cautions with relation to the 1930 figures were cited in chapter 4. Unfortunately, the figures for 1940 are missing, since the Census Bureau in that year used no classification that could be taken as an approximation of the Chicano population. For 1950, 1960, and 1970, the "Spanish surname" identification is used as such an approximation, since the overwhelming majority of persons of Spanish surname in the Southwest are of Mexican origin. The charts present two types of information. One is occupational distribution, which shows the percentage of Chicanos to be found in each type of occupation in each census year. The second set of figures, enclosed in parentheses, represents an "index of relative concentration" (IRC). This index shows the representation of Chicanos in each occupational category in comparison to the overall population. Thus an index of 0 would mean that no Chicanos are to be found in that occupational group. An index of 1 would mean that Chicanos are represented in that category in the same proportion as the general population, which is to say that if 30 percent of the population are laborers, then 30 percent of Chicanos would also be laborers. An index of .5 indicates that the Chicano representation in that category is only half of what it would be if they were represented equally, so that, for example, only 4 percent of Chicanos are professionals compared to 8 percent of the general population. A figure of 2 means that Chicanos are represented in that category at twice the rate of the general population; for example, 40 percent of Chicanos and only 20 percent of the general population are laborers.

TABLE 13

SOUTHWEST OCCUPATIONAL DISTRIBUTION AND
RELATIVE CONCENTRATION OF CHICANOS, 1930–70, BY SEX*

(Occupational Distribution in Percentages, Relative Concentration
Indicated in Parentheses)

Occupational Level	1930		1950		1960		1970	
	M	F	M	F	M	F	M	F
Professional & technical	0.9	2.9	2.2	4.6	4.1	5.5	6.4	7.6
	(.18)	(.18)	(.25)	(.31)	(.33)	(.42)	(.39)	(.46)
Managers, proprietors & officials	2.8	2.4	4.4	3.9	4.6	2.5	5.2	2.4
	(.28)	(.63)	(.35)	(.49)	(.36)	(.48)	(.43)	(.53)
Clerical					4.8	20.4	6.6	27.8
⎫	3.4	10.1	6.5	2.39	(.69)	(.62)	(.86)	(.72)
⎬	(.37)	(.33)	(.47)	(.58)	3.6	7.6	3.9	6.1
Sales ⎭					(.47)	(.93)	(.50)	(.77)
Craftsmen & foremen (skilled)	6.8	.6	13.1	1.4	16.7	1.2	20.8	2.2
	(.47)	(1.06)	(.66)	(.75)	(.81)	(.97)	(1.02)	(1.30)
Operatives (semiskilled)	9.1	21.9	19.0	28.1	24.1	24.8	25.4	23.1
	(.92)	(2.18)	(1.16)	(1.54)	(1.35)	(1.29)	(1.11)	(2.50)
Laborers (unskilled)	28.2	2.8	18.7	1.4	15.2	1.1	12.1	1.5
	(2.50)	(2.53)	(2.22)	(1.69)	(2.12)	(2.35)	(1.85)	(1.80)
Service	4.0	38.4	6.3	27.8	7.5	26.1	10.5	26.2
	(.68)	(1.36)	(.98)	(1.42)	(1.15)	(1.40)	(1.25)	(1.27)
Farm laborers	35.1	19.7	24.7	6.2	16.8	3.9	8.1	3.0
	(2.62)	(3.10)	(3.89)	(2.47)	(4.16)	(3.20)	(3.42)	(4.78)
Farmers & farm managers	9.8	1.0	5.1	.3	2.4	.2	.9	.1
	(.59)	(.38)	(.64)	(.58)	(.61)	(.36)	(.48)	(.52)
Occupation not reported	—	—	—	2.4	—	6.6	—	—

*Data for 1930 for "Mexican gainful workers 10 years and older." Data for 1950 and 1960 for Spanish-surname workers 14 years and older. Data for 1970 for Spanish-surname workers 16 years and older.

Sources: Briggs et al., *The Chicano Worker*, p. 76; U.S. Census Report, 1930, 1950, 1960, 1970.

TABLE 14

TEXAS OCCUPATIONAL DISTRIBUTION AND
RELATIVE CONCENTRATION OF CHICANOS, 1930–70, BY SEX*

(Occupational Distribution in Percentages, Relative Concentration
Indicated in Parentheses)

Occupational Level	1930		1950		1960		1970	
	M	F	M	F	M	F	M	F
Professional &	0.8	2.9	1.6	3.8	3.1	5.3	5.4	7.4
technical	(.24)	(.21)	(.18)	(.31)	(.33)	(.40)	(.33)	(.47)
Managers, proprietors &	3.4	2.6	4.4	4.3	4.5	2.8	5.3	2.5
officials	(.40)	(.61)	(.36)	(.78)	(.35)	(.60)	(.41)	(.60)
Clerical					4.6	15.9	6.4	25.8
	3.7	8.7	6.5	23.5	(.71)	(.55)	(.91)	(.74)
	(.37)	(.39)	(1.18)	(.66)	3.8	9.3	4.3	7.2
Sales					(.52)	(1.11)	(.58)	(.88)
Craftsmen &	7.3	0.4	12.4	1.2	14.7	1.0	21.8	2.2
foremen (skilled)	(.61)	(1.20)	(.63)	(1.00)	(.40)	(1.04)	(1.00)	(1.21)
Operatives	6.1	16.4	16.3	21.5	22.3	20.3	24.2	19.7
(semiskilled)	(.80)	(2.13)	(.90)	(2.10)	(1.27)	(2.25)	(2.00)	(2.12)
Laborers	23.6	2.3	18.8	1.4	14.6	1.2	13.1	1.8
(unskilled)	(2.02)	(2.14)	(2.00)	(2.30)	(2.56)	(2.54)	(1.83)	(1.70)
Service	4.2	39.7	6.5	33.5	7.3	32.2	9.7	31.2
	(1.01)	(1.25)	(1.18)	(1.20)	(1.75)	(1.22)	(1.33)	(1.31)
Farm laborers	35.0	25.9	25.4	8.1	14.2	5.7	8.4	2.3
	(2.17)	(1.78)	(3.36)	(2.49)	(3.50)	(4.10)	(3.08)	(3.83)
Farmers &	15.9	1.2	5.1	.4	3.2	.2	.8	.1
farm managers	(.60)	(.28)	(.36)	(.41)	(.50)	(.38)	(.25)	(.37)
Occupation not reported	—	—	1.0	2.4	6.9	6.1	—	—

*Data for 1930 for "Mexican gainful workers 10 years and older." Data for 1950 and 1960 for Spanish-surname workers 14 years and older. Data for 1970 for Spanish-surname workers 16 years and older.

Sources: U.S. Census Report, 1930, 1950, 1960, 1970.

TABLE 15

NEW MEXICO OCCUPATIONAL DISTRIBUTION AND
RELATIVE CONCENTRATION OF CHICANOS, 1930–70, BY SEX*

(Occupational Distribution in Percentages, Relative Concentration
Indicated in Parentheses)

Occupational Level	1930 M	1930 F	1950 M	1950 F	1960 M	1960 F	1970 M	1970 F
Professional & technical	0.5 (.15)	3.6 (.18)	2.9 (.34)	8.8 (.56)	6.0 (.44)	8.3 (.51)	9.7 (.52)	10.0 (.52)
Managers, proprietors & officials	1.3 (.20)	2.8 (.70)	4.4 (.41)	3.7 (.52)	5.2 (.40)	2.9 (.54)	6.8 (.56)	3.3 (.66)
Clerical					6.3 (1.08)	23.1 (.75)	7.7 (1.17)	30.0 (.88)
{ Clerical & Sales }	1.8 (.28)	6.1 (.37)	6.5 (1.51)	27.5 (.83)				
Sales					3.6 (.64)	7.8 (.97)	3.5 (.61)	6.7 (.91)
Craftsmen & foremen (skilled)	4.6 (.45)	0.3 (1.10)	12.9 (.75)	.8 (.86)	16.5 (.82)	.7 (.75)	19.4 (.99)	1.8 (1.10)
Operatives (semiskilled)	19.2 (1.93)	9.0 (.57)	14.8 (1.00)	9.0 (1.36)	19.9 (1.16)	8.0 (1.60)	19.7 (1.98)	10.0 (1.90)
Laborers (unskilled)	20.7 (1.53)	1.6 (2.20)	19.0 (2.03)	.6 (1.40)	15.0 (2.25)	.44 (1.23)	12.1 (1.83)	1.1 (1.54)
Service	3.0 (.90)	67.2 (2.02)	6.9 (1.34)	40.0 (1.60)	10.9 (1.89)	41.7 (1.62)	14.4 (1.62)	36.5 (1.46)
Farm laborers	35.1 (1.56)	5.2 (1.32)	14.3 (1.55)	1.8 (.67)	8.9 (2.23)	.5 (1.06)	4.7 (1.74)	.5 (1.61)
Farmers & farm managers	13.9 (.56)	4.2 (.70)	13.0 (1.03)	.8 (.63)	3.4 (.72)	.2 (.33)	1.4 (.51)	.1 (.19)
Occupation not reported	—	—	2.3	7.0	3.6	6.4	—	—

*Data for 1930 for "Mexican gainful workers 10 years and older." Data for 1950 and 1960 for Spanish-surname workers 14 years and older. Data for 1970 for Spanish-surname workers 16 years and older.

Sources: U.S. Census Report, 1930, 1950, 1960, 1970.

TABLE 16

COLORADO OCCUPATIONAL DISTRIBUTION AND RELATIVE CONCENTRATION
OF CHICANOS, 1930–70, BY SEX*

(Occupational Distribution in Percentages, Relative Concentration
Indicated in Parentheses)

Occupational Level	1930		1950		1960		1970	
	M	F	M	F	M	F	M	F
Professional & technical	0.3 (.08)	1.0 (.04)	1.9 (.16)	5.6 (.37)	4.1 (.33)	6.6 (.45)	7.4 (.42)	9.9 (.55)
Managers, proprietors & officials	0.4 (.04)	0.4 (.09)	2.9 (.16)	2.9 (.48)	3.2 (.25)	1.6 (.32)	5.0 (.40)	1.8 (.42)
Clerical ⎫	0.9 (.07)	3.5 (.11)	4.4 (.66)	20.0 (.50)	4.1 (.62)	17.3 (.53)	6.4 (.90)	27.8 (.75)
Sales ⎭					2.7 (.38)	5.0 (.64)	3.2 (.42)	4.4 (.57)
Craftsmen & foremen (skilled)	2.2 (.15)	0.3 (.39)	9.0 (.50)	1.3 (.97)	12.6 (.68)	1.3 (1.17)	18.3 (.96)	1.6 (.96)
Operatives (semiskilled)	14.7 (1.19)	6.3 (.75)	22.1 (1.33)	20.0 (2.35)	26.0 (1.64)	17.6 (2.64)	25.8 (2.75)	15.6 (2.36)
Laborers (unskilled)	25.3 (2.54)	3.4 (3.26)	22.1 (2.83)	2.1 (3.10)	20.2 (2.96)	1.1 (2.36)	13.3 (2.24)	1.9 (2.10)
Service	1.7 (.35)	41.6 (1.42)	5.0 (.83)	39.3 (1.76)	8.5 (1.38)	39.8 (1.76)	14.5 (1.65)	36.2 (1.67)
Farm laborers	48.8 (3.52)	41.5 (15.33)	20.7 (3.00)	5.7 (1.66)	10.9 (3.32)	1.5 (3.21)	4.2 (2.01)	.8 (1.37)
Farmers & farm managers	5.7 (.32)	2.1 (.89)	7.6 (.50)	.6 (1.32)	2.8 (.44)	.1 (.31)	1.2 (.33)	.2 (.27)
Occupation not reported	—	—	1.4	3.1	4.2	8.0	—	—

*Data for 1930 for "Mexican gainful workers 10 years and older." Data for 1950 and 1960 for Spanish-surname workers 14 years and older. Data for 1970 for Spanish-surname workers 16 years and older.

Sources: U.S. Census Report, 1930, 1950, 1960, 1970.

TABLE 17

ARIZONA OCCUPATIONAL DISTRIBUTION AND
RELATIVE CONCENTRATION OF CHICANOS, 1930–70, BY SEX*

(Occupational Distribution in Percentages, Relative Concentration
Indicated in Parentheses)

Occupational Level	1930		1950		1960		1970	
	M	F	M	F	M	F	M	F
Professional & technical	0.6 (.15)	3.4 (.19)	1.6 (.21)	4.3 (.28)	2.5 (.23)	5.8 (.39)	5.9 (.36)	7.4 (.42)
Managers, proprietors & officials	2.9 (.34)	3.3 (.92)	3.7 (.28)	4.6 (.63)	3.8 (.29)	2.4 (.48)	5.0 (.41)	1.8 (.39)
Clerical	4.1 (.39)	14.8 (.62)	6.1 (1.28)	28.4 (.86)	2.6 (.50)	18.2 (.59)	4.8 (.74)	24.3 (.69)
Sales					2.7 (.36)	10.1 (1.18)	3.6 (.48)	7.0 (.87)
Craftsmen & foremen (skilled)	7.9 (.47)	0.5 (1.32)	13.0 (.78)	.6 (.76)	13.5 (.65)	.6 (.63)	21.0 (.99)	1.9 (1.09)
Operatives (semiskilled)	26.1 (1.57)	13.1 (.82)	25.4 (1.57)	14.6 (1.51)	21.7 (1.34)	17.1 (2.15)	25.3 (2.59)	21.3 (2.13)
Laborers (unskilled)	26.5 (2.30)	1.5 (2.04)	17.2 (2.97)	.5 (1.42)	13.7 (2.10)	1.0 (2.09)	14.5 (2.00)	1.6 (2.25)
Service	3.0 (.60)	55.0 (1.76)	5.5 (.92)	37.7 (1.44)	4.9 (.89)	35.3 (1.46)	9.4 (1.05)	30.3 (1.42)
Farm laborers	26.4 (1.62)	7.9 (1.92)	23.9 (2.42)	6.4 (2.03)	27.9 (4.04)	3.4 (4.35)	9.5 (3.08)	4.0 (5.78)
Farmers & farm managers	2.5 (.23)	0.6 (.26)	1.7 (.21)	2.3 (.16)	.6 (.34)	.1 (.26)	.4 (.39)	.2 (1.27)
Occupation not reported	—	—	2.3	2.5	4.2	6.0	—	—

*Data for 1930 for "Mexican gainful workers 10 years and older." Data for 1950 and 1960 for Spanish-surname workers 14 years and older. Data for 1970 for Spanish-surname workers 16 years and older.

Sources: U.S. Census Report, 1930, 1950, 1960, 1970.

TABLE 18

CALIFORNIA OCCUPATIONAL DISTRIBUTION AND
RELATIVE CONCENTRATION OF CHICANOS, 1930–70, BY SEX*

(Occupational Distribution in Percentages, Relative Concentration
Indicated in Parentheses)

Occupational Level	1930		1950		1960		1970	
	M	F	M	F	M	F	M	F
Professional &	1.0	3.0	2.6	4.7	4.5	5.2	6.5	7.2
technical	(.17)	(.17)	(.12)	(.33)	(.33)	(.37)	(.31)	(.43)
Managers, proprietors &	1.9	1.8	4.5	3.5	4.2	2.3	4.9	2.3
officials	(.16)	(.55)	(.25)	(.55)	(.34)	(.49)	(.31)	(.49)
Clerical					4.8	24.2	6.7	29.2
	3.2	13.6	6.4	23.7	(.68)	(.70)	(.82)	(.75)
	(.19)	(.36)	(.75)	(.57)	3.2	6.0	3.7	5.5
Sales					(.40)	(.76)	(.41)	(.68)
Craftsmen &	7.0	1.4	13.9	1.8	16.6	1.5	20.4	2.3
foremen (skilled)	(.35)	(1.63)	(.50)	(1.27)	(.79)	(1.27)	(1.02)	(1.43)
Operatives	8.1	40.8	21.6	41.2	24.4	32.4	26.9	27.9
(semiskilled)	(.70)	(3.56)	(1.00)	(3.13)	(1.50)	(2.83)	(2.44)	(2.89)
Laborers	37.6	4.7	17.7	1.6	13.0	1.2	11.0	1.4
(unskilled)	(3.57)	(3.86)	(1.75)	(2.70)	(2.32)	(2.94)	(1.73)	(1.82)
Service	4.2	27.5	5.5	16.9	6.5	16.8	10.8	20.3
	(.57)	(1.09)	(.62)	(.85)	(1.13)	(.94)	(1.12)	(1.09)
Farm laborers	35.7	7.1	23.4	5.1	15.9	3.1	8.4	3.9
	(3.61)	(8.32)	(3.60)	(3.91)	(5.15)	(4.49)	(3.97)	(5.79)
Farmers &	1.3	.1	2.7	.2	1.9	.1	.4	.1
farm managers	(.19)	(.07)	(.50)	(.34)	(1.02)	(.54)	(.82)	(.71)
Occupation not reported	—	—	0.0	1.3	6.3	7.1	—	—

*Data for 1930 for "Mexican gainful workers 10 years and older." Data for 1950 and 1960 for Spanish-surname workers 14 years and older. Data for 1970 for Spanish-surname workers 16 years and older.

Sources: U.S. Census Report, 1930, 1950, 1960, 1970.

The formula for computing the relative concentration can be presented as

$$IRC = \frac{\dfrac{\text{Spanish surnames in the } i\text{th occupation}}{\text{All persons in the } i\text{th occupation}}}{\dfrac{\text{Spanish surnames in all occupations}}{\text{All persons in all occupations}}}$$

The advantage of using the index of relative concentration is that changes in the distribution of Chicanos in the occupational hierarchy over time can be readily seen. The percentage figures can also be used for this purpose, but can be misleading because the overall occupational distribution changes over time too; for example, the percent of Chicano clerks may be increasing but the percent of the total population who are clerks may also be increasing, and thus no relative gain is made. The index of relative concentration controls for this type of change.

In examining these figures, it should also be kept in mind that a higher proportion of Chicano males than females is considered as being ''in the labor force,'' which means that one is paid for one's labor. Housewives, for example, whose work is not compensated with a wage, are considered not in the labor force, and hence are not included in these statistics. The proportion of Chicanas in the labor force has been increasing, however. A simple computation from the respective censuses indicates the following percentage of Chicanas in the Spanish-surname labor force:

1930	14.5 percent
1950	21.7 percent
1960	26.6 percent
1970	33.2 percent

Several observations can readily be made from these charts. The differences in male–female occupational patterns are quite marked, with females more highly represented in clerical and sales positions and service occupations. Males, on the other hand, are more highly represented in the craftsmen and laborer categories and also in managerial positions, although at a much lower level.

The decline in agricultural occupations is also dramatically indicated in the figures, to the point where only a small percent of the Chicano population is now working in the fields. This decline is apparently continuing, and is matched by an overall decline in the number of such occupations in the economy as a whole. Interestingly, the relative concentration of Chicanos in farm work has risen as the absolute number has declined.

Some state-to-state variation can also be seen from the figures, as, for example, in the relatively high percentage of Chicanos in New Mexico in the professional and technical field.

For our purposes, however, the most significant trend is the tendency for the Chicano population to improve its standing in the occupational hierarchy over time. This relative upgrading has been slow but quite consistent over the four census years covered. In charting this trend, it is particularly unfortunate that the data for 1940 are missing, since it is impossible to distinguish the situation in the 1940s from that in the 1930s. The general supposition has been that Chicanos' occupational standing may have slipped during the 1930s but gained significantly during the 1940s. If this is so, the 1940s gain more than compensated for losses during the 1930s.

A more detailed look at the occupational categories shows a consistent percentage gain in the professional and technical field, for the Southwest as a whole and for each individual state. More significantly, the relative concentration has also tended to rise. In the managerial category, on the other hand, there is no clear trend, and the female representation here has declined since the 1930s.

In the typically "white collar" occupations, there seems to be a consistent upward trend in Chicano and Chicana representation in the clerical field, but the same does not seem to hold true in sales. The most recent figures indicates a decline in the number of Chicanas holding sales positions.

The various "blue collar" fields show somewhat different situations. In the craftsmen category, which is dominated by males, there has been a clear trend toward greater representation, to the point that Chicanos are now at a level of parity with the general population. In the less desirable operatives category, Chicanos have been overrepresented for some time. The heavy Chicana representation here is accounted for by the large number who occupy such positions as laundry operatives. In the non-farm laborer category, which is largely a male preserve, the relative concentration of Chicanos has been high since 1930, and is now declining.

The heterogeneous "service" category, which includes everything from domestic servants to barbers and police, but in which most of the workers are relatively low-paid, Chicano males have been increasing their representation while Chicanas have declined, although they are still overrepresented.

Data for relative incomes of Spanish-surname persons also show improvement over time. According to one study, the income of Spanish-surname persons in the Southwest was 57.2 percent of Anglo income in 1949, and 61.6 percent in 1959 (Grebler, Moore, and Guzmán, 1970, p. 190). Another study presents table 19 as an indication of changes from 1959 to 1969.

While the overall relative income remained virtually stable for the Southwest during the 1960s, an increase in most of the states was offset by a decline in California, where Chicano incomes have been the highest in the

TABLE 19

MEDIAN INCOME OF SPANISH–SURNAME FAMILIES
AS A PERCENT OF ANGLO INCOME,
SOUTHWEST, 1959 AND 1969

	1959	*1969*
Southwest	65%	66%
Arizona	68	74
California	79	73
Colorado	67	69
New Mexico	57	67
Texas	52	58

Source: Briggs, Fogel, and Schmidt, *The Chicano Worker*, p. 59.

past. Why the incomes should have declined in California at the same time that there was some occupational upgrading is not clear.

On the whole, then, the available evidence on occupational stratification indicates that there has been some integration of the Chicano population into the regular class structure since 1930. Another way to put it would be that the segmentation line has become weaker over time, although it has by no means disappeared. Several factors seem to have combined to produce this effect.

Urbanization is one such factor. The proportion of the Chicano population that resides in urban areas has risen steadily in recent decades. On the basis of census reports, the Spanish-surname population of the Southwest was 66.4 percent urban in 1950, 79.1 percent urban in 1960, and 85.5 percent urban in 1970 (Grebler, Moore, and Guzmán, 1970, p. 113; 1970 Census of Population, Subject Reports, *Persons of Spanish Surname*, p. 21). Concentration in the cities has given Chicanos access to a greater range of occupations. It has also had the effect of diffusing Chicano workers among a much larger number of employers. As documented in earlier sections of this work, Chicanos prior to 1930 were heavily concentrated in certain work areas, particularly agriculture, railroads, and mining. The high proportion of Chicano workers hired by such employers gave them a high stake in perpetuating a segmented labor market, and they erected a system of controls to maintain those divisions. As Chicanos have become less concentrated in the urban area, the stake that any given employer has in maintaining racial segmentation has declined, and the system of controls has become relatively weaker. It may also be the case that such a system of controls is inherently more difficult to enforce in the city than in the countryside, given the greater complexity of the urban economy and the lower visibility of the work force. In the rural areas a system of social sanctions can be brought to bear on employers who deviate from established norms, because there are fewer of them and knowledge of what each is doing is greater. Thus both the lesser concentration of Chicano workers and the greater complexity of the urban economy have contributed to their integration into the class structure. Harold Baron has made a similar point with regard to Black workers:

> Although in the metropolitan centers special advantage was taken of the new Black workers regarding pay, work conditions, and job security, no distinctive *form* of economic subsystem was erected upon the special relations with this labor force. Accordingly, no important sector of the capitalist class developed a direct stake in the racial control of labor comparable to that of the nineteenth century planter class. [Baron, 1975, p. 189]

This is not to say that urban employers had no stake in developing and perpetuating such a system, but simply that their stake was lower and thus the system of controls weaker.

The recurrent *labor shortages* that have been associated with American wars have also played an important role in allowing Chicanos and other racial minorities entry to the industrial labor market. In her study of industrial employment in Texas, Margaret Brookshire quotes from a Fair Employment Practices Committee (FEPC) document to the following effect:

> For eighteen months after Pearl Harbor, Mexican-Americans found little employment in war industries. Their utilization was confined to common labor, mainly in construction jobs. . . . However, after 1942, increased shortage of manpower and efforts of FEPC induced industry to use Mexican-Americans in other than common labor jobs. [Brookshire, 1954, p. 29]

Apparently, many of the initial gains were in war-related industry (Brookshire, 1954, p. 35; Loomis, 1942, p. 34; Loomis and Loomis, 1942, pp. 385–86). Scott Greer, writing of the Los Angeles labor market, also makes reference to Black and Chicano job gains during World War II, although he notes that some of the gains were lost after the war, as the buffer role came into operation. Still, it is clear that the situation did not go all the way back to what it had been prior to the war. Some of the gains stuck (Greer, 1959, p. 31). The effects on the San Antonio labor market are reported by another researcher in these terms:

> The shortage of skilled workers during World War II is generally recognized as by far the greatest single factor in opening this level of employment to Mexican-Americans. Employers, who reluctantly turned to

persons of this ethnic group, found them quite capable of mastering skilled jobs, and they also found that they could be worked satisfactorily alongside Anglos. By 1963, Mexican-Americans were commonly found throughout plant departments and engaged in substantially all types of skilled occupations. [Landoldt, 1965, p. 216]

The first two of these factors affecting class integration are of course linked, as the labor shortages were a major factor in pulling Chicanos into the cities. It is also important to keep in mind that the long period of economic expansion that the United States underwent from the Second World War through the 1960s has also played a role in allowing Chicanos entry into the urban labor markets.

The accelerating *interpenetration of government and economy* that was described earlier is a third major factor, with two components. One is its effect on *unionization* and the other is the implementation of *antidiscrimination policies*. With regard to unionization, a variety of sources indicate that it has had a significant impact on the advancement of Chicanos. In speaking of the meat packing industry in Texas, Pauline Kibbe has this to report in the mid-1940s:

> At those packing plants in which labor organizations have been established and collective bargaining agreements consummated, discrimination against both Latin Americans and Negroes has been greatly reduced. . . .
>
> In the unorganized packing plants where labor agreements do not exist, Latin American workers are not given the same job opportunities, nor do they receive the same rates of pay as do the Anglo Americans employed. One of the large packing companies operating in Texas has the unenviable record of using race prejudice to defeat the organizational efforts of the workers. So far, its tactics have been successful. [Kibbe, 1946, p. 162]

Robert Landoldt indicates a similar effect on a flour mill in San Antonio, and notes that Chicano workers there are receptive to unionization (Landoldt, 1965, pp. 163, 216). More extensive data are available from Margaret Brookshire's study of Nueces County, Texas, in the 1950s—the same area that had been studied earlier by Paul Taylor. Her research indicated that both in the chemical industry and in the primary metals industry the introduction of unionization had had an impact on the employment patterns of Chicanos (Brookshire, 1954, pp. 101, 122–35). She summarizes the situation here as follows:

> In some industries, such as primary metals, and in some plants within the chemical industry, the Mexican-American appears to be integrated into the plant work pattern in such a way that he is economically indis-

tinguishable from his fellow employee. His employment and advancement pattern in these cases follows the established procedure of the plant usually in accordance with the provisions of a collective agreement. (Ibid., p. 268]

The attitude of the unions toward the Chicano is of particular interest here, since unions have often been seen as a barrier to Chicano mobility into the skilled worker category. The historical pattern that seems to emerge from the various studies is one where Chicanos have been systematically underrepresented in certain types of unions, in particular the construction and building trades and the railroad brotherhoods (Landoldt, 1965, pp. 123ff.; Kibbe, 1946, p. 162; Brookshire, 1954, pp. 190, 195). Even so, it does not appear to be solely union policy that determines the racial composition of the organization. Scott Greer, in an extensive study of labor unions in the Los Angeles area, believes that

it seems highly probable, on the basis of this data, that the relative exclusion of Mexicans and Negroes from unions at certain job-levels is more clearly the result of hiring practices in industry than of the ethnic policy of unions. [Greer, 1959, p. 28]

In this connection, it is important to assess the specific roles of unions and management in hiring and promotion. There appears to be general agreement among students of this subject that the unions have had an impact not primarily through influencing who will and will not be hired, but in setting conditions for promotion, such as seniority, that make racial discrimination more difficult. The managerial role is the key to the initial hiring decision. Thus Brookshire states for the chemical industry:

In establishing the proportion of Mexican-Americans in each plant in the industry, managerial decision apparently plays a major role, for management has retained the hiring prerogative in all union contracts in the industry and has this prerogative in the plants not unionized. [Brookshire, 1954, p. 100]

More generally,

In most manufacturing and nonmanufacturing industry, managerial policy plays a dominant role in determining what proportion of the labor force of the plant is Mexican-American, subject to many influences such as the condition of the labor market and employee attitudes. [Brookshire, 1954, p. 252]

The dominant role of the management prerogative is also brought out in interplant variation within the same industry. Brookshire makes note of two chemical plants under the same management, one with 75 percent Chicano employees and another with none (ibid., pp. 115–16). Another researcher on

Texas industries has also noted that employers in the same field will vary from very few Chicano employees to a very high proportion (Meyers, 1951, p. 23).

Scott Greer is in agreement with the general observation made above. He observes that for Los Angeles

> the chief agency of change in the ethnic composition of the unions is the supply and character of labor in relation to effective demand. Once men are working, the union must organize them, no matter what their ethnic identification. [Greer, 1959, p. 29]

> Only in protecting seniority did the unions have an effect on labor market composition. [Ibid., p. 31]

He also notes that the dispersion of racial minorities in a job hierarchy is facilitated by the presence of industrial unions, as opposed to craft unions (ibid., pp. 36–39). Greer ties together the effects of labor shortages and unionization on minority occupational integration in the following model:

> The integration of an ethnic minority in an urban labor force moves through these steps. First, there is an expansion of job opportunities beyond the ability of the "preferred," non-ethnic labor force to fill them, followed by the recruitment of ethnic workers. These workers enter at the lower levels and, if the union-management barriers hold, are segregated there—a small and constant part of the workforce. If, however, the work is organized by industrial unions and the labor shortage continues the management resistance is likely to disappear, and ethnic workers will continue to increase until they are necessarily upgraded. [Ibid., p. 39]

Greer points out that Chicano workers were in the Los Angeles industrial labor force before unions became important, and that "when ... the wave of industrial unionism reached Los Angeles in the late 1930's and early 1940's, they became members of the industrial unions which, in many cases, would have failed without them" (ibid., p. 29).

The major impact of unions on racial minority employment, then, seems to be in making occupational stratification more difficult for management to perpetuate, in helping to eliminate the buffer role that racial minorities have historically played, and in setting conditions of uniformity that make impossible a policy of dual wages. Unionization, in turn, is historically a product of workers' struggles to organize themselves, but in the United States their successful recognition as bargaining agents during the 1930s and 1940s was largely a result of the crises provoked by the Depression and the war, and the greater government regulation of the economy that these in turn produced.

The other aspect of the increased state role in the economy that is of concern here is antidiscrimination policies. There are scattered references in the literature to the effects of these policies. Pauline Kibbe refers to one case where the national Fair Employment Practices Committee (FEPC) intervened to upgrade Chicanos occupationally at a Shell Oil plant in Texas, in this case over the opposition of the local union as well as the company (Kibbe, 1946, p. 161). Meier and Rivera note the intervention of the National Labor Relations Board in the matter of dual wages during the Second World War (Meier and Rivera, 1972, p. 184). Robert Landoldt feels that FEPC directives made a difference in the hiring practices of Kelly Air Force Base, the largest employer in the San Antonio area, in the postwar period (Landoldt, 1965, p. 93). Margaret Brookshire cites a large number of cases brought before the FEPC charging discrimination against Chicanos (Brookshire, 1954, p. 39). Nevertheless, she feels that the public sector's antidiscrimination policies have played a secondary role compared to private-sector factors such as the labor market (ibid., p. 273). It is difficult to gauge the importance of these policies, since they may exert an indirect as well as direct effect. Still, the general feeling one gets is that the antidiscrimination policies, including the affirmative action plans that became fashionable during the 1960s, are a distinctly secondary factor. A Special Report of the 1970 San Bernardino County Grand Jury into fair employment practices revealed the following.

> The department heads and/or their representatives who were interviewed were asked about policies regarding affirmative action and the County policy of equal employment opportunity. Few indicated any knowledge of this area. . . . No apparent effort has been made to disseminate this policy to employees, and several department heads in referring to affirmative action expressed the view that there was no need for these kinds of programs. [Special Report, 1970, p. 5]

A study by Jerolyn Lyle has found that industries which hold government contracts and are thus required to file affirmative action plans are actually worse off in terms of hiring workers with Spanish surnames than other firms. "This would appear to indicate that . . . programs to ensure equal employment opportunity in firms with government contracts were not accomplishing their goals" (Lyle, 1973, p. 14). More information on the workings of affirmative action plans in the private sector is provided in the appendix to this book.

Two other factors, related to each other and to urbanism, may have played a significant role in the limited occupational integration that has taken place: *education* and *assimilation*. Greater access to the educational system in the cities is part of the overall pattern of weakened controls that Chicanos encountered in becoming more urbanized. While the theme cannot be developed in detail here, numerous references in the literature make clear that education for Chicanos in rural areas has been deliberately circumscribed as a means of maintaining a low-wage labor force. Agricultural employers have often played a direct role in this by sitting on school boards, although their influence is also felt more indirectly. In the cities, with lower stakes in the racially segmented labor force for individual employers, educational access has been greater. In addition, Chicano children in the urban areas are not taken out of school to work in the fields part of the year, as is often the case in rural areas out of sheer economic necessity. Associated with greater formal education is greater cultural assimilation, as in the use of the English language. Increased assimilation is also a generational phenomenon. The proportion of the Chicano population represented by the second, third, and later generations has been increasing over time, and this also has a tendency to increase the degree of assimilation (Grebler, Moore, and Guzman, 1970, p. 106). Brookshire and Landoldt both argue that the combined effects of education and assimilation have contributed to greater Chicano representation in apprenticeship programs and in retail trade (Brookshire, 1954, p. 204; Landoldt, 1965, p. 241). The urbanism-assimilation link has also been made by D'Antonio and Samora in discussing Chicano mobility in health-related occupations (D'Antonio and Samora, 1962, p. 24). As a partial assimilation has proceeded, it has become more difficult to maintain a segmentation line that is based not only on race but on ethnicity, and hence culture.

A final factor that can be discussed in connection with class integration is *occupational upgrading,* a general phenomenon in the American economy which consists of a shift in the occupational structure toward jobs that have higher status and generally require higher educational and skill levels. This is reflected in table 20. These trends, and particularly the growth of professional and technical workers and the decline of blue-collar workers since 1940, have often been cited as making the occupational integration of racial minorities more difficult than would otherwise have been the case. This is probably true, and this development thus represents a counterforce to the factors making for integration that have been listed above. Still, it appears that in some occupational areas it may have a limited beneficial effect on Chicanos. Landoldt cites as one factor facilitating the entrance of Chicanas into the nursing field in San Antonio the ''shortage of Anglo girls willing to endure the rigorous training, hard work and relatively low remuneration of nursing'' (Landoldt, 1965, p. 258). It may be that as the occupational structure has shifted upward, certain fields, such as nursing, have suffered a relative downgrading in status and are not as desirable to Anglo workers as they once were, thus allowing entrance to racial minorities. The gains thus made are of course limited by the relative downgrading of the field.

The various factors that have been outlined above that enter into the model of integration into the class system can be diagrammed as in figure 6.

All of this having been said, it is necessary to point out the limits of class integration in the cities. In every historical period there has been a kind

TABLE 20

CHANGES IN THE U.S. OCCUPATIONAL STRUCTURE:
NUMBER OF WORKERS IN EACH CENSUS CATEGORY,
1900–1970 (IN THOUSANDS)

	1900	1920	1940	1950	1960	1970
Managers, officials, proprietors, farm owners and managers	7,460 25.6%	9,245 21.9%	9,132 17.7%	9,530 16.1%	10,400 15.5%	9,998 12.7%
Professional and technical	1,234 4.3	2,283 5.4	3,879 7.5	5,081 8.6	7,475 11.1	11,322 14.4
Independent professional and technical	320 1.1	420 1.0	570 1.1	654 1.1	873 1.3	1,200 1.5
Professional and technical workers	910 3.1	1,860 4.4	3,310 6.4	4,427 7.5	6,602 9.9	10,100 12.9
Clerical and sales workers	2,184 7.5	5,443 12.9	8,432 16.3	11,365 19.3	14,184 21.2	18,548 23.6
Service workers	2,626 9.1	3,313 7.9	6,069 11.8	6,180 10.5	8,349 12.5	9,724 12.4
Manual workers	10,401 35.8	16,974 40.2	20,597 39.8	24,266 41.1	24,211 36.1	27,452 34.9
Craftsmen and foremen	3,062 10.5	5,482 13.0	6,203 12.0	8,350 14.2	8,560 12.8	10,027 12.8
Operatives	3,720 12.8	6,587 15.6	9,518 18.4	12,030 20.4	11,986 17.9	13,811 17.6
Non-farm laborers	3,620 12.5	4,905 11.6	4,875 9.4	3,885 6.6	3,665 5.5	3,614 4.6
Farm workers	5,125 17.7	4,948 11.7	3,632 7.0	2,578 4.3	2,057 3.1	1,400 1.8
Total	29,030	42,206	51,742	58,999	66,681	78,408

Source: Szymanski, "Trends in the American Working Class," *Socialist Revolution* (July–August 1972), p. 107.

FIGURE 6

FACTORS INFLUENCING CLASS INTEGRATION

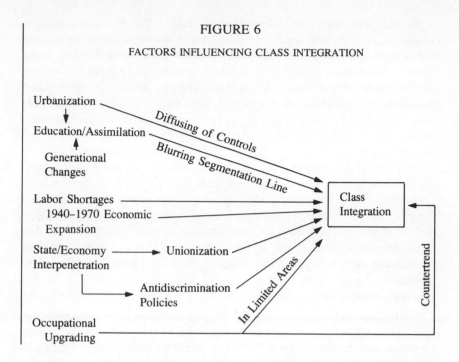

of ceiling which defined what kinds of jobs were normally deemed suitable for Chicanos in a given area. Over the years, the ceiling has shifted upward in a very gradual manner. Whereas at one time it was placed at the laborer and service category, it later was raised to cover operatives, and still later came to include craftsmen. There it seems to rest for the time being, as Fred Schmidt makes a point of stressing (Schmidt, 1970, pp. 2, 32). This is not to say that there are no Chicanos in the higher-status categories, as the census statistics clearly indicate there are. It *does* mean that Chicanos are systematically underrepresented at the higher levels, and the situation is made somewhat worse than the broad occupational statistics indicate by the fact that Chicanos tend to be concentrated in the lowest positions within each occupational category (Fogel, 1967, p. 119).

In part, this situation is created by continuation of the traditional practice on the part of employers of job typing. This takes place both through typing Chicanos *into* certain kinds of jobs and typing them *out* of others. One researcher, in a study of the Texas State Employment Commission's Austin office, found it not uncommon for the office to refer Chicano workers only to low-status jobs because of employers' expressed preference for Anglo workers for white-collar jobs (Crain, 1948, pp. 55, 74). An example of typing into a job category comes from Brookshire's study: "The Mexican-American woman is preferred to a 'white' woman laborer; employers hold the opinion that at the wages paid a better Mexican-American than 'white' worker can be found" (Brookshire, 1954, p. 154). Landoldt notes that Chicanas dominate the San Antonio cigar, candy, and apparel industries because of their reputed manual dexterity; and they were retained when the plants mechanized (Landoldt, 1965, p. 215). On the other hand, the San Antonio telephone company, the city's largest private employer, typed all non-menial jobs as "Anglo" and all menial jobs as "Black" (ibid., p. 245). The Texas petroleum industry generally hired Chicanos only for the hardest and most strenuous jobs, reserving the better jobs in this relatively high wage field for Anglo workers (Kibbe, 1946, pp. 159–60; Brookshire, 1954, p. 140). Various researchers have also reported that in positions requiring customer contact, such as in sales, employers were especially likely to discriminate against Chicanos and other racial minorities (Greer, 1959, p. 28; Brookshire, 1954, p. 225). Lest it be thought that such job typing is a thing of the past, Landoldt's 1965 study provides examples.

In a primary metals plant,

> Mexican-Americans had advanced as far and as rapidly as Anglos, with the exception of top supervisory jobs. That only one Mexican-American had attained such advancement was attributed to lack of confidence of many in this ethnic group regarding their supervisory abilities, and also to their educational limitations. [Landoldt, 1965, p. 198]

Of eighteen plants studied, it was found that there were no Chicanos at an administrative level and that 42 of the 45 supervisors were first-line supervisors.

> Officials at eight of the companies volunteered their convictions that Mexican-Americans were generally lacking in one or more of the following supervisory qualifications: mental capacity, judgment, emotional stability, ambition, and worker acceptance. [Ibid., p. 219]

Eleven of the eighteen employed no Chicano clerical workers.

At the business and professional levels, the situation remained particularly acute. According to a 1975 report, "The number of U.S. firms owned by Mexican-Americans is almost insignificant—less than one percent of all firms and representing less than two-tenths of one percent of the gross receipts of all firms" (Schmidt and Koford, 1975, p. 101). Ruth Tuck has one of the best summary statements on the continuation of a trend noted in an earlier section of this book:

> The Mexican-American business or professional man finds himself in a position not very different from that of the Negro of the same status, in that he must depend on his own group for his income. If he (or she) is

hired as a teacher, it is for a "Mexican" school. If he operates a store, it is for Mexican-Americans; if a newspaper, it is for them, too. Social workers carry Mexican case-loads; doctors and lawyers find their most dependable source of income among their own group.... A subtle form of segregation, it is perhaps more injurious than all the rest, because it closes—or limits sharply—the way out at the top of the semi-caste. [Tuck, 1946, p. 182]

Ozzie Simmons found much the same pattern in his study of McAllen in the Lower Rio Grande Valley of Texas in the 1950s. The small Chicano-owned businesses were confined to the barrio and a Chicano clientele, whereas the larger stores were almost all Anglo-owned and catered to Anglo and Chicano alike (Simmons, 1952, pp. 145–49).

The Mexican American representation in such types of business as auto repairs, beauty shops, barber shops, cafes and restaurants, grocery stores, and service stations reflect the dominant-subordinate relation in that all of these enterprises are wholly dependent on colonia clientele and were able to develop and survive because of the opportunities presented by a Mexican group concentrated in one area. [Simmons, 1952, p. 216]

The most striking characteristic of the Mexican American businessman is that he must depend on his own group for his patronage, and that he is even further limited to those enterprises which do not compete with Anglo business or which offer services more conveniently located for colonia residents. Anglo American businessmen, on the other hand, enjoy all of the Anglo patronage and most of the Mexican as well. In San Antonio, where Mexican American business exists on a much larger scale than in McAllen, a glance at the membership list of the Mexican Chamber of Commerce reveals that the same pattern of dependence on the group itself prevails. [Ibid., p. 223]

A balanced view of the present situation of Chicanos in the economy, then, must recognize the changes that have been taking place since the Second World War, while recognizing the limitations and historical continuities imposed by institutionalized segmentation.

THE 1970s

There are three types of developments affecting the status of Chicano and Mexicano workers that can be analyzed for the current decade. One of these, the most recent turn of the cycle concerning the undocumented worker, was discussed in the previous section. The other two have to do with occupational trends during a period of relatively high unemployment, and with what I see as a possible emergence of a marginal sector of the Chicano population.

Occupational trends for the last few years can be seen in table 21. These figures are not strictly comparable to the census data presented earlier, since they are based on self-identification as being of "Mexican origin" in surveys of a relatively small number of people. In addition, the available figures are for the United States as a whole, rather than for the Southwest only. Still, they provide some general impressions. From the data for 1971 through 1976, few clear trends emerge. There seem to be small gains in the professional and managerial categories, but the considerable fluctuation and the small samples upon which the data are based should be kept in mind. While it is true that there seems to be no overall trend toward a more equal distribution, neither does there appear to be a downward trend, as one might have postulated from the high levels of unemployment that prevailed during the decade and the potential effects of the buffer role. A clearer picture will probably not emerge until data from the 1980 census are available.

The Reemergence of Marginality

In chapter 3, I described the appearance of a transitory marginal group of Chicanos who had been displaced from their traditional agricultural roles but for whom the new forces of production had not developed to the point of being able to reabsorb them. As the new economy developed, those Chicanos were incorporated into the productive process in the colonized sector. In more recent years there has developed an integrated or at least substantially integrated sector, described earlier in this chapter. At this point I wish to advance the hypothesis that along with this development there has occurred a reemergence of a marginal sector, this time possibly permanent. Before elaborating the hypothesis, however, I would like to go deeper into the concept of marginality and its relationship to the reserve labor force, which is one aspect of the colonized sector.

Karl Marx, in the first volume of *Capital*, described the existence in nineteenth-century capitalism of a relative surplus population, also referred to as an industrial reserve army. This was a population which was often out of work, but whose existence was functional for the development of the capitalist economy in that it provided the labor reserve needed during periods of capitalist growth, which typically proceeded unevenly (Marx, 1967, p. 633). It also exerted a downward pressure on wages. Marx described various forms which this reserve army took, and the methods by which it was constantly reproduced. One of the underlying assumptions of the concept was that the labor requirements of the capitalist economy would continue to expand, so that the portion of the population which was not economically functional at a given period would become so in another period.

In recent years a body of analysis has developed which questions this assumption. One of the seminal sources of this argument is found in Baran

TABLE 21

U.S. OCCUPATIONAL DISTRIBUTION
FOR THE MEXICAN-ORIGIN POPULATION, 1971–76, BY SEX (IN PERCENTAGES)*

Occupational Level	Male						Female					
	1971	1972	1973	1974	1975	1976	1971	1972	1973	1974	1975	1976
Professional & technical	4.5	4.7	4.8	5.2	7.6	5.5	3.6	5.4	5.2	4.5	6.2	6.0
Managers, proprietors & officials	5.2	5.6	5.3	5.7	6.2	5.6	1.6	3.6	3.8	1.6	2.2	3.2
Clerical	6.1	4.5	4.1	5.0	6.2	4.9	26.2	26.6	26.7	27.5	28.2	30.1
Sales	2.3	2.7	2.5	2.7	5.0	2.1	4.6	4.6	5.6	4.0	5.4	4.8
Craftsmen	19.5	20.9	20.0	19.2	2.6	19.1	1.8	0.6	1.6	1.6	1.5	3.0
Operatives	27.6	27.0	28.4	26.9	18.3	29.0	26.9	21.6	25.5	29.3	25.3	22.2
Laborers	15.0	14.7	14.0	14.2	28.1	14.3	0.2	1.2	1.4	1.2	1.9	1.7
Service	11.5	11.8	12.1	9.3	14.2	10.9	32.8	33.4	27.5	26.1	28.3	20.8
Farm laborers	8.2	7.8	8.4	11.5	10.4	7.8	2.0	2.8	2.7	4.2	1.1	2.5
Farmers & farm managers	0.1	0.5	0.4	0.4	7.7	0.6	—	—	0.2	—	—	0.1

*Figures for 1971 and 1972 for 14 years and older. All other years for 16 years and older.
Sources: Current Population Reports, *Persons of Spanish Origin in the United States*, 1973–76.

and Sweezy's neo-Marxist work, *Monopoly Capital* (1966). In that work they elaborate a general theory of contemporary monopolistic or oligopolistic American capitalism, based on the theory that the dynamics of this system can best be understood in terms of the tendency to produce surpluses which create a number of stubborn problems. The surpluses of which they speak consist of surpluses of value, of industrial capacity, of commodities, of capital itself, and of labor. As the capacity of the system to produce these surpluses increases, a number of compensating mechanisms come into play. For example, the tendency to develop a surplus of labor is in part met by expanding the area of public civilian employment and the number of persons in the military. Some writers have argued that these long-term trends toward the production of a surplus work force have been aggravated by trends toward automation in the economy (Seligman, 1965). Another factor that is sometimes cited is the internationalization of the American corporation and the associated trend to export industrial plants to low-wage foreign areas, the so-called "runaway shops." The Border Industrialization Program along the U.S.–Mexico border is one example of such a development, in which plants which would otherwise be located in areas such as the Southwest are instead set up in Mexico in order to make use of Mexican labor directly, without first having to lure it to the United States. (For descriptions of this program, see Baerrensen, 1971, and Fernández, 1977.)

José Nun has followed up this general line of thought by differentiating the Marxist concepts of relative surplus population and the industrial reserve army (Nun, 1969). According to him, some of the surplus population plays a functional role in the economy, along the lines described by Marx, and can properly be seen as an industrial reserve army, providing elasticity to labor supply and maintaining a downward pressure on wages. However, under existing and foreseeable conditions, another portion of the surplus population is superfluous to the real labor needs of the economy, given that there is no longer a tendency for the expansion of the labor needs of capitalism over time. This portion he calls the "marginal mass."

Before discussing whether there is a marginal sector of the Chicano population, it would be well to evaluate the plausibility of the general marginality argument. The argument has been fueled by statistics showing that official unemployment in the industrialized countries of the West is now at its highest level since the Great Depression ("Western World Joblessness Hits 17.1 Million, Highest in 40 Years," Los Angeles *Times*, Nov. 29, 1975). In large part, however, the argument is based on the assumption that the level of unemployment in the United States is considerably higher than the official statistics indicate. The official rate counts only those workers who are actively looking for work, and it has been frequently criticized for not including persons who have worked in the past but have become discouraged at not being able to find work and have stopped looking. The official statistics have also been criticized for not counting as unemployed those persons who are only working part-time, many of whom would like to work more.

When corrections are made for these two factors, the unemployment rate often doubles. Thus a special Census study of the New York City central urban area found that the official unemployment rate there was 8.1 percent, but when adjustments were made for the two factors cited above, it rose to 13.3 percent (Braverman, 1974, p. 399). In a similar computation, the 1976 unemployment rate for the United States was found to jump from 5.8 to 11.8 percent ("What's the Real Unemployment Rate?" *Dollars and Sense,* April 1976, p. 12). Since the concept of the discouraged worker is based on psychological factors, however, there is some dispute about the extent of this phenomenon (see e.g., Flaim, 1973).

There is, however, a much more ambitious argument, made most notably by Baran and Sweezy but also by others. This argument is that the official and expanded unemployment rates are only the tip of the iceberg, and that the bulk of the relative surplus population is made up of several components that have increased notably since the Depression and the Second World War. One source of this is in persons who are now members of a greatly expanded military service, as compared to the pre–World War II situation. Another component is in the much larger number of young people who are in college and would otherwise be in the work force. Baran and Sweezy also argue that the vast expansion of government employment since the Depression is in large part an attempt to take up the slack in labor demand in the private sector (Baran and Sweezy, 1966, chap. 6). The part of government employment which is most obviously related to unemployment is the part that clearly consists of "make work," such as the public service programs explicitly aimed at reducing unemployment. Another obvious component consists of government-funded training programs. But Baran and Sweezy go on to argue that many public jobs, not in either of those categories, are in fact jobs that are not needed by the economy for economic reasons, and have in fact been created to ease social tension associated with high unemployment rates.

A related argument links the trend toward an earlier retirement age with the growth of a relative surplus population. A recent newspaper article noted some of these trends:

> Early retirement is not happening simply because people want it. It is happening because powerful institutions see it as being in their own best interest. Corporations are sliding the mandatory retirement age down to 62, 60 and even 55 because it suits their productivity needs.
>
> The proportion of older people in the work force is declining rapidly. Two decades ago, nearly half of all men over 65 were still in the work force—employed or looking for jobs. Now, only a fourth are. It will be

close to a fifth by 1980, the Census Bureau estimates. Furthermore, there is a slow but perceptible decline in the percentage of men between 55 and 64 remaining in the work force. ["Retiring Early—Rosy Dream or Nightmare?" Los Angeles *Times,* Apr. 4, 1973]

Of course, even if these arguments are accepted in whole or in part, it is not the case that all of the observable or disguised unemployment represents a condition of marginality. A substantial part of it would constitute a reserve labor force, to be drawn upon or shifted around if the labor market so required. The distinction between the reserve army and the marginal mass is not one that can be unambiguously tied to specific individuals. It is, as José Nun has pointed out, an analytical distinction and can only be made at a conceptual level (Nun, 1969, p. 202). It could possibly be expressed in terms of percentages, but this would require an in-depth study and a more exact method of estimation, which, to my knowledge, are not in existence. Nevertheless, it seems clear that if the level of obvious and hidden unemployment is on the scale indicated by some of these writers, only a small percent of it could be considered a true reserve labor force. The rest would have to be considered marginal.

If the marginality hypothesis is accepted, it would follow that racial minorities in the United States constitute a disproportionate share of that sector of the population. Some writers have argued that the Black population is in the process of becoming in large part superfluous to the economic needs of the United States. Sidney Willhelm, for example, develops such an argument, tying his formulation closely to the advance of automation and the consequent reduction in labor needs (Willhelm, 1971, chap. 6). Scattered bits of statistical information also tend to bear out the marginality hypothesis for Blacks. Christopher Gellner notes that Blacks are more likely than Whites to enter the labor market as economic conditions improve, thus indicating that a higher proportion of Blacks are discouraged workers (Gellner, 1975, p. 27). More significantly, Richard Freeman finds that the ratio of Black to White labor-force participation rates has declined for both males and females in the period 1948 to 1972, although he does not interpret this finding (Freeman, 1973, p. 72). Since the labor-force participation rate measures the extent to which a group is represented in the labor force, a decline in the Black–White ratio is consistent with the idea that Blacks are finding it increasingly difficult to find jobs. Journalistic accounts also point in the same direction. A 1976 article touches directly on many of these points:

In February of this year, while national unemployment stood at 7.6%, the unemployment rate among blacks 16 to 19 years old was 35.2%, according to the Labor Department's Bureau of Labor Statistics. For whites in the same age group, the jobless rate was only about half as high—17.1%.

But unemployment among black teen-agers may often be as high as 50%, some researchers say, if those . . . who are too discouraged to look for work are counted.

The shortage of job opportunities has led some observers—economists, social workers and civil rights spokesmen—to conclude that many jobless black teen-agers have become a permanent underclass within the economic system—human surplus material in America's highly technological society.

. . . A complicating factor in the black teen-age unemployment picture is the number of "hidden unemployed"—those who have given up looking for work and are not counted by Bureau of Labor Statistics as part of the labor force.

There are many thousands of such "discouraged workers" among black teen-agers and adults, Robert Hill, chief researcher for the National Urban League in Washington, D.C., said.

Robert Hill believes that, if the former job-seekers who have given up were counted, during the third quarter of 1975 . . . about 758,000 black teen-agers were out of work.

This puts black teen-age unemployment "around 50% nationally and that's still a conservative figure," Hill said. ["Permanent 'Underclass' of Jobless Blacks Feared," Los Angeles *Times,* Apr. 5, 1976]

The impact on Chicanos of these developments is likely to be much the same, given the similar structural position of Chicanos and Blacks in the economic system. Scattered evidence supports the idea of Chicano marginality, although it is by no means conclusive. The unemployment rate of Chicanos continues to be considerably higher than that of Anglos, although not quite as high as that of Blacks. In 1977, the official "Hispanic" unemployment rate in the United States was 10.0 percent, while for the "White" population as a whole the rate was 6.2 percent (U.S. Commission on Civil Rights, 1978, p. 27). The labor-force participation rate of Chicanos appears to be high, but this is largely because of the age distribution of the Chicano population. As one researcher has demonstrated, the labor-force participation rates of Spanish-origin males in all age groups over 25 are lower than those of Anglo males. The labor-force participation rates for Chicanas are also lower than those for Anglo women (ibid., pp. 4–5).

Disguised unemployment is also a factor that needs to be taken into account here. As Schmidt and Koford have written,

Changes made by the Bureau of Labor Statistics in the definition result in a significant amount of present unemployment being masked, deferred, or ignored. For example, now all enrollees in the Neighborhood Youth Corps' out-of-school programs and some other manpower programs count as employed, although such enrollees established their eligibility for the programs by being unemployed. At the same time, members of the Job Corps were simply counted as "not in the labor force."

In this connection it is interesting to point out that in the manpower work and training programs administered by the U.S. Department of Labor the number of Mexican-American enrollees is two and three times the number of Anglos in some states and exceeds that of Anglos in each state. The total enrollment of Mexican-Americans was 68,748, compared to 52,025 Anglos, as of June 30, 1972. [Schmidt and Koford, 1975, p. 95]

Another indicator of possible marginality is cited by these same authors:

In the Southwest the difference in the proportion of Mexican-American and Anglo families who received public income assistance is indeed great. The percentage of Anglo families ranges from 2.0 in Arizona to 5.9 in Colorado, whereas for Mexican-American families it goes from 8.4 percent to 14.9 percent in the same states. [Ibid., p. 97]

Yet another researcher has concluded that Chicanos improved their income position from 1950 to 1970, but in the process moved into jobs that were, on balance, declining in importance in the economy. On the basis of that trend, he feels pessimistic about the future economic mobility of Chicanos (Kane, 1973, p. 395).

CHAPTER **6**

The Role of the State

Just because you're paranoid doesn't mean they're not really out to get you.

—Popular saying

WHAT HAS BEEN THE ROLE of the state in creating, maintaining, or changing the structure of inequality that characterizes the situation of Chicanos in American society? That is the question this chapter addresses.

The role of the state in advanced capitalist societies has received much attention in recent years, but, as with most other theoretical topics, there is little agreement on appropriate approaches or definitions. The concept of the state itself, which seems deceptively simple, is subject to considerable variation. In Max Weber's classic formulation, the state is that institution in society which reserves to itself a monopoly on the legitimate use of physical force within a given territory (Gerth and Mills, 1946, p. 78). Marxists generally add a functional component to this: The state is seen as an institution which arose historically in order to ensure the domination of one class over other classes (Engels, 1972; Lenin, 1975). Violence is, of course, one element in this domination, but by no means the only element. Another variation derives from the relationship one sees between the state and such institutions as the bureaucracy, the courts, and the legislature. Some writers simply equate the state with the totality of these concrete public institutions. Others employ a more abstract and analytic conception. Erik Wright, for instance, sees the state as follows:

"Structure" is a much broader and more complex notion than "organization"... when the state is regarded as a "structure," it is no longer conceived of as a tightly bounded instrument (organization)... rather, it is conceived of as a complex network of institutions, organization, and social relationships. [Wright, 1974–75, p. 107]

Alan Wolfe follows a similar approach:

There is the problem of whether the state... represents an actual reality which can be identified or whether it has a conceptual utility only. It does have an existential reality which can be easily identified. This is

157

what is often called government. Yet that thing called the government can only do what it is supposed to do if behind it is an apparatus responsible for the reproduction of the social system within which the government operates. That other thing, which cannot in fact be directly touched or seen, is the state. The state is therefore a process which becomes embodied in certain structures. Those structures are overthrown by a revolution, the hidden authority relationships behind them need more time and effort before they will wither away. [Wolfe, 1974, pp. 149-50]

Whereas this analytical approach is more satisfactory for certain purposes, for the current task references to the state will for all practical purposes mean the various concrete institutions which make up the government: the executive, the bureaucracy, the legislature, the judiciary, the military, the police, etc. For present purposes, also, we will not define the state in functional terms, leaving that matter open to empirical investigation.

There are also various answers that are given to the question of what role the state plays in modern societies, particularly with respect to conflicts of interest between different groups. The first step in my analysis will be to summarize the most important theories. After that I will review some of the empirical material presented in earlier chapters in light of these theories.

The first version of the role of the state in resolving conflict of interests stems from *pluralist* theory. Pluralist theory is widely diffused in the writings of American social scientists (see, e.g., Dahl, 1956 and 1967; Lowi, 1969; Key, 1961; Rose, 1967; Burns and Peltason, 1966; and other American government textbooks). This theory is based on the concept of the United States as a pluralist society, that is, one in which there are no clear-cut class divisions but rather a multiplicity of fragmented and cross-cutting cleavages. The view of the political system as pluralist follows from this vision of society. The political system is seen as an arena in which the various groups in the society carry on a process of competition and bargaining, with no one group being able to establish a clear preponderance of power. Control of the state is thus dispersed as groups act as checks against each other. The state is basically a neutral institution which registers the outcome of the process of political competition, and the policy decisions emanating from the state reflect the shifting coalitions that are formed among the competing groups around each political issue. A central assumption of this theory is that no one group dominates, and that all significant groups in the society are able to affect the policy process somewhere along the line by organizing themselves and following the rules of the political game. This key assumption is often stated baldly in the leading political science textbooks, although the more serious analytic works generally impose limitations on it. Thus Dahl, after stating that "a central guiding thread of American constitutional development has been the evolution of a political system in which all the active and legitimate groups in the population can make themselves heard at some crucial stage in the process of decision" (Dahl, 1956, p. 137), goes on to mention that "if a group is inactive, whether by free choice, violence, intimidation, or law, the normal American system does not necessarily provide it with a checkpoint anywhere in the process" (p. 138). Still, this qualification comes at the end of the cited work and the implications of this exception are not further developed or integrated into the general theory. The bulk of the literature in this tradition conveys the impression that the exceptions are minor and do not significantly contradict the major themes of free access, countervailing power, and state neutrality.

A variation of the pluralist theory can be found in the writings of Grant McConnell, who sees the United States as a pluralist society but one in which certain important institutions of the state have largely fallen under the control of interest groups, particularly those composed of large corporations (McConnell, 1966).

A second theoretical position, that of the *power elite,* is associated with the work of C. Wright Mills (Mills, 1956). Mills conceives of the United States as essentially a mass society in which powerful interest groups play a role, but in which they are largely unresponsive to the public will. Mills' main thesis is that American society has become increasingly dominated by the heads of three large bureaucratic hierarchies: the corporations, the executive branch of government, and the military. Mills sees these three hierarchies as at least partly autonomous but also tightly interlocked, with the corporate sector of the elite as the most powerful. Mills clearly differs from the pluralists in his view of the state, but he also differs from Marxist theories in not adopting a class analysis. Classes, for Mills, are just social groupings. While he does not deal directly with the question of clashes of interests and their resolution, the implication of this analysis is that the corporations are regularly able to secure their interests through their extensive control of the state. In his view, no other "private" sector of society is able to match the power of the corporations, and thus there is no countervailing power. William Domhoff has provided a variation of this approach in attaching central importance to an upper social class which controls the various components of the power elite primarily through placement of some of its members in key positions, but also through the formation of high-level policy-planning associations and the manipulation of public opinion (Domhoff, 1967, 1970, 1974).

A third concept of the role of the state is provided by the *Marxist* tradition, with variations. The Marxist view of American society differs fundamentally from that of pluralists and power elitists, in that the basic divisions of interest are perceived as following class lines. Classes, in turn, are defined by the relationships that people have to the means and the process of production: capitalists own the means of production and hire labor power; workers do not own the means of production and sell their labor power; the petty bourgeoisie rely for their living primarily on their own labor power; and so on. Classes in themselves are ultimately analytic categories, not formal institutions, although they may take concrete form when a class that is conscious of itself as a class organizes itself accordingly. Social formations (parties, interest groups), then, may correspond to classes, or they may be organized on other bases (segments of classes or narrower interest groupings). In any case, classes are seen as providing the most fundamental definitions of people's interests in the society, whether or not those interests are directly perceived by the members of that class. Thus all workers have an interest in higher wages and better working conditions, and ultimately in overthrowing class society and its relations of domination and subordination. Capitalists have an interest in keeping wages low and appropriating as much of the value produced by the workers' labor as possible, and ultimately in maintaining the class society in existence.

The Marxist concept of class is fundamentally different from the prevailing American social science view which takes classes as mere social strata, defined on the basis of level of income, degree of education, or even self-perception. The great advantage of the Marxist definition is that it forms part of a broad theory of historical social change, based on the conflict of classes, whereas the strata concept is simply a descriptive category. In addition, the Marxist concept does a better job of grouping people according to their interests.

Among Marxist analysts of politics there is general agreement that the state in capitalist society serves the interest of capitalists as a class, and is not a neutral arbiter of the interest-group process. Beyond this, however, there is significant disagreement. Two major areas of contention are explored below. (This discussion draws upon Miliband, 1965, 1969, 1972, 1973; Poulantzas, 1972, 1973a, 1973b, 1975, 1976; Gold, Lo, and Wright, 1975; Esping-Andersen, Friedland, and Wright, 1976; Wright, 1974–75; Wolfe, 1973, 1974; Lenin, 1975; Bridges, 1974; Block, 1977; Mollenkopf, 1974; Sardei-Biermann, Christiansen, and Dohse, 1973; Offe, 1972, 1973.)

The first area of disagreement has to do with *the degree to which the state is directly controlled by the capitalist class.* Some Marxist writers in the past have written as if the state were a direct instrument in the hands of the capitalist class, to be manipulated at will in pursuit of their interests (the *instrumentalist* position; see Perlo, 1975, for a recent example). The prevailing view now, of which Nicos Poulantzas has been a leading exponent, is that of the relative autonomy of the state. This does not mean that the state does not serve the interests of capitalists, but that it is not controlled by capitalists in a direct manner. Miliband, who is sometimes characterized as an instrumentalist, has provided a good short statement against instrumentalism:

> A simple illustration of the point [the relative autonomy of the state] is the common interpretation of the most familiar of all the Marxist formulations on the state, that which is to be found in the *Communist Manifesto,* where Marx and Engels assert that "the modern State is but a committee for managing the common affairs of the whole bourgeoisie." This has regularly been taken to mean not only that the state acts on behalf of the dominant or "ruling" class, which is one thing, but that it acts *at the behest* of that class, which is an altogether different assertion and, as I would argue, a vulgar deformation of the thought of Marx and Engels. For what they are saying is that "the modern state is but a committee for managing the *common* affairs of the *whole* bourgeoisie": the notion of the whole bourgeoisie implies the existence of separate elements which make up that whole. This being the case, there is an obvious need for an institution of the kind they refer to, namely the state; and the state *cannot* meet this need without enjoying a certain degree of autonomy. [Miliband, 1973, p. 85n.]

The state, then, is concerned with serving the general class interests of capitalists and, ultimately, in ensuring the existence of a class society, although it will serve particular interests where doing so does not contradict the broader aim. But in order to properly fulfill the broader role, the state cannot be tightly controlled, for several reasons:

1. The capitalist class is not completely united on policy issues. As members of the same class they share fundamental interests, but on particular issues their interests may be in conflict. The state must be able to make a judgment as to how particular policy demands will affect the more fundamental class interests.

2. An agency is needed that can take a long-range view and calculate overall effects. During the 1930s, for example, the state acted to grant certain concessions to workers because the immediate costs of such concessions were outweighed by the long-run benefits of preventing more radical alternatives from gaining support.

3. A crucial role performed by the state is that of preserving the legitimacy of the social order. In order to better perform this function, the state must present the *appearance* of being neutral. Direct control by capitalists would make it much harder to preserve this appearance.

An instrumentalist view of the state makes it difficult to explain many actions of the state, especially those which are resisted by capitalists organized in interest groups. A noninstrumentalist perspective is better able to reconcile these actions with a general Marxist analysis. In passing, it may be mentioned that many state actions which are commonly thought to have been resisted by capitalists as a whole were in fact not so resisted (see Weinstein, 1968; Kolko, 1967).

A second area of contention among Marxists has to do with *which factors primarily account for the correspondence that exists between state actions and capitalist interests.* While Marxists agree that such a correspondence exists, there is some dispute about the nature of the mechanisms that effect the correspondence. Several possibilities exist:

1. Capitalists, because of their great command of resources, are able to use those resources to exercise preponderant influence through the interest-group process. This would include campaign contributions, lobbying, the control of information, and related activities. This process is open to all interest groups, but capitalists are able to use it to best advantage because of their superior resources. While this avenue of influence is universally acknowledged to exist, it would be most effective in securing the particular interests of capitalist groups, but not necessarily the interests of the class as a whole.

2. The second mechanism has to do with the control that the capitalist class exercises over the ideological apparatus of the society, such as the media. Given that the media are themselves large capitalistic enterprises, and dependent on other capitalists for their advertising revenues, it should not be surprising that they function to create a climate of opinion conducive to the realization of capitalist interests. This comes about not only through direct ideological manipulation, but through affecting the consciousness of the public, as in reinforcing deep-seated values supportive of the capitalist system: competition, materialism, individualism, etc. The resources available to the capitalist class are thus used not only to influence the political process directly but to create a supportive ideological atmosphere.

3. Capitalists can exercise control over the political process by placing members of their class in key political positions. This position is most closely identified with William Domhoff, who began as a power elitist but whose writings have increasingly reflected a Marxist perspective. It is also found in Miliband's writings. This position is often associated with the instrumentalist position, since it seems to imply direct control by capitalists and thus the use of the state as an instrument on their behalf. Other Marxists have argued that this is not a sufficient explanation. Nicos Poulantzas goes so far as to argue a contrary viewpoint:

> The *direct* participation of members of the capitalist class in the State apparatus ... even where it exists, is not the important side of the matter. The relation between the bourgeois class and the State is an *objective relation*. This means that if the *function* of the State in a

determinate social formation and the *interests* of the dominant class in this formation coincide, it is by reason of the system itself: the direct participation of members of the ruling class in the State apparatus is not the *cause* but the *effect,* and moreover a chance and contingent one, of this objective coincidence.

. . . It can be said that the capitalist State best serves the interests of the capitalist class only when the members of this class do not participate directly in the State appartus, that is to say when the *ruling class* is not the *politically governing class.* [Poulantzas, 1972, pp. 245-45]

4. The fourth possibility is already suggested in the Poulantzas quote just cited, and is generally discussed under the heading of the *structuralist* perspective. This perspective begins from an analysis of functional relationships in the society, and seeks to demonstrate that the very function of the state is to serve the general interest of the dominant class, as by creating unity among capitalists and disunity among workers. Thus Poulantzas speaks of the *capitalist state* as counterposed to *the state in capitalist society.* However, this perspective has been criticized for not specifying the exact mechanisms that ensure that the state will always accept this to be its function (Gold, Lo, and Wright, 1975, p. 38). It would seem that the logical argument to pursue from this point would be that the way in which the institutions of the state are structured bias the state toward the pursuit of capitalist interests. However, this argument has only been touched upon in the Marxist literature, and it appears that little has been done on this topic since the writings of Lenin. Lenin suggested that there were several structural aspects of the state that ensured its response to capitalists rather than workers: the high salaries paid top officials, guaranteeing that they would identify themselves with the wealthy; the appointment rather than election of administrators, insulating them from popular control; and the separation of the legislative from and administrative function, which prevented any mass participation in administration, where the real power of the state resides in modern capitalist societies (Lenin, 1975; Wright, 1974-75).

5. The fifth possibility is that the actions of the state correspond to the interests of capitalists because the interests of the state itself correspond to those of capitalists. According to this argument, the state under capitalism must identify with the interests of capitalists because to do otherwise would imperil the state of the economy through loss of confidence on the part of investors. With a decline in the economy, the tax revenues of the state also decline, and thus its resources. Also, a decline in the economy creates hard times, which are then blamed on the incumbents, who run the risk of being voted out of office. This is a type of structural argument as well, since it relies on the structure of the political economy rather than on the direct exercise of influence (Miliband, 1969, pp. 147-51; Bridges, 1974, pp. 172-73; O'Con-

nor, 1973, p. 8; Block, 1977, pp. 15ff.). The ultimate outcome of this situation is that the interests of the capitalist class become identified not only with
the interests of the state but are represented as constituting the national interest
as well.

From the preceding analysis we can abstract four general approaches to
conceptualizing the role of the state in relation to interests in the society. They
can be characterized as in figure 7.

One of the limitations of the Marxist perspectives up to this point is that
they have not been very specific in describing the various kinds of interest
conflicts that are possible in capitalist societies, or in specifying their likely
outcomes. One writer who has made an attempt in this direction is Alan
Wolfe, and before we review the materials on Chicanos and the state, it would
be well to summarize his discussion.

Wolfe presents several interest-conflict situations. The most important
is where there is a conflict between a privileged group and another group that

FIGURE 7

FOUR CONCEPTS OF THE ROLE OF THE STATE

	View of Society	Correspondence of State Action to Capitalist Interests	Degree of Direct Control of State by Capitalists	Mechanisms Through Which Such Control Is Achieved
Pluralist	Pluralist	Low	Low	Interest group
Power elite (non-Marxist instrumentalist)	Bureaucratic elitist	High	High	Placement in Key Positions
Marxist instrumentalist	Class	High	High	Placement and interest-group process
Marxist structuralist	Class	High	Low	Structure of the state and the society

challenges those privileges. He argues that in general the state will support the privileged group, although he notes two exceptions as follows.

> In those situations where the state intervenes against a group from the dominant class, it can be established as a general principle that such intervention will be the result of popular pressures that are too strong to ignore, that the intervention will be as symbolic as possible, and that the sanctions involved may even be beneficial to those interests over a period of time. [Wolfe, 1973, p. 30]

> Aid given by the state to groups outside the ruling class will be given only so long as the privileges of the ruling class are not significantly threatened; indeed, such aid will be given when the provision of no aid at all would more significantly hurt the dominant groups. [Ibid., p. 38]

Under the first heading Wolfe places antitrust legislation, and under the second the New Deal legislation that resulted in the recognition of unions, such as the Wagner Act. Wolfe presents two other types of situations, which are less important for our purposes than the first:

> When the state intervenes between two groups neither of which is in the dominant class, such intervention is designed to favor the group that those in power would like favored; the unfavored group, if it mounts a challenge to this policy, will be repressed. [Ibid., pp. 44]

> The last possibility . . . is the one that occurs when the state is a party to conflict among groups, all of whom belong to the dominant class. In those situations . . . the goal of state intervention is to favor neither group (assuming relatively equal power) but to bring the groups together around a compromise before this conflict has any effect on less powerful groups that might be able to take advantage of a major rupture. [Ibid., p. 51]

With these models and propositions before us, it is possible to review some of the material presented in earlier chapters for evidence bearing on these various formulations of the role of the state.

THE ROLE OF THE STATE:
CONQUEST AND EXPROPRIATION

The state claims a monopoly on the legitimate use of violence, and it was in exercising its control of violence that the American state had its first impact on the Southwest. The role of the state in the conquest of the Southwest was outlined in chapter 2, and there is no need to repeat the argument here, except to emphasize that the conquest was made on behalf of the interests of the dominant classes in the society, and that it was legitimized as a response to a Mexican attack and in terms of Manifest Destiny. In making use

of the Manifest Destiny appeal, the state succeeded in presenting the interests
of the dominant classes in the society as the national interest, and thus enlist-
ing substantial popular support for its expansionist policy.

The second major exercise of state power affecting Chicanos was in the
formal and informal expropriation of the land that began after the conquest
and continued into the twentieth century. This process was also described in
chapter 2. As Paul Gates has emphasized in his various writings, the resulting
pattern of land concentration was primarily of benefit to large Anglo landholders, members of the emerging dominant class in the Southwest who organized agriculture along capitalist lines. The specific methods by which this
was done are instructive examples of the role of the state in conflicts of
interest between more powerful and less powerful groups.

The most obvious examples of the state role in this regard are in the
setting up of special legal organs to rule on land-grant claims, such as the
California Land Commission, established in 1851, and the Court of Private
Land Claims, set up for New Mexico in 1891. The evidence reviewed in
chapter 2 indicates that the way in which these institutions proceeded seriously biased the outcome against the original claimants, and particularly the
Chicanos. This was so not only because the procedures put the burden of
proof on the claimants, but because of such factors as the language of the
courts, the location of federal land offices, and the application of Anglo legal
precepts to grants made under a different legal system. By letting a major part
of the burden of dispossession fall on such seemingly impartial institutional
mechanisms, the facade of state neutrality could be more easily maintained
while still obtaining the desired result in the end. At the same time, it is true
that the need for the state to preserve the aura of legitimacy and neutrality
served as a partial obstacle. Dispossession at times was slow, taking decades
to work itself out in some areas. Particular decisions of the courts also favored
the original claimants where their case was particularly strong, so that a
variety of mechanisms had to be used to achieve the desired end. A pluralist,
working with a short time perspective, might well have come to the conclusion that his model was validated by the procedures. Observation of the results
over a long period gives a better indication of the underlying processes at
work.

The actions of the federal government were, of course, only one side of
the coin. The other side consisted of the activities of regional and local
governments. The imposition of fixed land taxes, in keeping with the requirements of capitalist agricultural development, was a major factor in most
areas in dispossessing the former landholders, again in the form of impartial-
ity and uniformity. Manipulation of the tax rates, however, was apparently
not unknown. The operations of the Santa Fe Ring and other political-
economic combinations are one of the best illustrations of the way in which

the direct control of state institutions by the dominant economic interests served to further the expropriation and reconcentration of land.

It should be kept in mind that in facilitating the transfer of land, the state acted not only on behalf of capitalist class interests but on its own behalf. A great deal of the land that was taken over in New Mexico went not to private interests but directly into the public domain. That the state is an institution with its own interests should not be overlooked, however much those interests coincide with those of the dominant class because of the way in which society is structured.

In the initial expansion of the American social order into the Southwest, then, the military and judicial institutions of the state played a leading role in first gaining and then consolidating control over the territory. The historian Fehrenbach goes so far as to call the law the "chief instrument of dispossession" in the Southwest (cited in chap. 2), although, of course, military control had to be established first.

THE ROLE OF THE STATE
IN THE REGULATION OF LABOR:
IMMIGRATION AND THE LABOR RESERVE

As seen in earlier chapters, the state has played a major role in the regulation of the labor supply for Southwestern employers. One way in which it has done this is through regulating the reserve role played by Mexicano workers and other Third World groups. Immigration policy provides an extended case study for evaluating the state role in this respect.

One way of looking at immigration policy is as an arena of interest-group conflict, in accordance with the pluralist approach. Over the years a number of interest groups have struggled to preserve or change the status quo. Among these groups have been agribusiness associations, organized labor, small farmers, nativist groups, and various agencies of the state itself. As a result of these struggles, a series of measures have been taken by the state, depending on the relative power the various groups were able to muster, and on other circumstances. Thus Congress passed the Chinese Exclusion Act in 1882, the Alien Contract Labor Law in 1885, the Immigration Act of 1924, and so on. A number of administrative decisions have also resulted from these conflicts, such as the Gentlemen's Agreement with Japan in 1907. Many such decisions have represented victories for forces seeking immigration restrictions, with employers on the losing side. The history of immigration policy, then, would seem to support the pluralist perspective and the view of the state as neutral, especially when each law or administrative decision is viewed in isolation. However, there are other factors that point to a very different conclusion, one which sees the state as a labor regulator on behalf of agribusiness interests. These considerations are the following.

1. Restrictionist victories have generally succeeded in cutting down on one or another source of cheap labor, but other sources have always been available. In recent years, when cheap labor has been unavailable through regular channels, employers have increasingly relied on undocumented workers from Mexico. *The state has collaborated in this policy through inaction,* that is, by not enforcing vigorously the restrictions against Mexican workers' crossing the border. The role of the Border Patrol and the set of understandings and informal procedures that have developed around that role were described in chapter 5.

2. This support-through-inaction has been supplemented by a long string of *positive state actions* on behalf of agricultural employers. The bracero program, originally instituted in 1942 as an administrative agreement in response to a wartime situation, and then formalized by Congress during the Korean War, is an outstanding example. The "drying out" of "wetbacks" is another. The "amiable fiction" under which green-card commuter workers are considered residents of the United States is yet another. Furthermore, it has generally not been necessary for employers to wage major public campaigns to secure these victories from the state, as the proponents of immigration restrictions have had to do. Rather, the persistent bias of the state certainly appears to have been acting in their favor, subject to being overturned only on the basis of concerted efforts by their opponents. (See Divine, 1957; Reisler, 1976; Craig, 1971.)

3. The state's role has not been limited to facilitating the movement of this type of worker into Southwestern labor markets. It has also acted to complete the reserve cycle, by returning the Mexicano workers to Mexico during periods of labor surplus. This happened after World War I, during the Depression, in the early 1950s, when braceros were available, and appears to be happening again in the 1970s.

The overall pattern that emerges from a long-term perspective, as opposed to the short-term perspective that pluralists favor, is one in which the normal and routine actions of the state favor the interests of employers, and in which organized labor and other interests have to struggle mightily to win even partial victories. These victories, which can be seen as grudging concessions to extraordinary mobilizations, have always been temporary and incomplete because of the other, routinized actions and non-actions by which the state has favored agribusiness. From this model, we can predict that the pattern will continue until such time as the state concludes that a major threat, such as to the territorial integrity of the country, overrides the interests of Southwestern employers.

What factors account for the long-term dominance of employer interests in this area? While it is not possible to give a complete answer from the limited information available, it seems evident that the *pattern of institutionalized access* which employers enjoy is in large part responsible. Perhaps the best evidence on this score comes from the carefully researched studies of Ernesto Galarza. He has described the manner in which the associations formed by labor employers came to be a regular part of the policymaking process with respect to the bracero program. A national organization, the Special Farm Labor Committee, was constituted as a federal advisory body, composed of representatives from the farmers' associations, and one of its subcommittees was charged with making recommendations relating to the bracero program to the Department of Labor (Galarza, 1964, p. 119). Public Law 78, which institutionalized the bracero program, required the secretary of labor to consult agricultural employers and workers, but the resulting consultation was extremely one-sided.

> Federal officials had in fact consulted employers on many subjects other than the supply of workers available and the wages being paid before Public Law 78 was enacted. The consultants were the representatives of the farmers' associations, combined into state and national committees such as the Special Farm Labor Advisory Committee and the Subcommittee on Mexican Labor. . . .
>
> In November 1947 Labor Department officials met with employers' representatives prior to the Mexican negotiations to receive suggestions as to proposed amendments. The following year the Department arranged regional meetings to discuss with growers draft proposals and invited a delegation to stay with the American officials at the same hotel for daily reviews and briefings. . . . Consultation of this type continued after 1959 for the purpose, among others, of drawing up contracts that would be acceptable to farm organizations.
>
> These courtesies enabled the growers to participate indirectly in working out the terms and provisions of the basic legal documents of the program. . . . Growers' approval was sought in advance for drafts of bills and resolutions introduced in the House and the Senate. . . .
>
> Consultation with organized labor, by contrast, was perfunctory, forced and intermittent. The Department of Labor's commitment to equality in consultation was never honored. . . . A federal Labor Advisory Committee was appointed by the Secretary of Labor. Its meetings were sporadic, its agenda screened and untimely. No drafts of agreements or contracts were ever submitted to it for advance study or comment. [Galarza, 1964, pp. 121–23]

While Congress has by no means been unresponsive to the wishes of employers, it seems from the available evidence that the bureaucratic institutions of the state have been far more reliable in the pursuit of agribusiness interests. The privileged access which employer groups have had to the bureaucracy appears to have been the decisive factor in their struggles to influence the policymaking and policy-implementing processes. While it is not possible to pinpoint from the available studies the exact source of these privileges, and thus not possible to choose between instrumentalist and structuralist types of explanations, the pattern is certainly inconsistent with pluralist assumptions of state neutrality and countervailing power.

The numerous specific defeats suffered by employers, however, are clearly inconsistent with the instrumentalist view of the state, although not with the structuralist perspective, given that employer interests have prevailed in the long run.

OTHER ASPECTS OF LABOR REGULATION

Another way in which the state has cooperated in the regulation of the agricultural labor supply has been through the schools. While this is a special topic that would require a full-scale study to investigate properly, scattered references can be found to it in the literature on Southwestern labor. Thus Paul Taylor, in his investigations, found that in Colorado beet growers were frequently members of the rural school boards, and were not interested in strictly enforcing the attendance laws for the children of their Chicano workers. "This indifference usually rests on the feeling that assistance of children of school age is essential to prompt performance of beet labor operations, coupled with unconcern over the interrupted schooling of children, many of whom are, after all, of an alien race" (Taylor, 1929, p. 195).

Government relief programs have also been used as labor market regulators. During the 1930s in Colorado, for example, much of the sugar beet labor supply was on relief in the off months, since there was little alternative employment. As noted in chapter 5, growers were able to secure the collaboration of relief authorities so that their workers would be forced off relief in time for the beet harvest (Schwartz, 1945, p. 117). Carey McWilliams makes reference to this same practice (McWilliams, 1942, p. 120). The use of the welfare system for this purpose is completely consistent with the depiction of the working of this system in the work of Frances Piven and Richard Cloward (Piven and Cloward, 1971).

In regulating migratory field labor, it appears that the responsible government agencies also felt called upon to represent the interests of the employers. The President's Commission on Migratory Labor, writing in 1951, described the attitude of the Farm Placement Services of the U.S. Employment Service:

> The Employment Service conceives its functions as rather narrow and limited. Moreover, its activities are marked by a certain one-sidedness

in favor of corralling supplies of migratory farm workers to meet growers' labor demand regardless of effects on the workers. Thus, the Service has tended to disregard the effects on workers of attracting or directing over-supplies of labor into certain crop areas.

In organizing and depending for advice on the Special Farm Labor Committee composed wholly of farm employers and their representatives, [the Farm Placement Division] acted as if, in bringing together employment opportunities and seasonal and migratory farm workers, only the advice of employers was needed, and the public and the worker had no interest in the matter. [President's Commission, 1951, pp. 100–1]

NON–SPECIFIC EXAMPLES

There are numerous cases where state activities have had important effects on Chicano and Mexicano workers indirectly, as by-products of policies adopted toward more general issues. The case of union recognition during the 1930s has already been discussed, and is dealt with specifically by Wolfe and other analysts in terms quite compatible with the alternatives he proposes. Since this case was discussed in earlier chapters, there is no need to go into it further. The other side of this coin is the long history of state repression of agricultural workers in their attempts to organize. (Much has been written on this topic. Good descriptions can be found in Jamieson, 1945; McWilliams, 1971; Reisler, 1976; and Kushner, 1975.) Here, as in other areas, state actions have as a rule favored the interests of employers; only under unusual circumstances has an agency of the state intervened on the side of the workers. Since these activities have taken place within a broader context of class conflict and have not been aimed exclusively or primarily at Chicanos, they will not be further analyzed here.

There is, as well, a more general aspect to this topic that is forcefully brought out in a recent survey of racial divisions in the Arizona copper industry. In this study, Jiménez notes the rigid exclusion of Chicanos from the political arena during Arizona's territorial period in the nineteenth century, to the point that there were no Chicano officials at any level of territorial government during this period (Jiménez, 1977, p. 18). Jiménez points out that this very exclusion denied to Chicanos the possibility of using the apparatus of the state to challenge the subordinate status that they were assigned within the mining industry and other sectors of the Arizona economy.

STATE ACTION ON BEHALF OF CHICANOS

All of the specific instances described above are cases in which the state has favored the interests of members of the dominant class at the expense of

Chicanos and Mexicanos. Are there instances where state action has gone the other way? Examples are not easy to come by, but of those that could be mentioned perhaps the equal opportunity and affirmative action statutes are the most notable. However, given the limitations on these policies (noted in chap. 5 and in the appendix), it would be safe to say that this falls well within the bounds of the second exception to the general proposition cited by Wolfe in cases of interest conflict between privileged and less privileged groups. This exception has two stipulations. One is that the interests of the dominant class not be significantly threatened, and given the limited effect of these policies this would certainly seem to be the case. The other is that the provision of no aid would more significantly hurt the dominant groups. Given the context in which these policies have been adopted, a strong argument could be made for this provision also. These policies derive largely from crisis situations, such as the Second World War and the urban uprisings of the 1960s, and have been essentially concessions made to ensure domestic tranquility in the face of external and internal threats. Thus they in no way demonstrate a bias in favor of racial minorities in the manner in which the other state actions described above demonstrate a state bias in favor of capitalist interests.

THE ROLE OF THE STATE: CONCLUSION

The materials on Chicanos in the economy were not written to test the various theories of the role of the state, and the attempt to apply them to this task in an ex post facto manner can be only partly successful at best. Still, some things can be said on the basis of these materials. The pluralist perspective is surely the weakest in understanding the Chicano experience, positing, as it does, a low correspondence of state action to capitalist interests and a neutral state role. The other three approaches are all preferable to pluralism in this respect. The Marxist structuralist perspective appears superior in that it better accounts for the imperfect control of the state by the dominant class, on the basis that this control is primarily exercised indirectly through the structure of the state rather than through direct control, as the power elite and Marxist instrumentalist positions assume. The various mechanisms of control are, of course, not mutually exclusive, and the most satisfactory formulation may be one that sees the particular interests of capitalists satisfied through the interest-group process and through placement of their own members in state positions, while the general interests of capitalists as a class are attended to through the mechanisms stressed by structuralists. The position taken by Poulantzas, that the state best looks after the general interests of capitalists when it is not directly controlled, may in fact be correct, but this in itself does not mean that all of these factors do not significantly affect the outcome of the policy process. Rather, it may help account for the fact that the state looks after both the particular *and* the general interests of capitalists, and that the two sometimes get in the way of each other. The currently vacillating attitude of the state toward undocumented workers from Mexico may serve as an example of this. The particular interests of Southwestern employers in cheap labor call for a lenient attitude, whereas the broader class interests call for tightening-up in order to avert future political challenges based on a potentially radical or separatist Chicano/Mexicano population in the Southwest. The state, responding to both types of interests, will in all likelihood adopt a compromise that will satisfy neither interest completely.

The propositions put forth by Wolfe are generally supported by the evidence from Chicano economic history, and serve to make somewhat more explicit the way in which the state responds to various situations by furthering the interests of groups from the dominant class while striving to maintain legitimacy and preserving its own neutral image.

A more rigorous test and more detailed formulation of the role of the state with respect to Chicanos will have to await studies specifically geared to that end.

CHAPTER 7

A Theory of Racial Inequality

> *Do not obtain your slaves from Britain because they are so stupid and so utterly incapable of being taught that they are not fit to form a part of the household of Athens.*
>
> —Cicero to Atticus,
> 1st century B.C.

SINCE THINGS ARE NOT always what they seem, social phenomena that appear uncomplicated often require considerable theoretical explanation. Racial inequality is no exception. The most widely held ideas about the causes of racial inequality in the United States turn out, on close examination, to be quite unsatisfactory. In order to develop a satisfactory theory, however, it is first necessary to describe and analyze existing theories. These fall into three broad categories, which will be considered in turn: deficiency theories, bias theories, and structural discrimination theories.

DEFICIENCY THEORIES OF RACIAL INEQUALITY

The contention of these theories is that racial minorities occupy an inferior economic, social, and political status because of some deficiency within the minority groups themselves. There are at least three different varieties of deficiency theory, each stressing a particular type of deficiency.

Biological Deficiency Theory

This category encompasses the classic racist theories associated with such writers as de Gobineau, Houston Chamberlain, and Madison Grant, in which racial inequality was attributed to genetic and thus hereditary inferiority on the part of certain races. These theories, while still commanding considerable overt and covert popular support, have been held in scientific disrepute for several decades (Benedict, 1959). Still, some observers have seen a resurgence in recent years, as in the work of the educational psychologist Arthur Jensen. In his lengthy article "How Much Can We Boost IQ and Scholastic Achievement?" (1969) and in a more recent book (Jensen, 1973), he deals

174

with the question of differences in the measurement of IQ between Blacks and Whites. Jensen speculates that a substantial part of these differences may be due to biological inheritance. Apparently he feels that if a biologically produced intellectual deficiency could be demonstrated, this would contribute to explaining social inequalities between Blacks and Whites (Jensen, 1969, p. 79). In spite of the notoriety that Jensen's work has achieved, it is difficult to take it very seriously as an explanation of generalized minority inequality in the United States. One reason for this is that there are serious methodological problems with his writings, such as the heavy reliance on IQ test scores, universally acknowledged now as very imperfect measures of anything that could be considered general intelligence. (See Block and Dworkin, 1974, for an extended critique.) Another is that even if racial differences in intelligence could be conclusively demonstrated, their effect on social inequalities would still be highly problematic. In fairness to Jensen, it should be noted that he is very cautious and tentative in his speculations, far more than some of his supporters and mass media popularizers.

The problems encountered in Jensen's work are characteristic of the entire field of intelligence measurement, as brought out in a recent survey of the literature by Loehlin, Lindzey, and Spuhler (1975). In addition to the many pitfalls of definition and measurement, attempts to separate out the effects of heredity and environment on test scores have achieved little or nothing that could be considered conclusive, and many studies hopelessly confound such variables as race and class. Some quotes from this survey give an indication of the status of this type of research.

> The studies we have reviewed . . . provide no unequivocal answer to the question of whether the differences in ability-test performance among U.S. racial-ethnic subpopulations do or do not have a substantial component reflecting genetic differences among the subpopulations. [Ibid., p. 133]

> All in all, while the existence of some amount of cultural bias in some IQ tests for some intergroup comparisons can hardly be doubted, we are a long way from being able to assess with confidence the precise importance of such biases for particular group comparisons. [Ibid., p. 71]

> The majority of the variation in either patterns or levels of ability lies within U.S. racial-ethnic and socioeconomic groups, not between them. Race and social class are not very powerful predictors of an individual's performance on tests of intellectual abilities. [Ibid., p. 235]

In general, then, there is no persuasive evidence for the thesis that racial groups differ in intelligence, much less that such purported differences can tell us something about social inequality, and such theories receive little support from the scientific community. Other types of deficiency theories (described below) generally receive considerably wider support.

Theories Based on Deficiency in Social Structure

This type of theory argues that minority racial groups in the United States are held back by problems in the social structure of those groups. One highly influential work which applies this approach to American Blacks is Daniel Moynihan's report, titled *The Negro Family: The Case for National Action* (Moynihan, 1965; reprinted in Lee Rainwater and William Yancey, 1967, which includes a number of critiques; see also Ryan, 1971), written at the height of the public debate on race that took place in the 1960s. Briefly, Moynihan argues that historical factors have created a weak family structure among Blacks and that this weakness creates emotional and attitudinal problems, such as emotional instability and male role confusion. It also brings about a social "tangle of pathology" (drugs, crime, etc.). This situation results in low educational achievement and a general condition of inequality—poverty, unemployment, low-status jobs. A vicious circle is set up, with economic problems reinforcing the weak family structure. Moynihan acknowledges that prejudice and discrimination exist, but he assigns these factors a distinctly secondary and diminishing role. A diagram of this model can be seen in figure 8. (Moynihan does not present his ideas in a formal model, so I have tried to construct one for him by reading his work carefully. The possibility of misinterpretation, of course, exists. It is unfortunate that virtually none of the analysts of racial inequality attempt a rigorous formulation of their ideas.)

A study which falls within this same category of theories and relates specifically to Chicanos is D'Antonio and Form's *Influentials in Two Border Cities* (1965). D'Antonio and Form describe a condition of political powerlessness of the Chicano residents of El Paso, Texas. This powerlessness they attribute to such structural deficiencies among Chicanos as a lack of political organizations, a "low level of social integration," and factionalism.

Cultural Deficiency Theories

These theories find the source of minority inequality in one or more cultural traits of the group in question. The emphasis here is on attitudes and values rather than social structure, although the two types of factors are often linked together in the models. One of the most widely discussed proponents of this view in recent years is Edward Banfield. Banfield draws some inspiration from the "culture of poverty" school to argue, in *The Unheavenly City*, that inequality in the United States is largely attributable to a "lower class culture," consisting of such traits as a present rather than future orientation, a lack of work discipline, and so on. Individuals who share this "culture" do poorly in school, and their low educational attainment creates conditions of poverty and powerlessness, which interact with each other and create a vicious circle to perpetuate educational inequalities. While it is not only racial minorities that participate in the "lower class culture," they are overrepresented there because of historical reasons, including past racial discrimination. Prejudice and discrimination are acknowledged to exist today, but they are not stressed in Banfield's work. An attempt to construct a formal model of Banfield's concepts is presented in figure 9. A critique of Banfield's ideas on grounds of internal inconsistency and lack of evidence can be found in Franklin and Resnik's *The Political Economy of Racism* (1973, pp. 159-72).

Banfield's work, while widely discussed, is not necessarily typical of the cultural deficiency tradition, which has been applied to Chicanos with a vengeance. A more representative and quite influential work is that of Herschel Manuel, who is concerned to explain educational nonachievement among Chicano children. It is difficult to present his ideas systematically, since his presentation is rambling and connections are not always explicitly made. In addition, he seems to want to cover his bases by at least mentioning several types of factors. Still, his argument goes something like this:

Cultural deficiencies, including a language handicap and such values and attitudes as fatalism, present rather than future orientation, dependency, and a lack of success orientation lead directly to problems in the schools. At the same time, the low economic level of most Chicano families creates an environment of "cultural disadvantage," a vague term intended to encompass such disparate items as experiential deprivation and a lack of material resources (adequate clothing, books, etc.). Poverty combines with a high incidence of "culture conflict" between Anglos and Chicanos in their communities to produce personality problems such as feelings of inferiority and insecurity. These factors also contribute to poor school performance, which in turn aggravates feelings of inadequacy in another example of a vicious circle (Manuel, 1965, p. 189). This model is set forth in figure 10.

Manuel, with many other analysts of Chicano education and psychology, draws inspiration from a long line of writings which picture Chicano culture as highly traditional and nonadapted to the requirements of upward mobility in an industrial society. Perhaps the most influential of these studies have been done by Florence Kluckholn (Kluckholn and Strodtbeck, 1961). Her characterization of Spanish American culture, based on one small village in New Mexico, is often made the basis of sweeping and stereotypical generalizations about Chicano culture, and Manuel's work is no exception. For a review of this tradition, see Vaca (1970). The use of the Kluckholn and Strodtbeck study for this type of interpretation is particularly ironic, since it dealt with possibly the most isolated group of Chicanos in the Southwest, and even here rapid attitudinal change was shown to be taking place in response to

FIGURE 8

THE MOYNIHAN MODEL

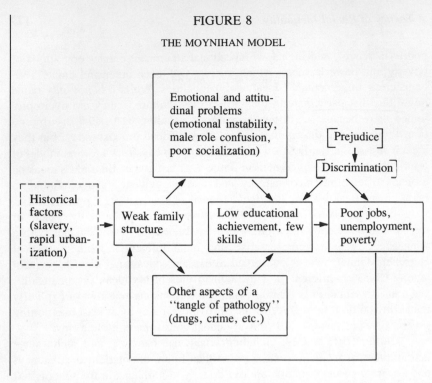

Note: Factors in brackets indicate items given less importance. Factors enclosed in broken lines are characterized as having importance in the past but not the present.

FIGURE 9

THE BANFIELD MODEL

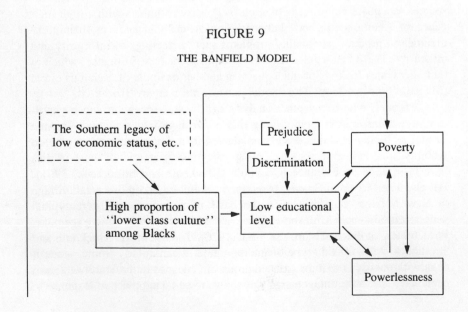

FIGURE 10

THE MANUEL MODEL

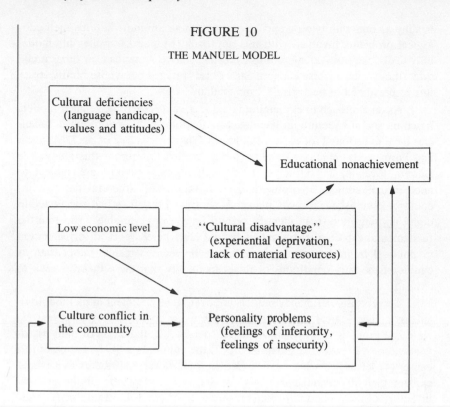

changing economic and political conditions (Kluckholn and Strodtbeck, pp. 201, 209, 256–57).

Evaluation of Deficiency Theories

Biological theories of racial deficiency are largely discredited, and recent attempts at revival, such as those based on IQ testing, are embroiled in complex disputes over methods. Even if racial IQ differences could be demonstrated, nothing would have been established with respect to social inequality.

The more popular deficiency theories are based on social structure and culture. The Moynihan model, based on the structure of the Black family, has been subjected to numerous criticisms, such as his use of aggregate statistics rather than ethnographic research as a way of characterizing family structure. Critics have pointed out that aggregate statistical measures are crude and provide no means for ascertaining the social meaning of family patterns. Aggregate statistics on "broken" families are taken as an indicator of family pathology, for example, even though a family with a single parent may be as healthy as one with two parents. However, there are more serious methodological problems involved with this approach. Moynihan applies his model only to Black families, and not to Chicano, Native American, or other racial minorities which are also economically disadvantaged but whose family structure is presumed to be "strong" rather than "weak."

As an approach to explaining racial inequality, then, deficiency models based on social structure are inelegant methodologically—different deficiencies have to be found for each racial group. The same is true of the D'Antonio and Form study mentioned above (for a detailed critique of this study, see Barrera, Muñoz, and Ornelas, 1972). All of these studies are subject to another methodological problem: even if the social structural deficiencies could be established, it could plausibly be argued that they had succeeded in doing nothing more than identify certain intervening variables, and that the fundamental causes of racial inequality lie elsewhere. Social disorganization or political fragmentation might as easily be seen as results rather than as causes of the very conditions of racial inequality that these theories seek to explain.

The cultural deficiency models are even more deficient in methodological rigor. The logical process at work seems to go something like this: (1) Here is a group which is disadvantaged socially; (2) the cause of their disadvantage must lie with the group itself; (3) the culture is a likely source of this cause; (4) let us see what we can find in their cultural attributes that would explain their disadvantaged status. A search is then made of the cultural inventory of the group until some presumed traits are discovered that hold the group back from achievement and social mobility. These, then, constitute the explanation.

Given such an approach, it is not difficult to see why the researcher is always able to come up with appropriate explanations. The cultural apparatus of any people is so complex that presumably negative traits can always be discovered, and especially if the researcher relies on cultural stereotypes or on small, atypical samples of the racial minority group. Even if such negative cultural traits could be firmly established, the possibility that there may be offsetting positive cultural traits never seems to enter the minds of cultural deficiency theorists. From a strictly logical standpoint, in order to establish any validity for this approach one would have to take a more or less complete cultural inventory of *both* the disadvantaged group and the majority non-disadvantaged racial group that serves as the basis for comparison. Negative and positive traits would have to be established for both groups. Only if this were done and a clear balance in favor of the more advantaged group emerged could an argument be made with any degree of plausibility. Needless to say, none of the cultural deficiency studies has begun to follow such a procedure, or even an approximation of it. The most sophisticated of these studies, by

Kluckholn and Strodtbeck, is marred by the atypicality of the communities studied.

Another argument that can be made against these theories is that the cultural characteristics they point to can in many cases be considered as deficiencies only within a given institutional framework. Let us grant that a monolingual Spanish-speaking child will have difficulty in a monolingual English-speaking school. This is a "deficiency" only because the society has failed to provide a bilingual educational system for that child to attend. Given such an educational system, the "deficiency" here is not in the minority racial group but in the educational system itself.

Furthermore, the cultural deficiency school suffers from the same general methodological problem as the social structural school, that of theoretical inelegance. Different cultural traits have to be found in each cultural group to serve as deficiencies, whether the group be Black, Chicano, Puerto Rican, Filipino, or any of hundreds of Native American groups. It would seem to be rather astonishing that all of these groups should have cultures deficient with respect to Anglo culture. Rather than accept this inelegant approach, it seems far more plausible to consider these theories as legitimizing myths, reflections in the social sciences of the ideologies that have historically served to justify the relationship of inequality between European and Third World peoples. Even though the specifically biological assumptions of the earlier theories have been rejected by most contemporary social scientists, the basic inclination to "blame the victim" (to use William Ryan's phrase) lives on.

If the arguments so far are not sufficiently convincing, one more can be added. Deficiency explanations of racial inequality are superfluous in that all of them assume that equal opportunity exists and has existed for the minority races in American society, and that they have failed to seize the opportunity because of their own deficiencies. Yet all of the material presented in earlier sections of this book demonstrates that such opportunity has not been present for Chicanos, and similar demonstrations can be made for other groups as well. The lack of equal opportunity is so clear and so persistent in the historical record that it seems absurd to have to resort to deficiency arguments to explain racial inequality. Where improved opportunities have existed, even temporarily as during wartime, Chicanos have not been slow to respond. The works cited earlier by Charles Loomis serve to point this out for the very area of the Southwest where one of the most famous cultural deficiency studies was conducted. Margaret Brookshire stated the case quite clearly in her study of Neuces County, Texas:

> There was nothing to support a belief that separate treatment where it occurs is due to unique group response on the part of Mexican-Americans. Indeed, with the exception of the fact that the Mexican-American group continues to be Spanish-speaking, there emerges from

this study no distinct group characteristic which might affect the pattern of industrial employment of Mexican-Americans. . . .

These data . . . support the belief that Mexican-Americans generally avail themselves of existing opportunities in the same way that other workers do. [Brookshire, 1954, pp. 270, 271]

BIAS THEORIES OF RACIAL INEQUALITY

The second major category of theories of inequality consists of bias theories. These are theories which focus on prejudice and discrimination as the sources of minority inequality, and thus tend to put the responsibility on the Anglo majority rather than on the minorities. The Kerner Commission's condemnation of "White racism" is the most widely publicized effort in this direction in recent years, although the report also has thrown in a hodgepodge of cultural and social structural deficiency explanations (*Report of the National Advisory Commission on Civil Disorders,* 1968).

The classic work in this area, however, is the still-influential study by Gunnar Myrdal, *An American Dilemma,* published in 1944 (Myrdal, 1944). Myrdal's model is fairly simple in terms of the variables he sees as currently playing an important role, but more complex in terms of historical variables (this model is presented in figure 11). Basically, Myrdal explains the unequal status of Blacks as a function of racial discrimination, which in turn is a product of White prejudice. But he places great emphasis on the concept of the vicious circle (the principle of "cumulative causation"), arguing that the disadvantaged condition of Blacks reinforces the prejudice of Whites by confirming their low opinion of Blacks. In the historical section of his massive study, Myrdal argues that the social structure of the American South brought into being a set of interests based on slavery, and that these interests popularized racial ideologies as a means of justifying the subordinate position of Blacks. These racial ideologies are one source of contemporary White prejudice. The other source is also derived from the Southern social structure, and was mediated by a complicated set of notions having to do with sexual relations (Myrdal, 1944, p. 1142). Other factors that enter into Myrdal's theory are the interests that employers in general had in the past in creating divisions among their workers, and the continuing interest that White workers have in limiting job competition with Blacks. These factors are given secondary importance.

Myrdal's study is quite voluminous, and different parts of the work seem to stress different factors in explaining racial inequality. Because of this it is difficult to reduce Myrdal's ideas to a model. In certain passages he appears to stress the interests of Whites, and in others he dwells upon social deficiencies that have been created in Blacks by the long-standing pattern of

FIGURE 11

THE MYRDAL MODEL

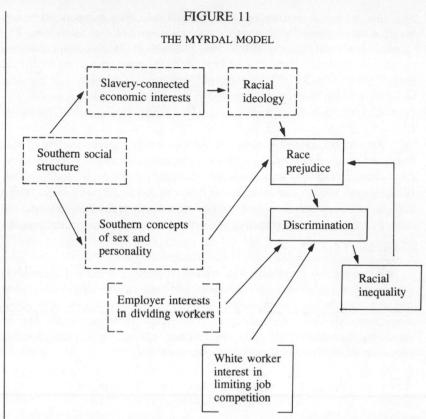

Note: Factors enclosed in solid lines are the major variables. Those enclosed in broken lines operated in the past but not in the present. Factors in solid brackets are minor variables currently operative, while those in broken brackets operated in the past but not in the present.

discrimination to which they have been subjected. He also makes use of the concept of "caste" in describing Black-White relations, although he is not consistent in the way he deals with this concept. Thus by referring to different parts of his work, one might be able to construct several different models of causation. In portraying his core model in the way I have, I have relied on those concepts which seem to be most essential to Myrdal's analysis. Central to that analysis is the idea that discrimination in most of the contemporary United States is primarily due to racial prejudice on the part of Whites, with other factors playing a secondary role.

Kenneth Clark, who was a staff member of the Myrdal study, provides a more recent version of bias theory (Clark, 1972). He also focuses on racial prejudice and discrimination, but he includes a deficiency component consisting of a set of ghetto "pathologies" that are reminiscent of Moynihan. The "pathologies" and the inequalities, both products of discrimination, are then pictured as mutually reinforcing. This could be seen as a type of hybrid model, since it includes both bias and deficiency variables, but the bias variables are seen as more fundamental in that the deficiencies are products of discrimination, present as well as past. This model is summarized in figure 12.

Another tradition of writing that falls under the general heading of bias theory is that of economists who perceive discrimination in the marketplace as a function of employer and employee "tastes" for discrimination (Becker, 1971; Arrow, 1971). These models will not be discussed further here, since they are relatively technical and operate under assumptions so far removed from the "real world" that their usefulness for my purposes is quite limited.

Evaluation of Bias Theories

While specific bias theories have their problems, the general approach is not so much wrong as incomplete. Generally, these theories begin with racial prejudice and do not inquire further into its origins. Most lack a historical perspective. Myrdal is an exception to this, and there is a great deal of interesting material in his study. His model will be reexamined after the discussion of structural discrimination theories.

STRUCTURAL DISCRIMINATION THEORIES
OF RACIAL INEQUALITY

The third major type of theories of racial inequality in the United States can be called structural discrimination theories. These theories locate the source of minority disadvantage in the social structure of the society as a whole. "Structure" here refers to the regular patterns of human interaction in the society. Structures can be either formal, in which case they would be considered institutions, such as schools, government, or corporations, or informal, as in the class structure. "Structure" is thus a broader concept than "institution." The type of theories described in this section consider racial discrimination to be built into the structures of the society. They differ from bias theories in that they do not locate the ultimate source of racial discrimination in the attitudes of prejudiced individuals. Discrimination, for these theorists, can exist quite apart from overt individual prejudice, since it is inherent in the social patterns of the society. The concept of "institutional racism," popularized in recent years, is consistent with the emphasis of these theories. Two major varieties of structural discrimination theory are described below, the caste-class school and internal colonial theory.

FIGURE 12

THE CLARK MODEL

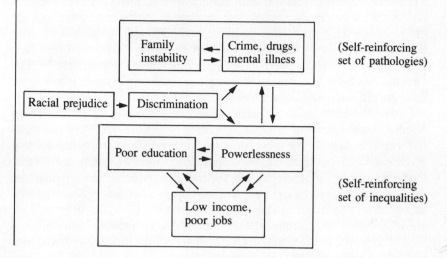

FIGURE 13

WARNER'S CASTE–CLASS DIAGRAM

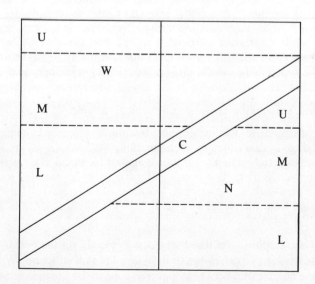

Source: Warner 1936, p. 235. *C* refers to the caste line, *W* and *N* to the White and Negro populations, *U*, *M*, and *L* to upper, middle, and lower classes.

The Caste-Class School

Application of the term "caste" to describe American race relations has a considerable history, but it is most closely identified with a series of studies done by W. Lloyd Warner and his associates in the 1930s and 1940s. Perhaps the best representative of this tradition is *Deep South*, published in 1941 (Davis, Gardner, and Gardner, 1941), but Dollard's *Caste and Class in a Southern Town* is also closely linked with this school (Dollard, 1957). The term has also been picked up by other writers, including Myrdal, whose main theoretical thrust was quite different.

For Warner and his associates, the social structure of the American South could be described as a combination of caste and class. They saw caste and class as both being ways of stratifying people in such a way that privileges, duties, obligations, and opportunities were unequally distributed. Caste, however, was characterized by endogamy (prohibition of marriage outside the caste) and by rigid barriers between the divisions. Class was seen as non-endogamous and as allowing social mobility (Warner, 1936, p. 234; Davis, Gardner, and Gardner, 1941, introduction [written by Warner].

The writers in this tradition clearly differentiated themselves from those in the bias tradition. Thus, according to Warner:

> One of the terms used in popular currency to express the feelings whites have for Negroes and Negroes for whites is "prejudice". The so-called "more liberal" whites say that certain of their members are "biased" or "prejudiced" against the other group, and some of the "more liberal" Negroes use these same terms when they refer to the attitudes of members of their own group. Both terms refer to the same social phenomena but, while expressive of certain of the attitudes felt by whites and Negroes about the other group, do not adequately represent the whole social situation to which they refer. [Davis, Gardner, and Gardner, 1941, p. 5]

Dollard sees prejudice as an intervening variable:

> We turn now to the mysterious but much discussed theme of race prejudice. In describing caste distinctions we have already indicated the factual material related to prejudice against Negroes. The major consideration seems to be that it is a defensive attitude intended to preserve white prerogatives in the caste situation and aggressively to resist any pressure from the Negro side to change his inferior position. [Dollard, 1957, p. 441]

Thus the emphasis on these works was clearly on the social structure and the discriminatory patterns institutionalized in that structure. Warner diagrammed the relationship between caste and class in the South in a much-cited diagram (figure 13).

In recognizing that there was considerably more to racial inequality than prejudice, the caste-class school was on the right track. However, its writings are subject to some severe limitations. Part of the problem is definitional. In using the term "caste" to describe race relations, they chose a concept which is closely identified with one particular society, India. Yet in that society caste is a very different phenomenon from anything found in the United States. Each caste, for example, is tied to a particular occupation, and caste lines are not racial or even ethnic in nature. In addition, caste divisions are justified on religious grounds, and have historically been imbued with a high degree of legitimacy. Racial divisions, on the other hand, are typically justified in terms of biology or cultural differences, and are imposed on the subordinate race rather than accepted as legitimate (Simpson and Yinger, 1958, pp. 356–57; Oliver Cox presents an extended discussion of the caste system in India and a critique of the caste-class school in his *Caste, Class and Race,* 1970). Since these distinctions are not of minor importance but have important implications for the dynamics of the system, the use of the concept of caste for the United States is unwarranted.

Secondly, it is difficult if not impossible to construct a model based on these writings, since the lines of causality are unclear. The studies seem to be largely descriptive in nature, and lack of a historical perspective makes it hard to figure out why this system came into existence or why it remains so persistent today. One possibility is that the system of racial division is simply a matter of historical continuity with the social structure that existed under slavery. Another is that the system is actively maintained by Whites because it serves their interest to do so. Dollard, in fact, devotes considerable attention to the ways in which the system benefits the White "middle class," but he does not really say that that is why the system continues in force. The discussion in *Deep South* has a very strong emphasis on the control of sexual relations, but again, it is never actually stated that this is the underpinning of the system.

Finally, this tradition's treatment of class relations is unsatisfactory. Part of the problem is conceptual lack of clarity. Initially, they describe class as a means of unequally distributing the rewards and responsibilities in the society. Elsewhere they state that " 'social class' is to be thought of as the largest group of people whose members have intimate access to one another. A class is composed of families and social cliques" (Davis, Gardner, and Gardner, 1941, p. 59n.). Yet in Warner's diagram and in the text generally, class is a matter of how people think of their social status in relation to other people in the society. The other difficulty is that the authors of *Deep South* clearly found their conceptual framework inadequate for describing the workings of Southern society. In chapter 10 they suddenly introduce the concept of the "economic group," which is thought of as a large informal group of persons (1) who exhibit similar attitudes and dogmas with regard to property and money and the distribution of these possessions among the members of society, and (2) whose incomes, economic possessions, and economic functions usually fall within certain limited and characteristic ranges. [Ibid., p. 237]

It seems that the reason for the introduction of this concept is that their class concept does not serve to group people together adequately on the basis of their *interests,* and thus on the basis of their behavior based on the pursuit of their interests. At one point in their study they note the common interests of White and Black employers:

The evidence at hand leaves no doubt that a strong solidarity exists between the leading white and colored business and professional men with regard to the manipulation of the caste sanctions. . . .

A certain amount of co-operation exists . . . between parallel economic groups, across caste lines. This intercaste solidarity is especially strong between the two upper economic groups. [Ibid., pp. 474–75]

This kind of commonality of interests and behavior would never be suspected from an examination of Warner's caste-class diagram, which clearly separates the White upper class and Black upper-class. It appears that the authors are groping for, but refuse to embrace, something similar to the Marxist concept of class.

Colonial Theories

During the 1960s a number of factors converged to popularize the idea that race relations in the United States could be described as a form of "internal colonialism." These factors were largely political events and trends rather than developments within social theory itself. As Robert Staples has noted, "After assimilation concepts were put to a reality test by the civil rights movement during the sixties and found wanting, a more nationalist orientation emerged" (Staples, 1976, p. 37). One direction that this took was toward the concept of internal colonialism. As the civil rights movement evolved into the Black Power movement, the political imperative switched to organizing along racial and ethnic lines, rather than continuing to work primarily in multiracial groups. From this perspective, it was natural to use the national liberation movements of the Third World as models, and to see racial minorities in the United States as occupying a similarly colonized position.

For this type of organizing to succeed, moreover, it was necessary to develop a different attitude among the minority population. To the extent that deficiency explanations of inequality had been internalized by the minority groups in the United States, a "colonial mentality" existed that had to be broken before effective resistance could become possible. Here, then, was another parallel with colonial situations abroad, and the writings of Fanon and Memmi, with their discussions of the psychology of colonialism, were eagerly seized upon by American political activists (Fanon, 1963; Memmi, 1965).

The decade of the 1960s was also the period of heavy American involvement in the Vietnam War, and as that war dragged on, more and more political activists began to describe the United States as an imperialistic country. If the United States was an imperial power abroad, it was much easier to think of it as an imperial power domestically as well, with its internal Third World colonies. Given this political atmosphere, it is not surprising that many of the early popularizers of this term were writers who were political activists. Stokely Carmichael, Tom Hayden, and Huey Newton wrote articles and books during this period which dealt with American racial minorities, using a colonial framework (Carmichael and Hamilton, 1967; Hayden, 1968; Foner, 1970).

At about the same time, the concept began to be employed by some social scientists. While it is true that the idea of the internal colony had appeared in a few analytic works in the early 1960s (Harold Cruse used it in a 1962 article [reprinted in Cruse, 1968]), it was during the late 1960s that it began to be taken more seriously. Robert Allen made use of the colonial framework in his analysis of Black politics, published in 1969 (Allen, 1969). But it was in the essays of Robert Blauner, the first of which also appeared in 1969, that the concept received its first systematic exposition (these essays are reprinted in Blauner, 1972). Blauner used the concept for several purposes. It became a means of criticizing a number of academic writings which treated America's racial minorities within the same framework as European ethnic immigrants. In this tradition, Blacks were the latest wave of immigrants to arrive in the urban centers of the United States, only this time from the American South rather than from Europe. The assumption was that Blacks, Chicanos, and other racial minorities would fit into the pattern of assimilation and upward mobility that had been established by the White ethnic groups. Blauner argued that the experiences of Third World groups and of White ethnic immigrants were, and would continue to be, significantly different. The Third World groups, Blauner insisted, had been subjected to a system of discrimination which was structurally rooted to a much greater extent than that experienced by European immigrants. Blauner also made use of the colonial framework to explain certain aspects of Black politics in the 1960s, including community control, cultural nationalism, and urban uprisings (ibid., pp. 95–104).

Since the late 1960s the term has been used by a number of writers for different purposes, but my interest in the concept is limited here to its usefulness as a theory of racial inequality. Before dealing with this question, however, it is necessary to consider whether the term "colonial" is appropriately applied to race relations in the United States, and what its connotations might be.

The Nature of Colonialism

The term "colonialism" is applied to a very heterogeneous collection of situations, so that it is difficult to see what, if anything, they have in common. Given this fact, it is not surprising that there is no agreement on the definition of the term. Even if we restrict our attention to European expansion since the fifteenth century, we find very different types of relationships described as colonial. The earliest colonies were founded in the New World and on the coasts of Africa and southern Asia. The British and the French established settlement colonies in North America, pushing out or killing the native inhabitants. The Spanish had "mixed" colonies in the New World, with a substantial minority of European settlers and relatively large indigenous populations. The Portuguese in Brazil had a large colony, with Portuguese settlers, native Americans, and many slaves imported from Africa. In Africa and Asia, the Portuguese had commercial colonies, restricted to the coastal areas, designed for trade, and with few European settlers and little territory under their direct control (Fieldhouse, 1966, chap. 2).

There was considerable variation in the manner in which the colonies were settled. Originally, most of the colonies were established by private interests, and only later did the European states come to be the main sponsors of colonization. There was variation over time as well. According to Fieldhouse, the first period of European expansion lasted from the fifteenth century to the early nineteenth century, and was centered in America (ibid., p. 100). The second period, beginning later in the nineteenth century and continuing strongly into the twentieth, was largely based on Asia and Africa. The nature of most of the colonies differed in the two major periods.

> The reasons for which a particular dependency is acquired normally determine its character and functions as a colony. The old empire had consisted almost entirely of territories which were occupied by European settlers because they wanted to live there and make use of local resources. They were governed as far as possible as if they were part of the sovereign's European dominions, on the assumption that colonists were full subjects with the same rights and interests as those in the metropolis. [Ibid., p. 75]

> In the last resort, it was neither "mercantilism" nor political subordination that produced the special character of the American colonies, but the fact that they were colonies of European settlement. There were similar colonies in the modern period in Canada, Australasia, South Africa, and, with some differences, in Central Africa and Algeria. But

apart from these, the modern empires were alien, consisting of colonies which lacked any organic connexion with their metropolitan states. Europe reproduced herself in America as she seldom did again. American colonies were not commercial artifacts but extensions of Europe herself, differing little from the inner ring of European colonies which had been occupied first and had acted as stepping stones to the west—Ireland, the Azores, Canaries, Madeiras and Iceland. All were organic European societies. [Ibid., p. 99]

It is the colonies of the later period that generally come to mind today when we speak of colonialism, since they are the most recent. Even here, there was much variation in the nature of the colonies and in the manner in which they were governed. The British, for example, favored a policy of "indirect rule," in which the traditional political authorities in an area played a central role in governing the colonies. The French also made use of traditional political authorities, but they were much more subordinate to the colonial officers from the European metropolis. Under the French, the colonial subjects were encouraged to assimilate to French culture, and their eventual goal was to make French citizens out of the indigenous peoples (Crowder, 1964; see also a number of articles in Cartey and Kilson, 1970).

There is another type of situation which is commonly referred to as colonial, that of neocolonialism. Kwame Nhrumah, in his detailed study of neocolonialism in Africa, defines it this way:

The essence of neo-colonialism is that the State which is subject to it is, in theory, independent and has all the outward trappings of international sovereignty. In reality its economic system and thus its political policy is directed from outside. [Nkrumah, 1966, p. ix]

Used in this sense, the concept has achieved considerable currency.

Raymond Betts, in his survey of European expansion, notes that

neo-colonialism is, or has been considered to be, synonymous with what some historians have called the "informal" empire first established by Great Britain in Latin America in the early nineteenth century and then enlarged upon by the United States in the heyday of dollar diplomacy. [Betts, 1968, p. 151]

Stanley and Barbara Stein, in their classic account of the continuity of the colonial heritage in Latin America, illustrate the point clearly:

The failure of Latin American movements for independence to create the bases of sustained economic growth through balanced agricultural, ranching, and industrial diversification only indicates the continued strength of a colonial heritage of externally oriented economies linked closely to essential sources of demand and supply outside the new national economies. [Stein and Stein, 1970, p. 135]

... The major consequence of the anti-colonial movements in Latin America between 1810 and 1824, the crushing of the ties of transatlantic empire, led—one is almost tempted to say, inevitably—to neo-colonialism. ... The absence of an autonomous, self-sustaining economy strengthened the heritage or heritages of colonialism in Latin America after 1824. This is the rationale that Latin Americans and others have evoked in calling post-colonial Latin American economy and society neo-colonial. [Ibid., p. 136–37]

It is by now obvious that those who profited most in the eighteenth century from west European colonialism in the New World were the English merchants and manufacturers, bankers and shippers. Their greatest harvest came in the nineteenth century when they enjoyed a dominant position in the trade of the area. ... The English had been the major factor in the destruction of Iberian imperialism; on its ruins they erected the informal imperialism of free trade and investment. [Ibid., p. 154–55]

The use of the term "neocolonialism" is thus well established in the literature. Its use is not intended to denote that the situation referred to is the same as that of "classic" colonialism, but that it is a variety of colonialism which maintains the essential character of colonialism while modifying the form of the relationship. The same relationship is sometimes characterized as the "imperialism of free trade," as in the widely cited article by Gallagher and Robinson (1953). In this article, they argue that it is artificial to treat British imperialism simply in terms of formal control of territory. Adoption of that restricted viewpoint has led some historians to focus on the post-1880 period during which British formal possessions increased rapidly, and to depict the earlier part of the century as anti-imperialist. In fact, Gallagher and Robinson contend, Britain was imperialistic during the whole century in terms of bringing new territories into its economic sphere of control. Where possible, such control was established through the "imperialism of free trade," in which free access to the other territory's economy led to control via British industrial competitive advantage. Only where the local authorities resist such informal influences and where the political and military situation makes it possible have the British exercised direct control.

In reviewing these uses of the term "colonial" it appears that settlement colonies differ fundamentally from all of the others in that only one "people" is involved in those situations, at least in any long-term way. All other situations involve at least two ethnic and/or racial groups, with one being dominant and the other or others subordinate. Because of this and because modern usage generally refers only to the nonsettlement situations, I will use the term to refer only to the second category, in which more than one group is involved. "Presently, in speaking about colonies or colonialism, allusion is made above all to the domination of some people by others" (González

Casanova, 1965, p. 29). To do otherwise would be to lump together situations so dissimilar that they would have very little or nothing in common. The term would thus lose all analytic precision.

The only other significant factor that all the nonsettlement colonies have in common is that the relationship was entered into by the metropolitan power because it was felt that it was in its interest to do so. These metropolitan interests could be of various types, but generally they boiled down to economic interests first and political-military interests second. Thus Furnivall notes:

> Ordinarily, the motive of colonial expansion has been economic advantage. Considerations of prestige and military strategy have played their part, but in the main economic considerations have prevailed. [Furnivall, 1948, pp. 3-4]

Fieldhouse lists land and trade as the most important motives for the original European expansion (Fieldhouse, 1966, p. 4). Balandier also assigns primary importance to economic interests (Balandier, 1966, p. 37). Gail Omvedt, in her theoretical treatment of European colonialism, distinguishes two major phases. The first she terms *commercial imperialism* of the mercantile era, in which the motives were precious metals, spices, and other goods for trade, as well as control of labor power for plantations. The second phase she calls *industrial imperialism:* "As European industries developed, their need was no longer for trade control of luxury goods but for a wide-scale procurement of raw materials and markets for the finished products of the new factories, and increasingly outlets for investment" (Omvedt, 1973, p. 2). I believe colonialism in general, then, can be defined as follows:

> Colonialism is a structured relationship of domination and subordination, where the dominant and subordinate groups are defined along ethnic and/or racial lines, and where the relationship is established and maintained to serve the interests of all or part of the dominant group.

This definition is similar to that of Gail Omvedt, who sees colonialism as "the economic, political and cultural domination of one cultural-ethnic group by another" (Omvedt, 1973, p. 1).

Certain other characteristics which are sometimes claimed as aspects of colonialism are in fact not universally so. These are

1. *Formal political domination.* Hans Kohn has this in mind when he states that "a colonial relationship is created when one nation establishes and maintains political domination over a geographically external political unit" (Kohn, 1958, p. 4). As noted above, to base the concept on the formal nature of the relationship is to miss the fact that very similar dynamics are at work in the "imperialism of free trade," or neo-colonialism, and this leads to a misreading of history.

2. *Geographical separation (noncontiguity) of metropolis and colony.* It is difficult to see why the colonial relationship should be dependent on the existence of space between metropolis and colony. At any rate, this is not true of instances cited as neocolonial, for example, the United States and Mexico.

The Nature of Internal Colonialism

On the basis of the preceding discussion, it is possible to advance a definition of internal colonialism:

> Internal colonialism is a form of colonialism in which the dominant and subordinate populations are intermingled, so that there is no geographically distinct "metropolis" separate from the "colony."

This definition is similar to that employed by González Casanova: "Internal colonialism corresponds to a structure of social relations based on domination and exploitation among culturally heterogeneous, distinct groups" (González Casanova, 1965, p. 33). Of course, the degree of intermingling can vary considerably from case to case. In Latin America there are many instances of regional concentration of Indian communities, as is also the case in the United States. Chicanos also form majorities in certain regions, such as northern New Mexico. Where the relationship of ethnic/racial subordination coincides with regional concentration, it is easier to see the internal colonial relationship in operation.

The reason for advancing this concept is that there seems to be a clear need for a term to describe a relationship where an ethnic and/or racial group is subjected to systematic structural discrimination within a single society. The widespread use of the term "caste" to describe race relations in the United States and other countries attests to this need. However (as discussed earlier), this term is inappropriate for various reasons. The term "plural society," originally used by Furnivall and later taken up by others, is also sometimes applied in these situations, but it has a disadvantage in that it stresses separateness rather than discrimination in the group relations (Furnivall, 1948; Kuper and Smith, 1971). In the absence of a superior term, the concept of internal colonialism is best suited to designate this kind of relationship. (Other advantages of the term and the model based on it are discussed later in this chapter.)

Two types of objections are generally raised to the use of this concept. The first is that a distinct metropolis and colony are essential to the concept of colonialism. In fact, this has often not been the case in "classic" colonial situations, at least in a formal, legalistic sense. Spain provides one example:

> Perhaps the most interesting feature of Spanish colonial government was that its institutions and concepts so closely resembled those of Old Spain. Spain did not innovate: she adapted. She was fortunate, in that

the Spanish Crown already consisted of a multiplicity of kingdoms and provinces linked to Castile only in the person of the King. It was therefore possible and natural to regard the colonies not as dependencies of Old Spain, but as sister kingdoms. [Fieldhouse, 1966, p. 16]

Portugal made no constitutional distinction between her colonies and the metropolis (ibid., p. 31). France considered Algeria to be an integral part of France. Other examples could be cited.

It is true that a distinction between metropolis and colony existed in an informal, sociological sense, even where it did not exist in a legalistic sense. But even here there are ambiguities. While Spain transferred colonial revenues to the Castilian treasury and regulated the colonial economies to serve Castilian interests, these practices were also pursued with respect to the other Spanish kingdoms in the metropolis (ibid., pp. 24–25). One can also cite the presence of metropolitan settlers in the colonies, such as French Algerians or Spanish *peninsulares* in Latin America. These settlers participated in the exploitation of the indigenous people, yet they too were often in a position to feel exploited by the authorities in the old country. Their presence has the effect of blurring the distinction between metropolis and colony. Even if the argument is granted, it serves not to invalidate the concept but simply to justify the designation of these situations as *internal* colonies (the modifier signifies that we are talking about a variety of colonialism and that there is a distinction to be made between it and classic colonialism). Internal colonialism is a variety of colonialism in that it shares with classic colonialism essential characteristics (ethnic/racial subordination, the serving of certain interests) even though there is no clear geographical distinction between metropolis and colony. In the same way, designating a certain relationship as neocolonial does not mean that it is exactly the same as classic colonialism, but only that the same general type of relationship exists. It is as much an analytic error to ignore similarities as it is to pretend there are no differences.

The second type of objection is that in a colonial relationship, the subordinate indigenous population is in a majority. As with the noncontiguity argument discussed earlier with respect to the definition of colonialism, it is difficult to see why this should be considered an essential characteristic. The important thing would seem to be the nature of the relationship, and a dominant-subordinate relationship between racial/ethnic groups can exist regardless of who is in the majority and who is in the minority.

One other point should be clarified with respect to the concept of internal colonialism. In some materials written by Latin American authors, the term "internal colonialism" is used to refer to a situation where one region of a country is in a dominant and exploitative relationship with another region of the same country, regardless of ethnicity. One could argue, for example, that the American South has historically been dominated by the Northeast. Such situations are common in Latin America. The term "internal colonialism," as defined here, is not intended to cover such cases, unless ethnic/racial subordination is involved. As Pablo González Casanova has noted, ascriptive criteria (in this case, race and/or ethnicity) make the dynamics of a situation quite different from one in which such criteria are absent (González Casanova, 1965, p. 33). The fact that there is sometimes a strong overlap between regional and ethnic/racial subordination tends to confuse this distinction, but it is important to keep it in mind for analytic purposes. (Stavenhagen, in his article on Mexico, describes a situation involving such an overlap [1965].)

The Internal Colonial Model

The concept of internal colonialism has been used for various theoretical purposes, but has not been systematically applied as a theory of racial inequality. To develop a model along these lines, I have drawn upon Blauner but supplemented his discussion with some additional elements. A diagram of the model is presented in figure 14.

The central dynamic role in this model is provided by the concept of interests, which Blauner stresses by way of contrast with bias theories. The interests here are those which originally gave rise to European colonialism, of which internal colonialism is an extension, as well as the contemporary interests of privileged groups (Blauner, 1972, pp. 21-22, 52-53, 58-60). The

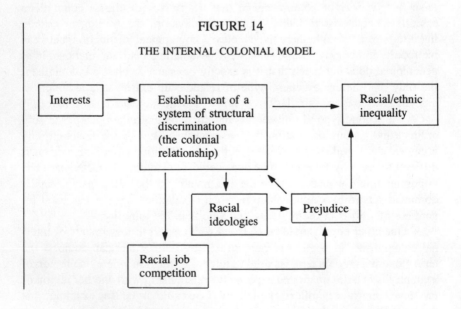

FIGURE 14

THE INTERNAL COLONIAL MODEL

system of structural discrimination that forms the essence of the colonial relationship exists first of all in the economic realm, but extends into political institutions, the educational system, and all forms of social structures. Blauner gives heavy emphasis to the workings of the labor market in the United States (ibid., pp. 57ff.). The persistence of racial/ethnic inequality in this society is the result of this historic relationship, which continues to operate today.

The other important factor in perpetuating this inequality is racial prejudice, both by leading to individual acts of discrimination and by providing support for the structural aspects of discrimination. Prejudice, however, is treated quite differently from bias theories. Although Blauner does not develop the theme, he expresses the belief that racial prejudice is largely a product of racial ideologies that were developed to justify structural discrimination (p. 21). The other mechanism leading to prejudice is not really discussed by Blauner, but I have incorporated it into the model based on other materials. A number of historical works have pointed to job competition between Anglos and racial minorities as increasing racial tension and thus prejudice, and certainly there are numerous instances where this situation prevailed between Anglos and Chicanos. Edna Bonacich has developed this theme in an article on the "split labor market" (Bonacich, 1972). What many writers who have touched on this theme seem to miss, however, is that the antagonism arises because of the institutionalized hiring practices of employers. That is, when employers attempt to undercut the wages of Anglo workers by creating a colonized labor pool, the Anglo workers resist. Anglo workers tend to see this as *unfair* competition, but rather than take their antagonism out on the employers and their manipulations, they often turn their wrath on the more immediate and usually more vulnerable targets, the colonized workers. This dynamic emerges quite clearly from the materials on Chicano economic history.

The theme of racial ideologies and their origins needs to be developed further here, as it is an aspect of racial dynamics that is frequently misunderstood, and it is an important part of the colonial model. First, it should be emphasized that racial ideologies are a modern phenomenon, and do not stretch back into ancient times, as is often claimed. It is true that ethnocentrism, or the belief that one's own ethnic group is superior to others, has been around for a long time. However, this belief has traditionally been justified on cultural grounds, often religious in nature, and not on the idea that the other groups are inherently and biologically inferior. It was not until biological thinking began to displace religious thinking in the eighteenth century that racial distinctions in the modern sense could be made, and it was not until the nineteenth century that full-blown racial ideologies were developed (Benedict, 1959, p. 108; Myrdal, 1962, p. 97; Cox, 1970, p. 329).

When racial ideologies began to emerge in Europe, they were tied in all instances to the advancement of certain interests. These were usually the justification of privilege based on social inequality, but the protection of national interests also played a role. Much of early race theorizing was not aimed at Third World peoples at all, but at Europeans, although contacts with the Third World influenced the general climate of opinion. In Ruth Benedict's words,

> European expansion overseas . . . set the stage for racism dogmas and gave violent early expression to racial antipathies without propounding racism as a philosophy. Racism did not get its currency in modern thought until it was applied to conflicts within Europe—first to class conflicts and then to national. [Benedict, 1959, p. 111]

Racial ideology became one way in which European aristocrats tried to fortify their class position in the face of radical challenges. These ideologies took the position that the aristocrats were descendants of the Germanic peoples (referred to as Teutons and later as Aryans) who had overrun the old Roman Empire. The common people, on the other hand, were depicted as descendants of other, inferior European stocks, including the Romans (ibid., pp. 112ff.). The aristocrats were thus the descendants of a race which had proved its superiority in the distant past, and which had subsequently been responsible for the advance of civilization. By virtue of this inheritance they were ideally suited to rule and to maintain their class privileges. Later on, racist ideologies were transformed in Europe in order to serve the interests of nationalism, as France and Germany struggled for supremacy on the continent (ibid., pp. 129ff.). This tradition of writing was also drawn upon in the twentieth-century United States by American nativists attempting to stem the flow of immigration from southern and eastern Europe. These ideas served to whip up some of the emotion that went into the restrictive immigration legislation discussed in earlier chapters of this book.

In England, the origins of racist ideologies can be traced back to the sixteenth century and the creation of the Church of England (Horsman, 1973). The English sought to persuade themselves, after their break with the Catholic church, that they were returning to a purer form of religion that had prevailed among the early Anglo-Saxon inhabitants of the island. As the English delved more deeply into their past, they began to idealize their past political as well as religious institutions, and to link them historically to the institutions that had existed among the Teutonic people to whom they traced their ancestry. In the early stages this school of thought was not explicitly racial, but seemed to assume that the superiority of the old institutions had simply been transmitted over the generations. In the nineteenth century, however, racial overtones became more characteristic. As Reginald Horsman has noted:

The flowering of the new science of man . . . gave a firm physical, "scientific" base to the long entrenched ideas of Anglo-Saxon excellence. The work of the early nineteenth-century ethnologists was decisive in giving a definite racial cast to Anglo-Saxonism . . . an essential shift in emphasis occurred when the arguments about the inferiority of other "races" assumed an importance as great or even greater than arguments about the excellence of Anglo-Saxons. [Horsman, 1973, p. 395]

At times the point of reference was broadened to include not just the "Teutons" or "Aryans" identified by researchers on language and history, but the "Caucasian race" identified by researchers on the physical characteristics of humans. Sometimes the concepts were merged, and Anglo-Saxons were held to be the superior branch of the superior race. There also developed a certain exchange of ideas with the United States:

The development of a belief in the different innate capacities of the various races . . . and of the superiority of the Caucasian race, was considerably helped in the 1830's and 1840's by an influx of ideas from the United States. A country in which a great many were intent on justifying the enslavement of the blacks and the extermination of the American Indians proved a fertile ground for the growth of racism. [Ibid., p. 397]

These ideas were used for various purposes in England. They served in the early period to support English nationalism, but it also appears that they were used to justify English domination of the Celtic peoples of the area, the Welsh, Scots, and Irish, who were sometimes identified with non-Germanic people who had been expelled from continental Europe by the Teutons (ibid., p. 391; Hechter, 1975, p. 342). The concepts of Anglo-Saxon superiority and the broader racial concepts of the period were also important justifications for overseas imperialism, as England and the other European powers divided up the world among themselves.

In the New World, racial ideologies also served to justify exploitative relationships. To the extent that these ideas developed in Latin America, they did so as means of answering critics of the enslavement and brutalization of the Indians (Cox, 1970, pp. 334–35). It was in the United States that racial theories really flowered, however. As Thomas Gossett puts it,

Although in the seventeenth century race theories had not as yet developed any strong scientific or theological rationale, the contact of the English with Indians, and soon afterwards with Negroes, in the New World led to the formation of institutions and relationships which were later justified by appeals of race theories. [Gossett, 1965, p. 17]

The delayed nature of the ideological response can be seen in the following manner:

> The importance of Negro slavery in generating race theories in this country can hardly be overestimated, but it must be remembered that there was a minimum of theory at the time the institution was established. The theory of any political or social institution is likely to develop only when it comes under attack. [Ibid., p. 29]

> Institutional arrangements that prove painful or inconvenient to a substantial part of the population are generally called into question, and they are sooner or later justified in a set of popular beliefs. Whenever conspicuous differences of rank lead to embarrassing questions, ideologies emerge to explain the gradation. [Shibutani and Kwan, 1965, p. 241]

This is the essential mechanism that is embodied in the model diagrammed in figure 14. Racial ideologies came about in large part because they were useful in justifying classic colonialism and the neocolonial and internal colonial relationships that grew out of it. Of course the process is complex, and many factors enter into it and help determine how strong or how weak the ideology will become. But the essential point is that ideologies develop and are perpetuated because of the interests they serve. Shibutani and Kwan describe the process this way:

> Most ideologies are not deliberately produced artifacts. . . . They develop through a selective process, being shaped over a long period through the contributions of thousands of individuals. Students of the sociology of knowledge have pointed out that ideas that tend to support or facilitate the pursuit of predominant interests tend to be accepted, while other, equally valid ideas pass unnoticed or are rejected. Ideas are not always accepted or rejected on the basis of evidence; in many cases the choice is in terms of their utility. In any situation of inter-ethnic contact thousands of remarks are made; most of them are uttered a few times and are forgotten. But ideas consistent with prevailing interests or justifying deeds that have already been committed seem strangely more appealing and "true." These views tend to be taken more seriously and are repeated. . . . Race ideologies are like other political ideologies; they emerge through a selective process and justify social institutions. [Ibid., pp. 248–49]

The American attitude toward Blacks is a clear case of this process, and is so depicted by Gunnar Myrdal. He notes that "when the Negro was first enslaved, his subjugation was not justified in terms of his biological inferiority" (Myrdal, 1944, p. 84). The origins of a systematic racial ideology in the United States can be traced to the need of pro-slavery interests to respond to criticisms based on the "universal rights of man," criticisms which mounted as revolutionary agitation developed in the late eighteenth century (Jordan, 1968, chap. 7). This racial ideology did not gain strength until three decades before the Civil War, as criticism of slavery became even more vehement.

> In the precarious ideological situation—where the South wanted to defend a political and civic institution of inequality which showed increasingly great prospects for new land exploitation and commercial profit, but where they also wanted to retain the democratic creed of the nation—the race doctrine of biological inequality between whites and Negroes offered the most convenient solution. [Myrdal, 1944, pp. 87–88]

After the war, the ideology survived and was intensified as a means of justifying the continued exploitation of the Black population. Myrdal also argues that the ideology became more prevalent in the North as a way of justifying the national compromise arrived at in the 1870s that allowed the South to continue its oppression of the Blacks (ibid., p. 88).

That, of course, is not the whole story. Racial ideologies become embodied in the thought of future generations who have no conception of the exact context in which they originated, and are thus transformed into broad-based racial prejudice even among people whose interests are not served by it. Oliver Cox described this process several decades ago:

> In our description of the uses of race prejudice in this essay we are likely to give the impression that race prejudice was always "manufactured" in full awareness by individuals or groups of entrepreneurs. This, however, is not quite the case. Race prejudice, from its inception, became part of the social heritage, and as such both exploiters and exploited for the most part are born heirs to it. It is possible that most of those who propagate and defend race prejudice are not conscious of its fundamental motivation. To paraphrase Adam Smith: They who teach and finance race prejudice are by no means such fools as the majority of those who believe and practice it. [Cox, 1970, p. 333n.].

Thus race prejudice may be said to take on "a life of its own" with the passage of time, as future generations are socialized to be prejudiced. Still, it is necessary to qualify the qualifier in order not to lose sight of the major point:

> It should be borne in mind that race prejudice is not simply dislike for the physical appearance or the attitudes of one person by another; it rests basically upon a calculated and concerted determination of a white ruling class to keep some people or peoples of color and their resources exploitable. If we think of race prejudice as merely an expression of dislike by whites for some people of color, our conception of the attitude will be voided of its substance. [Ibid., p. 349n.].

In accordance with the internal colonial model, prejudice is manifested in individual acts of discrimination, and serves as a support when aspects of structural discrimination are called into question. The recent controversies about busing and the Bakke decision can serve as cases in point.

Varieties of Internal Colonialism

While there is no clear-cut division of internal colonial theories into different varieties, there is one logical basis for such differentiation that at times emerges in the literature. This has to do with the way in which the interests at stake are depicted. In the United States, for example, it is possible to see all Anglos as benefiting from the system of structural discrimination, as Carmichael and Hamilton charge in their book *Black Power* (1967). On the other hand, one can also argue that only one part of the noncolonized population benefits from internal colonialism. Where the second point of view is accepted, the argument is usually that it is the dominant class among the noncolonized population whose interests are served by this system. Robert Allen analyzes internal colonialism from this standpoint (Allen, 1969). The first type of theory might be called "right" colonial theory and the second "left" colonial theory because of their political implications, but this is only for reference purposes. "Non-class differentiated" and "class differentiated" colonial theories are more accurate but more cumbersome labels. Some writers are difficult to classify as one or the other. Blauner, for example, is somewhat ambiguous on this question (notwithstanding Prager's "right" interpretation of his writing; see Prager, 1972–73). The implications of the "left" perspective will be dealt with below.

It should also be kept in mind that the practices associated with internal colonialism, as with all types of colonialism, can vary considerably in degree. The degree of inequality associated with colonialism is one of these variable dimensions. A situation such as exists in the Union of South Africa represents a very harsh example of internal colonialism (Wilson, 1973; Adam, 1971; van den Berghe, 1965, 1967). A situation such as the "Celtic fringe" in Britain represents a much milder case (Hechter, 1975). Colonized populations in the United States and Latin America represent a somewhat intermediate position. In the case of Chicanos, it is certainly the case that the existing system is less harsh than it has been at some points in the past, as brought out in earlier chapters. Rather than a sharp distinction between colonized and noncolonized racial/ethnic groups, there is what might be termed a continuum of colonialism.

Evaluation of the Internal Colonial Model

The model of internal colonialism as a theory of racial inequality has several advantages, but also an important limitation. One of the important advantages is its broad scope. It is not limited to the contemporary period, but incorporates a historical dimension that allows us to see more clearly the dynamics of racial inequality as they have developed over time. In this manner we can grasp causal connections that may be obscured in certain historical periods but stand out more strongly in others. One of the more important consequences of this is that the nature of racial prejudice is illuminated, in effect transcending bias theories and incorporating them within a broader framework. Most bias theories do not go into the question of the historical origins of prejudice. Myrdal does, but he is an exception, and in this respect his work converges somewhat with colonial theory. Still, there is an important distinction in that colonial theory stresses the operation of interests in the present and not just in the past, and puts more emphasis on the *structural* aspects of discrimination in the contemporary period.

With respect to deficiency theories, I consider colonial theory to be far more accurate historically and thus more persuasive theoretically as an explanation of racial inequality. In addition, it is more "elegant" in a methodological sense, in that it accounts for a much wider range of phenomena with a relatively small number of variables. Deficiency theories have to come up with different deficiencies for each situation, whereas colonial theories can account for a great deal of racial inequality within the same basic framework. Colonial theories do not completely rule out certain types of "deficiency" explanations of inequality. For example, there is little doubt that an oppressed racial group does not have the same opportunity to acquire education and skills that a dominant group does, and in this sense it could be said to be "deficient." But colonial theories put such factors in a completely different light by tracing their origins to structural discrimination and not to some inherent characteristic of the minority group itself. In addition, such factors are seen as distinctly secondary when compared to the overwhelming direct effects of structural discrimination.

Colonial theories also have the advantage of a broader comparative scope, as well as a broader historical scope, than most other theories. In putting the experience of U.S. racial minorities in a colonial framework, this school of analysis establishes important structural (and historical) similarities with minorities in other countries and with the Third World in general. The perception of these international parallels gives us a better perspective on the local situation and enables us better to evaluate the importance of the various factors involved in perpetuating inequality. It is no coincidence that most comparative analyses of race emphasize structural variables to explain racial stratification and inequality, even if they do not explicitly adopt a colonial perspective (Shibutani and Kwan, 1965; Schermerhorn, 1970; van den Berghe, 1967; Frazier, 1957; Rex, 1970; Wilson, 1973).

The major limitation of colonial theory as it has developed to this point is indicated in a passage of self-criticism from Blauner:

> This suggests a major defect of my study. It lacks a conception of American society as a total structure beyond the central significance that I attribute to racism. Thus my perspective tends to suffer from the fragmented character of the approaches to American race relations that I have just criticized. Conceived to a great extent within the confines of the middle ranges of theory, there is not systematic exposition of capitalist structure and dynamics; racial oppression and racial conflict are not satisfactorily linked to the dominant economic relations nor to the overall distribution of political power in America. The failure of Marxism to appreciate the significance of racial groups and racial conflict is in part responsible for this vacuum, since no other existing framework is able to relate race to a comprehensive theory of capitalist development. [Blauner, 1972, p. 13]

In order to see in more detail what the Marxist tradition does have to offer for the analysis of racial inequality, it is necessary to review some of these writings. After this I will present a partial synthesis of colonial theory and class analysis.

MARXIST ANALYSIS OF CLASS STRUCTURE IN CONTEMPORARY CAPITALIST SOCIETY

Marxist discussions of the nature of classes in advanced capitalist societies can become very complex, too complex for the purposes of this book. Nicos Poulantzas, for example, goes into considerable theoretical detail on this topic. A more concise and comprehensible alternative is provided in an article by Erik Olin Wright, titled "Class Boundaries in Advanced Capitalist Societies" (Wright, 1976). Wright presents the class structure of such societies as the United States as shown in figure 15.

According to Wright's analysis, capitalists, workers, and petty bourgeoisie comprise the three major classes within advanced capitalist society. Capitalists and workers are the classes particular to capitalist society. Petty bourgeoisie, while not without significance, are in a sense holdovers from an earlier, precapitalist mode of production. They are small, independent professionals and businessmen. The three other positions in his diagram are occupied by what he terms "contradictory locations within class relations." Persons who occupy these positions are not clear-cut members of the traditional classes, but occupy locations which are intermediate between two classes, in that they partake of some of the characteristics of both classes. Small capitalists occupy an ambiguous position between large capitalists and petty bourgeoisie. Where the petty bourgeoisie rely entirely on their own labor and that of their families to make a profit, and the large capitalist derives

FIGURE 15

CLASSES IN ADVANCED CAPITALIST SOCIETY

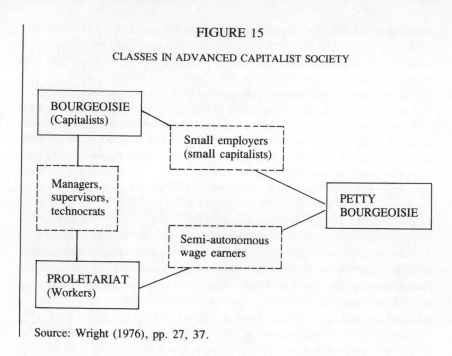

Source: Wright (1976), pp. 27, 37.

virtually all of his profit from the labor of a large number of employees, the small capitalist relies importantly on his own labor as well as that of a small number of employees.

The semi-autonomous employees include such persons as employed professionals and high-level technical workers such as researchers. They have in common with the workers the fact that they sell their labor and do not own the means of production. At the same time, they have greater autonomy in their work than the proletariat, and in this way they resemble the petty bourgeoisie.

The "contradictory location" between capitalists and workers is quite heterogeneous. At the bottom of this category are the foremen and line supervisors. They are close to the position of workers in that they sell their labor and are close to the production process, but they function in such a way as to control the labor of others. Above the foremen and line supervisors are the technocrats (technicians) and the middle managers. Above them, and closest to the bourgeoisie in the class structure, are the top managers, who do not own the means of production but who exercise considerable control over the process of production.

A somewhat different analysis is provided by Barbara and John Ehrenreich in their 1977 article, "The Professional-Managerial Class" (Ehrenreich and Ehrenreich, 1977). They do not deal with the existence of contradictory class locations. While retaining the conventional class divisions of capitalist, worker, and petty bourgeoisie, they argue that a new class has come into existence since the late nineteenth century, and they propose that this class be called the "professional-managerial class" (PMC). This "new" middle class includes many of the same people that Wright puts in the contradictory location between workers and capitalists, but also most of the semi-autonomous employees. It includes teachers, engineers, scientists, government workers, all except the top managers, technicians, culture producers such as writers, and other professionals. They argue that this new class of educated workers has come into existence as a result of developments in the structure of capitalist society, and that it has a common relationship to the system of production and shares a common life style. They state: "We define the Professional-Managerial Class as consisting of salaried mental workers who do not own the means of production and whose major function in the social division of labor may be described broadly as the reproduction of capitalist culture and capitalist class relations" (ibid., pt. 1, p. 13). By this they mean that the class functions in such a manner as to control, shape, and regulate the economic, social, political, and cultural relations that are necessary to perpetuate capitalist society and keep it running as smoothly as possible. Thus the Ehrenreichs propose a four-class framework which is relatively easy to work with and which I will adopt for constructing the model I describe later in this chapter. For other purposes it may be that Wright's scheme has certain advantages.

Marxist Theories of Racial Inequality

Given the extensive Marxist tradition of social theory, it is disappointing to find how little serious analysis there is of racism and racial inequality. The reason for this undoubtedly traces back to classic Marxist political economy, in which class divisions in capitalist society are heavily emphasized and there is an assumption that they will supersede other kinds of divisions, including those based on race and ethnicity. When Marxist scholar-activists like Lenin were forced to deal with the question of "national minorities," they generally did so in a pragmatic political manner that contributed little to our understanding of the linkage between class and race or ethnicity.

The American Marxist writings that do exist on the subject are marked by considerable heterogeneity, and there is certainly nothing that can be seen as *the* Marxist theory of minority inequality or race relations generally. In addition, these analyses do not seem to flow in any logical or direct manner from basic Marxist theoretical categories, so that it is not unusual for analysts who consider themselves Marxists to come to diametrically opposed conclusions on questions of race. Many leading Marxist scholars barely touch on the subject in their works.

One school of American Marxist thought holds that American capitalism no longer has any compelling need to perpetuate racial divisions. Eugene Genovese is one example. He argues that there is a strong historical connection between the subordination of Blacks and the development of American capitalism, especially during the nineteenth century. But he feels that since the First World War, the relationship between capitalism and racism has become less clear.

> With the decline of sharecropping and tenancy in the South, with ur-
> banization, and with substantial structural changes in the economy,
> American capitalism no longer needs or generates in the old way racial
> discrimination as an organized form of class rule. Since the blacks today
> are prepared to exact a high price for the conditions to which they are
> subjected, there is good reason to believe that the capitalists as a class
> and capitalism as a system would purge themselves of racism if they
> could. Racism, however, is so deeply rooted in American society that it
> cannot be torn up without fundamental changes in capitalism itself.
> [Genovese, 1968, pp. 59–60]

Baran and Sweezy likewise believe that the members of the American ruling class see it as in their interest to eliminate racial inequality, but their view is somewhat more complex than that of Genovese. They pose the problem very clearly:

> The conclusion seems inescapable that since moving to the cities, Ne-
> groes have been prevented from improving their socio-economic posi-
> tion: they have not been able to follow earlier immigrant groups up the
> occupational ladder and out of the ghetto. . . . What social forces and
> institutional mechanisms have forced Negroes to play the part of perma-
> nent immigrants, entering the urban economy at the bottom and remain-
> ing there decade after decade? [Baran and Sweezy, 1966, p. 263]

Their answer is that three sets of factors are responsible. The first is a number of private interests, including employers who benefit from divisions among their workers, ghetto landlords, marginal businesses that need cheap labor to survive, and White workers, who are protected from Black competition for jobs. The second is race prejudice, which is of historical origin but is reinforced in the contemporary world by the need of Whites to have a subordinate group on whom they can vent the frustrations and hostilities generated by class society. The third is the economy's declining need for unskilled and semiskilled labor. The position of the large capitalists who constitute the ruling class, however, is that any benefits they may derive from racial subordination are outweighed by the growing revolutionary threat posed by Blacks in the context of a worldwide anti-imperialist trend. Thus while this class has endeavored to further racial equality, it has been able to achieve relatively little because of its limited control of the system [ibid., pp. 263–71].

Michael Reich, on the other hand, argues in a widely quoted article that the contemporary capitalist class benefits substantially from the existence of subordinate racial groups. Reich argues that racial divisions in the society are carried over into the work force, and that divisions among workers sap their bargaining strength and thus keep both Black and White wages down, thus widening the gap between workers' and capitalists' income. He attempts to test this proposition by developing a measure of racism (the ratio of Black median family income to White median family income) and correlating it at the level of the metropolitan area with measures of inequality among Whites (e.g., the percent share of all White income received by the top 1 percent of White families). The correlations which result from this procedure support his argument, even with controls for various other factors (Reich, 1972).

(Of course the limitations of this kind of correlational test should be kept in mind. In essence all that Reich has shown is that there is a relationship between Black–White inequality and White–White inequality. Correlations do not show any direction of causation or even establish causation, since the demonstrated relationship could be a product of another, uncontrolled, factor.)

In general, then, it could be said that there is in fact no *tradition* of Marxist writing in America on race. The scattered Marxist theoretical works on this subject often seem unaware of other Marxist analyses, so that there is no accumulation of knowledge. In addition, the works frequently contradict each other. Perhaps one reason for this state of affairs is that many of the writers who have dealt with race have done so as a sort of sideline, with their main theoretical interests focused elsewhere. The only really substantial Marxist theoretical work to date on race in the United States is Oliver Cox's *Caste, Class and Race,* originally published in 1948 (Cox, 1970).

The perspective that Cox presents is in many ways compatible with the present work, although his data are based on the Black experience and mine on the Chicano. Cox's framework is essentially that of "left" colonial theory, and while he does not apply that terminology to the contemporary experience of Blacks, he places American race relations firmly in a colonial context. He develops the theme that modern race relations had their origins in the colonial systems developed by Europeans after the fifteenth century. He sees racism as an ideology developed to justify those systems, used by the capitalist "to keep his labor and other resources freely exploitable" (ibid., p. 333). He observes that "in the United States the race problem developed out of the need of the planter class, the ruling class, to keep the freed Negro exploitable. To do this, the ruling class had to do what every ruling class must do; that is, develop mass support for its policy. Race prejudice was and is the convenient vehicle" (ibid., p. 475). While the needs of the Southern agricultural capitalist were the most pressing, in Cox's view racial subordination serves the interests of capitalists as a whole in two ways: by providing a sector of workers who are more tractable and manipulable, and by keeping workers as a whole divided among themselves (ibid., p. 487).

While Cox's analysis provides valuable elements for a theory of racial inequality (and I have drawn upon his work to develop my own ideas), it has significant limitations. For a Marxist, his conception of class is certainly anomalous. He discusses the concept of social class in terms of groups of people who share a certain status, and he sees social class systems as peculiar to capitalism (ibid., p. 142). In addition, he distinguishes what he calls "political class" from social class, and characterizes the former concept in terms of organizations (ibid., p. 154). The term "social class," as he uses it, is closer to the non-Marxist conception of class as strata, and neither concept corresponds to what is generally accepted as the Marxist idea of class as defined most fundamentally by the relationship to the means and process of production. Perhaps in part because of this confusion over the notion of class, Cox nowhere works out a systematic relationship between class and racial divisions in American society. While valuable and suggestive, his work is by no means the last word on the subject. Nevertheless, it should have been taken far more seriously by later generations of Marxist writers.

Labor Market Segmentation and Class Fractions

The most valuable contribution of Marxism to the discussion of race is not so much in the explicit analyses of racism as in providing an understanding of the social and economic context in which racism operates. In addition to general class analysis, two lines of thought that have been developed in the last few years appear to be particularly helpful, that of *labor market segmentation* and that of *class fractions*.

The concept of labor market segmentation can be traced to the idea of the dual labor market. Certain researchers, most notably Doeringer and Piore (1971), posited the existence of two labor markets as a means of explaining persistent unemployment among racial minorities. In the primary labor market were found those jobs which offered security and stability, good pay and working conditions, the possibility for advancement, and a stable set of procedures in the administration of work rules. Jobs in the secondary labor market offered the opposite conditions, and were what might be termed dead-end jobs. The concentration of minority workers in the secondary labor market was seen as one reason for their high unemployment rates and other conditions of disadvantage. Most of the growing literature on this topic has dealt with elaborating this basic dichotomy and exploring its ramifications (for a review of this literature, see Torres, 1978).

More recently, other writers have taken up the concept and have attempted to generalize it by speaking of labor market segmentation, and arguing that several dimensions of segmentation exist, including race and sex. They have also introduced a historical perspective and placed the discussion in a Marxist framework (Edwards, Reich, and Gordon, 1975). They present the theme that in the latter part of the nineteenth century there were important trends in the United States that signaled a danger to the hegemony of the capitalist system. The labor force was becoming more homogeneous with the development of the factory system, and the growing proletarianization of the work force was producing labor conflicts that were increasingly taking on a class character and raising broader and more militant demands. Partly as a defense against these trends, capitalists devised an elaborate system of job stratification that involved the proliferation of job categories and the ranking of those jobs in a status hierarchy. The intent was to divide the work force and thus prevent class solidarity from coming about. Associated with this process was the creation of a segmented labor market, in which various segments or submarkets emerged, each with its own set of rules, working conditions, wages, and opportunities. The primary and secondary labor markets were thus created. Minorities and other relatively vulnerable groups (women, youth) were, and are, concentrated in the secondary sector and in less desirable jobs generally. David Gordon develops this theme in greater detail in another work. He feels that employers deliberately filled the worst jobs with people who were the least likely to establish solidarity with better-off workers.

> Gradually, as the composition of the American labor force changed, it became relatively easy for employers to reserve the most "secondary" jobs for teens, women and minority group workers with quite confident expectations that they would not identify with the more advantaged workers and develop a common consciousness about the disadvantages of their jobs. [Gordon, 1972, p. 74]

While these writers mention racial and sexual divisions, most of the work in this vein has continued to stress segmentation based on the structure of occupations. The dimensions of racial and sexual labor market division have largely remained theoretically unintegrated with the rest of their work, although they include descriptive studies of sexual labor segmentation in their collection of essays.

The discussion of class "fractions" in recent years is generally associated with the writings of Nicos Poulantzas, although others have also taken up the concept. Poulantzas argues that there are several types of divisions within classes, of which class fractions are the most important. As he states, "The Marxist theory of social classes further distinguishes *fractions* and *strata* of a class . . . on the basis of differentiations in the economic sphere, and of the role . . . of political and ideological relations" (Poulantzas, 1975, p. 23). He describes various fractions, such as the commercial and industrial fractions of the bourgeoisie, and clerks, office workers, and technicians as three fractions within the "new petty bourgeoisie." Fractions, according to Poulantzas, are significant in that they can "take on an important role as social forces, a role relatively distinct from that of other fractions of their class" (Poulantzas, 1973a, p. 28).

Francesca Freedman also discussed class fractions in a recent article, using the concept in a somewhat broader fashion than Poulantzas. She speaks of class fractions as "structural divisions . . . within a class," and states that such divisions can be based on many factors, including race and sex (Freedman, 1975, p. 43). However, most of her discussion of fractions within the American working class deals with fractions on the basis of the structure of occupations, much as Poulantzas does. Thus she is primarily concerned with distinctions such as skilled versus unskilled workers, industrial versus service workers, and so on. In a footnote at the end of her lengthy article she concludes: "For reasons of lack of space I have omitted the role of minorities and women in the capitalist economy, and therefore in the development of the working class. Many of the fractions we have dealt with here intersect with racial and sexual divisions (ibid., p. 81n.). The tendency to deal with racial and sexual divisions in footnotes and passing references is not unknown in Marxist writings on political economy.

Class Segmentation

The labor market segmentation approach is limited in that racial and sexual divisions in the labor force are relatively neglected. It is also limited in that it concerns itself only with the labor market and not with classes as a whole. Thus this tradition is largely confined to an examination of the working class. The class fraction approach is broader in its conceptualization, in that it is concerned with classes as a whole. However, it shares with the segmentation literature the relative neglect of race and sex, and in addition it does not appear to be as solidly grounded empirically. Both approaches see the divisions with which they are concerned as typically based on the structure of occupations in the economy, although Poulantzas adds political and ideological criteria as secondary factors. The divisions based on the structure of occupations are racially and sexually neutral, and presumably, they would exist in a capitalist economy even if the work force were entirely homogeneous racially and sexually.

What I am proposing is that there are two major types of intraclass divisions in a capitalist political economy, with each major division having subdivisions. These divisions I propose calling *class segments*. Type 1 consists of divisions based on the structure of occupations. This category can be called *structural class segments,* and can be further broken down as described above by Poulantzas and Freedman. Type-2 divisions are based on the characteristics of the workers themselves, and can be called *ascriptive class segments,* since they are based on ascribed characteristics of persons. Within this broad category are two major subdivisions, one based on race and/or ethnicity, and one based on sex. Racial and ethnic characteristics are, of course, more ambiguous and subject to social definition than sexual characteristics. The formal definition of this type-2 division is as follows:

> An ascriptive class segment is a portion of a class which is set off from the rest of the class by some readily identifiable and relatively stable characteristic of the persons assigned to that segment, such as race, ethnicity, or sex, where the relationship of the members to the means and process of production is affected by that demarcation.

My contention is that Chicanos have been incorporated into the United States' political economy as subordinate ascriptive class segments, and that they have historically been found occupying such a structural position at all class levels. While I have stressed in the definition the relationship to the system of production (i.e., the economic system), a person's class position is typically manifested in all institutions of the society (e.g., the educational system, the political system).

A SYNTHESIS OF INTERNAL COLONIAL
AND CLASS SEGMENTATION APPROACHES

Of the various theoretical models that have been set forth to explain the persistence of racial inequality in the United States, the internal colonial model is the most comprehensive and the one that most accurately reflects empirical reality. The particular variation that I favor is the class-differentiated or "left" version of that model. On the one hand, it is consistent with a view of capitalist society as class society, in which the dominant class exercises disproportionate influence on all aspects of the system. Colonialism historically has been established to serve the interests of merchants, industrialists, and would-be landowners, or of the state which ultimately safeguards the interests of the dominant classes. Internal colonialism is no exception to this rule. In addition, this model is consistent with the bulk of the material summarized in chapters 2, 3, 4, and 5 on the role of agricultural and industrial capitalists in the nineteenth-century continental expansion of the United States, and in structuring the subordinate labor force that came into existence in the Southwest on the basis of various racial minorities.

It is sometimes argued that Anglo workers have benefited from internal colonialism, and that their interests are also involved in perpetuating that system. However, this is true in only a very partial sense, and is untrue in a general sense. The argument is often supported by reference to antiminority sentiments and social movements among Anglo workers, based on job competition. However, a careful historical examination reveals that Anglo workers have been reacting to the racially segmented labor system created by employers precisely to undercut the wage standards, organizing efforts, and unity of workers as a whole. To the extent that employers have been successful in these efforts, Anglo workers have seen their enemies as the manipulated minority workers, rather than the manipulators. This misperception, essentially a type of false consciousness, has been encouraged by the racial ideologies developed to support the system, and by the general obscuring of class relations created by the hegemony of capitalist ideology. The impulse of Anglo workers has been to exclude the minority workers from the economy in order to solidify their own position. Only when this effort has been blocked have they gone along with the segmentation of the labor force.

Examination of the objective interests of the Anglo workers leads to the same conclusion. Anglo workers do benefit in a way from being spared the most undesirable work and from being cushioned against the worst dislocations of the economy (via the "buffer" role of the minority workers). However, they lose from the downward pressure exerted on wages by the segmented labor market, and from the use of minority workers as strikebreakers in their reserve role. Most importantly, the divisions created among workers by labor-force segmentation prevent the coming about of class consciousness and the ability of the workers to act in a unified manner to secure their interests. Members of the working class clearly have a much greater interest in uniting politically to change the system as a whole and to abolish classes than in competing with each other for limited gains.

Employers' interests, on the other hand, gain across the board from this system. Dual wage structures lower their labor costs. The buffer role allows the impact of recessions to be concentrated on the most vulnerable and politically least dangerous segment of the workers. The reserve role allows them to expand and reduce their labor force as needed, and to use the reserve labor force as leverage against demands of the employed workers. The most important aspect, however, has to do with the divisions that are created among the workers as a whole, since this allows capitalists to promote what is after all their ultimate interest, the perpetuation of class society itself.

Only two possible disadvantages to employers can be cited. One is the confinement of talented minority workers to jobs where their talents are not fully utilized, but apparently most employers are willing to bear this cost in order to gain the other advantages. In any case, most occupational positions require only that a job be done adequately, not that it be done in a superior manner. In the situation of labor surplus which appears to be a permanent aspect of the American economy, it is not difficult to find workers to perform most jobs adequately. The other disadvantage, which seems to impress some observers, has to do with political unrest among the minority populations, for example, the urban uprisings of the 1960s. From the perspective of the '70s, it appears that this threat has been satisfactorily blunted through the combined use of selective repression and cooptation (for a good analysis of this process, see Allen, 1969).

Having adopted a class-differentiated colonial perspective, it remains to spell out the nature of structural discrimination in more detail and to relate the model to the American class structure, beyond the specification of class interests outlined above. The relationship is diagrammed in figure 16, in which the internal colonial model is reproduced in its "left" variation and in which the class structure is modeled on the Ehrenreich analysis described earlier.

The diagram at the bottom of figure 16 represents an elaboration of the box in the top of the diagram labeled "Establishment of a System of Structural Discrimination." Classes are the most general structural elements in a society, and the existence of a system of institutionalized discrimination in the society can be thought of in terms of a set of segmented classes. Segmentation in each class exists to the extent that such institutionalized discriminatory practices exist. If there is none, there is no segmentation. The segmentation line is drawn in a broken manner to indicate that it is not necessarily an impervious line. That is, a member of a racial minority may be in the subordinate segment or in the nonsubordinate segment. Under the latter conditions, he or she would be integrated into the class on the basis of equality with all other nonsubordinate members of that class. All Chicanos are not necessarily in one of the subordinate segments.

The diagram is drawn in a particular manner to illustrate certain points. The class diagram is not drawn in the familiar pyramid fashion because Marxist classes are not strata arranged, one on top of the other, on the basis of income, even though there is a correlation between class and average income. The classes are all drawn the same size because what is portrayed here is the structural relationships, not the relative magnitude of the class memberships. The segmentation line is drawn all the way across the diagram because Chicanos are members of all classes in the United States, but form a subordinate segment within each class.

The central aspect of this diagram is the way in which interests are grouped. A Chicano in the subordinate segment of the working class is still a member of that class, and has interests in common with all members of the working class, for example, in higher wages, better working conditions, the right to bargain collectively, and, ultimately, the establishment cf a classless society. These interests are in opposition to those of other classes, particularly the capitalist class. At the same time, Chicano workers have certain interests

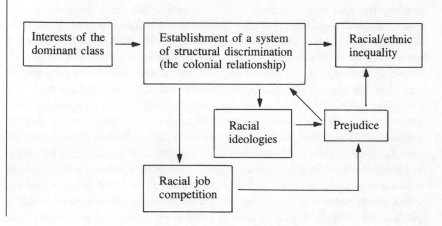

FIGURE 16

INTERNAL COLONIALISM AND CLASS SEGMENTATION

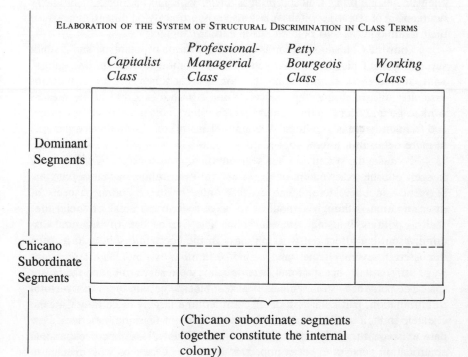

ELABORATION OF THE SYSTEM OF STRUCTURAL DISCRIMINATION IN CLASS TERMS

(Chicano subordinate segments together constitute the internal colony)

particular to them, such as the ending of racial discrimination, which, while of benefit to workers generally, would affect them more intensely.

The segmentation line, however, also cuts across class divisions, reflecting the fact that Chicanos in all classes suffer from institutionalized discrimination, even though it takes different forms for each class. This gives Chicanos as a group certain interests in common, based on the common experience of discrimination. Such interests would include equality in economic treatment, the end of housing and educational discrimination, and so on. Thus the various Chicano subordinate segments have certain interests in common, their colonial interests, and certain interests in opposition, their class interests. The different Chicano segments also constitute an internal colony in the sense that they share a common culture, at least in part, and this may be reflected in a shared interest in such things as bilingual-bicultural programs in the schools. Chicanos also constitute a colony with a certain coherence across class lines in the sense that they are liable to be in frequent contact with each other. Thus the bilingual Chicano teacher, a member of the professional-managerial class, comes in contact with Chicano parents from the working class. Chicano social workers are liable to have a largely Chicano clientele, as are other Chicano professionals. Chicano members of the petty bourgeoisie or (small) capitalist class also rely primarily on other Chicanos for their livelihood, as was pointed out in earlier chapters.

Thus the Chicano situation is complex in terms of interests, and it is not surprising that Chicano political patterns have somewhat of a shifting nature, with, at times, the segmentation division and, at times, the class divisions assuming an overriding importance. While it is not possible in the present work to go into detail on this pattern, it is familiar to most informed observers, and frequently creates political dilemmas. I intend to examine these patterns in more detail in a future work.

To make the system of class segmentation more concrete, it is necessary to spell out the exact nature of the structural discrimination that defines the segmentation line. Here, I can do that only for the economic aspects of discrimination, although it should also be done in other areas of social life, such as politics, housing, and education. The five aspects of structural discrimination that affect the working class in the economic sphere have been discussed in several chapters and should be familiar by now: labor repression, wage differentials, occupational stratification, the reserve role, and the buffer role. The petty bourgeois segment is also subject to certain types of structural discrimination, particularly in being confined to a largely or entirely Chicano clientele in their small businesses or independent professional practices. Few data exist on the Chicano professional-managerial class, but occupational stratification appears to be an important factor for Chicanos who manage to make it into this growing class. From personal observation, it seems that

Chicano professionals who work in bureaucracies are often hired only to deal with a Chicano clientele, much as Chicano white-collar workers have historically been employed. Chicano faculty in universities and colleges, for example, are often deemed employable primarily in ethnic studies programs, which are usually run on "soft" money and not considered a permanent aspect of the university. Chicano faculty are overwhelmingly in junior positions, and a kind of informal "revolving door" policy has come into being by which Chicano faculty are terminated when they come up for tenure, and their positions filled with other junior Chicano faculty. At the University of California at Berkeley, for example, the most recent figures indicate that total minority faculty in untenured positions rose from 6.9 percent in 1973 to 13.3 percent in 1976, but minority tenured faculty actually declined from 5.6 to 5.3 percent in the same period. In the latter year, "Hispanic" faculty (a category broader than Chicano) represented only 1.1 percent of the Berkeley faculty ("Fed Report Reveals State of Faculty Affirmative Action," *Daily Californian,* Aug. 8–10, 1977). These patterns reflect in part the existence of structural discrimination at lower levels of the public education system, so that few Chicanos reach the university level. But it also reflects certain institutionalized practices at the university level, such as culturally biased standards of evaluation, racially biased patterns of recruiting, and the habit of imposing disproportionate administrative responsibilities on junior Chicano faculty without weighing them seriously in the promotion process.

Class segmentation in the capitalist class must remain largely speculative because of lack of information, although the few data reported earlier on New Mexico tend to bear out the hypothesis. Still, this can be a theoretical advantage in that it allows us to make certain predictions from the model that can be checked empirically. If Chicano capitalists conform to the pattern of the petty bourgeoisie, they will be confined largely to small and perhaps medium-size enterprises, with a principally Chicano clientele. Their position will be maintained through certain institutionalized practices, one of which I predict will be the denial of credit to them by Anglo bankers on the same terms as credit is extended to Anglo businessmen. Other structural mechanisms will probably emerge from empirical studies.

It should be borne in mind that the diagram in figure 16 is not intended to depict the situation of all Chicanos. Chicanos in the marginal sector (discussed in chapters 4 and 5) are outside the class system in that they have no organic connection to the system of production. The diagram applies only to Chicanos in the colonized and integrated sectors—which is, however, most of the Chicano population. Also, the emphasis on the existence of segmentation should not obscure the fact that the segmentation line has been weakening at least since the Second World War. Continuation of that trend will mean that class divisions will become more salient as Chicanos become more integrated into the nonsubordinate part of the labor force. A reversal of the trend, or even a situation of stagnation, would undoubtedly lead to greater political mobilization along the colonial axis.

CONCLUSION

Chicano history could be said to start with the Mexican American War, an episode in the territorial expansion of Europe and European-derived societies that began in the fifteenth century. The manner in which the original Chicanos came about links Chicano history firmly with the history of other Third World people who have been subjected to the colonial experience in one or another of its forms. In this case, the imperial expansion of the United States resulted in internal colonialism, a condition which Chicanos have shared with other racial minorities. While the initial conquest affected only certain parts of the Southwest immediately and left others in a more or less peripheral state, the economic penetration which followed in the remainder of the nineteenth century eventually drew all parts of the area within the new order. As the interests of the American dominant class asserted themselves, the lands which remained under Chicano control were expropriated, in some cases rapidly and in others more gradually, and as likely as not under the color of law. It is perhaps in this expropriation that we can most clearly see the role the American state has played in creating and perpetuating the colonial status of Chicanos, although many other examples have been cited.

As part of that process of expropriation, but tied even more strongly to the exploitation of Chicano labor, a system of class segmentation was created in the nineteenth century that bound Chicanos to a structurally subordinate position in the society. With the waves of immigration that swept across the border in the early twentieth century, the numerical presence of Chicanos in the Southwest was greatly expanded. The structure of subordination, however, underwent only minor changes. During the Great Depression, thousands of Chicanos and Mexicanos were expelled from the Southwest as the labor market contracted. At the same time, important changes were made in the political economy of the United States, in particular the growing integration of the state and the economy. This development and others during the 1930s and 1940s set in motion a chain of events which have resulted in significant modifications in the class position of Chicanos in recent decades. Still, while some of these changes have resulted in a lessening of the harshness which has characterized the Chicano situation, the 1970s have brought some ominous trends. These include a new round of hysteria around the issue of un-documented workers, a broad-based backlash against minority demands, and a possible reemergence of marginality, this time on a more permanent basis. And while more Chicanos have become integrated or substantially integrated into the nonsubordinate part of the class structure, the segmentation line remains a major determining factor in most Chicanos' day-to-day reality. For the foreseeable future, the politics of the Chicano community can be expected to revolve around both class and colonial divisions in a complex manner whose outlines we can only dimly perceive in the current period of confusion and redefinition.

The Case of International Harvester

MOST OF THE MATERIAL on which this book is based is derived from studies of certain geographical areas or sectors of industry, or on broad statistical data. One way to supplement this type of information is through detailed case studies of particular corporations.

The case study described in this appendix is based on International Harvester, a large corporation typical of those which have come to dominate most sectors of American industry in the last century. In it I give a brief history of this corporate giant and summarize what is known about its use of minority labor, both Black and Chicano.*

In general, the historical patterns that we can observe at International Harvester are fully in keeping with the theoretical framework developed in the earlier sections of this book. The segmentation of its labor force was fully institutionalized at an early date, and this segmentation continues to be a prominent feature of the company's work force today. This case study is presented as a more detailed look at some of the aspects of class segmentation described throughout the book. Some of the more interesting aspects of this case have to do with the role of the schools in maintaining segmentation in the past, with the evidence of class consciousness among the corporation's managers, and with the attitude toward affirmative action.

INTERNATIONAL HARVESTER

The origins of International Harvester can be traced to western Virginia, where in 1831 Cyrus Hall McCormick developed a horse-drawn reaper. In 1847 McCormick moved to Chicago and built his own factory. This factory, known as the McCormick Works, was to remain for many years the sole manufacturing plant of the McCormick farm equipment company. By 1902 this plant was producing over a third of the United States' harvesting ma-

*This re-edited case study appeared as part of a longer article in *Review of Radical Political Economics* (Summer 1976), pp. 1–18. Copyright 1976 Review of Radical Political Economics. Reprinted by permission of the Union for Radical Political Economics.

chinery. In that year the McCormick company merged with the four next largest farm equipment companies to form International Harvester. This giant trust then produced 85 percent of the country's harvesting machinery. In 1914 legal action was brought against the company under the Sherman Anti-Trust Act, and it was eventually forced to break up. International Harvester Company remained in existence, and although reduced in scope it has continued as the largest company in the farm equipment industry. In recent years it has ranked among the top twenty-five corporations in the United States in volume of sales, which in 1973 amounted to over $4 billion. Throughout its history, the McCormick family has maintained a central position in management, and the current president is a McCormick. The mainstay of the company is in its lines of farm equipment and trucks, but it also operates its own steel plant (Wisconsin Steel Division) and manufactures industrial gas turbines (Solar Division). Its main plants are in the Midwest, but some are in the South. The Solar Division is located in San Diego.

Starting with 23 workers in 1847, McCormick employed 1,400 in 1884. In 1950 International Harvester had over 90,000 workers in all its divisions, and in 1970 over 100,000. Within the farm equipment industry generally, approximately two-thirds of the employees are blue-collar workers, with operatives, or semiskilled workers, comprising the single largest category (Ozanne, 1972, p. 13).

Trade unionism has had a long and turbulent history at McCormick and International Harvester. The earliest unions, based on crafts, appeared in the 1860s. In the late 1880s the Knights of Labor were strongly represented at McCormick. In 1886 striking McCormick workers were involved in conflicts with other workers and the police that led directly to the famous Haymarket Square bombing and the subsequent wave of anti-union repression. Union activity at McCormick and International Harvester rose and fell, as it did in industry generally, with changes in economic and political conditions. McCormick management was virulently anti-union, and succeeded time and again in smashing emerging unions. The tactics were a skillful blend of coercion and cooptation. On the coercive side was ample use of blacklists, police repression, and the firing of union activists. But the company also resorted to the shrewd use of bonuses, intracompany welfare programs, and company unions as the occasion demanded. After World War I, International Harvester was one of the members of the Special Conference Committee, a secret organization of ten of the largest corporations in the United States. The purpose of this organization was to deal with the threat of unionism and related labor matters. In this as in other ways, International Harvester proved itself to be a highly class-conscious corporation (Ozanne, 1967, pp. 157ff.).

International Harvester was successful in delaying the recognition of unions until 1941—several years after most of America's large industrial concerns. After the war there was a struggle for union dominance between the left-influenced Farm Equipment Workers and the United Automobile Workers, with the initially stronger Farm Equipment Workers losing out during the McCarthy era in the early 1950s. Since that time the UAW has been the largest union among International Harvester workers.

International Harvester and McCormick also have a long history of ethnic diversity in their work force. During the nineteenth and early twentieth centuries the succession of ethnic workers included Irish, Scandinavians, Germans, and Poles. World War I, however, signaled the end of large-scale European migration and the entrance of Black and Chicano workers in significant numbers into the International Harvester labor force. This trend was reinforced by the stringent postwar restrictions on immigration. Whereas Blacks had established a presence in Chicago industry earlier in the century, World War I marked a sharp rise in their level of industrial employment. For Chicanos, World War I marks their entry into the Chicago labor market.

It is important to keep in mind that even before this period the management of large industrial concerns was highly conscious of the ethnicity of their workers. During the nineteenth century, International Harvester had pursued a deliberate policy of encouraging ethnic diversity in its workers as a means of keeping them weak and divided. According to Robert Ozanne, "Harvester experience showed that the cohesiveness of nationality groups worked against the company in strike situations" (Ozanne, 1967, p. 184). In 1916, labor strife prompted President McCormick to write to his directors: "One of the advantages of building a new foundry organization will be that we will not have such a large percentage of Poles. It does not have a good effect to have so large percentage of one class of men" (ibid., p. 107). After World War I, the Industrial Relations Department of International Harvester compiled regular reports on the nationality and race of its employees (ibid., p. 184).

The policy pursued by International Harvester during this period was to leave racial hiring policies to the superintendents of the different plants. However, the central management carefully monitored the proportion of Black workers in the plants, and cautioned the superintendents if the level of Black employment reached a certain level. The various plants of International Harvester followed one of two patterns. Some excluded Blacks altogether. The others adopted a quota system, generally at about the 20 percent level (ibid.). The quota system appears to have been the product of two considerations. One was the desire to tap this pool of labor in a tight labor market; the other was the fear of ethnic solidarity.

One of the impacts of the postwar labor shortage was to put pressure on the exclusionary and the quota systems. The only alternatives to reduced output were to bid up the price of labor in the hope of attracting white workers from other industries, or to hire minorities. In this situation, International

Harvester management reluctantly decided to increase the hiring of minorities, rather than raise its labor costs by competing with other manufacturers for labor (Ozanne, 1968). By 1923, the level of Black labor at the central McCormick Works stood at 18 percent, and at the McCormick Twine Mill at 20 percent (Ozanne, 1972, p. 185). By 1929 it had risen to over 27 percent at the Twine Mill. Some plants, however, continued to employ no Blacks.

The Wisconsin Steel plant of International Harvester provided an interesting variation on this situation. The policy of Wisconsin Steel was to hire no Blacks at all. Confronted with the labor shortage, its solution was to hire Chicanos or Mexicans. In pursuit of this effort they recruited Chicano labor from as far away as Kansas City and Texas (Taylor, 1932, p. 37; Ozanne, 1967, p. 185). The figures for Mexican employment at Wisconsin Steel during the 1920s are given in table 22.

The Depression of the 1930s and the labor shortage it brought with it produced a sharp turnaround in the trend of hiring more minority labor. Minority workers were laid off at a greater rate than White workers, and the percentages of minority workers declined. At the McCormick Works, the proportion of Black workers dropped from 18 percent in 1923 to 10.3 percent in 1940. At the Tractor Works it declined from 9 percent in 1923 to 6.5 percent in 1940. The McCormick Twine Mill saw a drop from 27.5 percent in 1929 to 18.8 percent in 1940 (Ozanne, 1972, pp. 185, 192).

With the labor shortages of World War II, the situation was turned around once again. Federal antidiscriminatory and fair employment practices legislation combined with the labor shortage to end the complete exclusion of

TABLE 22

MEXICAN EMPLOYMENT AT WISCONSIN STEEL IN THE 1920s

Year	Mexican
1921	.3%
1922	.6
1923	14.2
1924	14.8
1925	19.7
1926	21.8
1927	21.0
1928	19.5

Source: Paul Taylor, *Mexican Labor in the United States: Chicago and the Calumet Region* (Berkeley: University of California, 1932), table 3.

Black workers that still existed at many International Harvester plants. In 1940 Blacks constituted 4.5 percent of all the workers employed in International Harvester plants. By 1944 the number had risen to 11.6 percent. In 1950 it was 12.8 percent, in 1960 9.3 percent, and in 1970 11 percent (Ozanne, 1967, p. 192, and 1972, p. 84). Thus it would appear that there has been little change in the overall level of Black employment since the end of the Second World War. One factor that has contributed to the stagnation of the level of Black employment has been the recent trend of closing plants in the large urban centers, such as Chicago, and opening others in suburban and outlying areas.

Considerable variation in the levels of Black employment has continued at the different plants. The highest levels were reached at the McCormick Twine Mill before its closing in 1953. This plant, traditionally operated by female labor, reached a peak of 75.6 percent Black employment in 1951. The McCormick Works, which closed in 1961, employed 28.7 percent Black employees in 1960 (Ozanne, 1967, p. 192).

One of the most striking aspects of Black employment at International Harvester has been its relative concentration in certain types of work and certain occupational levels. The two work sectors in which Black employment was initially concentrated were the foundries, or metal casting shops, and the twine mills. The foundries were the places with the most arduous working conditions; the twine mills were areas of low-wage employment, almost entirely female. In 1924, for example, Black employment at the Tractor Works foundry was 35 percent, and in the McCormick foundry 29 percent. In the twine mills it was 24 percent (ibid., p. 184).

The typical minority employee was hired at the level of laborer, or unskilled worker, and there seems to have been a definite conception on the part of management as to what type of work minorities were suitable for. A special report on minority employment was initiated by President McCormick in 1925. Some representative quotes are: "In some instances the Negro is held to be suitable for semi-skilled work. . . . Steel mills are more satisfied with Mexicans for common and semi-skilled labor. . . . The Mexicans at the steel mills are developing into semi-skilled tradesmen but none are employed in mechanical or electrical trades" (ibid., p. 187).

Taylor presents the figures for two large steel plants in the Chicago area in 1928, and while the figures are not specifically for International Harvester, they are probably indicative of the general pattern in the steel plants of the area (see table 23).

Of interest in these data are not only the sharp differences between minority occupational patterns and overall patterns, but the very similar patterns for Chicano and Black workers.

A more recent study of the farm equipment and construction machinery

TABLE 23

	All Employees		Mexican Employees		Colored Employees	
	Number	%	Number	% of All Mexican Employees	Number	% of All Colored Employees
Skilled	8,101	36.7	38	1.8	128	4.7
Semi-skilled	5,704	25.9	397	19.1	438	16.2
Unskilled	8,256	37.4	1,646	79.1	2,150	79.2
Total	22,061	100.0	2,081	100.0	2,716	100.0

Source: Taylor (1932), p. 157. Data for Gary Works and South Works, Illinois Steel Company.

industries in the United States indicates that these patterns persist in modified form today. According to Ozanne, "In plants visited by the author or by other Industrial Research Unit personnel (and these were larger companies), it was found generally that Negro craftsmen tended to be concentrated in the foundries in such crafts as molders and coremakers, rather than being broadly distributed throughout the plant" (Ozanne, 1972, p. 62).

A review of occupational statistics presented in the same study reveals the following patterns for five large companies (not specified by name) in the farm equipment and construction machinery industries. In 1970 35.5 percent of these companies' employees were classified as white collar (all non-blue-collar categories), although only 8.9 percent of their Black employees fell into this classification. Of the 8.9 percent, the overwhelming majority were in the lowest white-collar category, that of office and clerical workers. At the highest level, that of officials and managers, only .9 percent of the employees were Black, compared to 8.2 percent of all employees. Some 11.5 percent of the Black employees were classified as craftsmen (skilled workers), 60 percent as operatives (semiskilled), 14.4 percent as laborers, and 5.2 percent as service workers. Black employees were overrepresented in proportion to their overall numbers in the bottom three categories, and underrepresented in all of the higher categories (ibid., p. 52). Several factors are also noted in the study that make these figures even bleaker. Thus Ozanne states that "the designation 'craftsmen' covers such a broad category of jobs that it conceals the fact that the Negro penetration into truly skilled trades has been almost negligible. Furthermore, the future for this category is not bright because of the almost universal failure to enroll a sufficient number of Negroes in the apprentice-ships'' (ibid., p. 53). Furthermore, "within the operatives classification, we observed a definite tendency for blacks to be overconcentrated at the lower ranges'' (ibid., p. 64).

At the white-collar level, the same study notes that Blacks have been almost completely excluded from sales positions, and that "in the offices Negro employment is generally only tokenism. Firms in communities of high Negro population have failed to do much better in the proportion of Negroes hired for their offices than firms in communities of low Negro population. This probably indicates that until recently the main offices actually have been neglected in the firms' equal opportunity policy'' (ibid., p. 60).

On the matter of differential pay rates (different pay for the same work), there appears to be little evidence. From the information presented by Taylor for Mexican workers in the Chicago of the 1920s, it seems that such practices existed but they do not appear to have been a major factor in the employment of minority labor (Taylor, 1932, pp. 78-79).

Another aspect of minority employment in the Chicago of the 1920s is touched upon in a comment by an employer from a large foundry: "We now have a good labor market, so we can replace the Mexicans with more desir-able labor'' (ibid., p. 92).

Up to now the discussion has been concerned with the main Interna-tional Harvester plants in the Midwest. Harvester's plants in the South deserve special comment. The three plants that have been studied are the Louisville Works, producer of tractors since 1946; the Memphis Works, where mechani-cal cottonpickers and other farm implements have been made since 1948; and the Evansville Works, which has manufactured refrigerators since 1946. The Louisville plant began with 4.2 percent Black workers, employed 14.1 per-cent in 1950, reached a peak of 20.9 percent in 1955, and declined to 11.9 percent in 1960—the last year for which published figures are available (Ozanne, 1967, p. 192). The Evansville plant had 4.4 percent Black workers in 1946 and 8.2 percent in 1950 (Hope, 1955, p. 35). The Memphis plant started with 12.2 percent Black workers in 1947 and had reached a level of 23.2 percent in 1949 (Ozanne, 1967, p. 192). In 1968, its percentage of Black employees was still at essentially that same level (Ozanne, 1972, p. 84).

A study of these three companies, covering the late 1940s and early 1950s showed a sharp pattern of Black concentration at certain occupational levels and in certain types of work. The basic pattern was that Blacks were greatly overconcentrated in unskilled labor and greatly underrepresented in skilled and white-collar occupations. At the Louisville Works, for example, in 1951 Black daywork production workers consisted of 54.8 percent unskilled and 2.8 percent skilled workers. Whites in the same category were 25.9 percent unskilled workers and 29.5 percent skilled (Hope, 1955, p. 43). The same author divided the production process into three stages, and found that Blacks were concentrated in the first stage, consisting of primary fabrication of parts from raw materials. Whites were more evenly distributed throughout the three stages, with the second stage being the finishing and assembling of parts and the third stage inspection, packing, and shipping (ibid., p. 47). Blacks were almost totally excluded from clerical, technical, and managerial employment (ibid., p. 132). The author concluded, on the basis of his study, that International Harvester's officially stated policy of equal employment opportunity would soon produce significant occupational advancement for Blacks. And yet a study based on 1969 data described the situation in the Memphis plant in the following terms:

> The plant is still characterized by lily-white and overwhelmingly black departments. Of the roughly 300 men in the truly skilled trades, there was but one Negro, an electrician who was on layoff in January 1969 because he had only 50 days' seniority in the electrical department. In welding, in 1969, there were roughly 3 Negroes out of 100, none of them with substantial seniority. In the machine department there were only 6 Negro machine operators out of 75 operators and inspectors, the most senior Negro having only six months' seniority. Among 279 foremen, 3 were Negro, 2 of them appointed in 1967, and the first in 1965. There were no Negro apprentices. Of 450 workers in the foundry, approximately 325 were Negroes, concentrated as usual in the hottest places, the forge shop, and pouring the molten metal. (Ozanne, 1972, pp. 84–85]

John Hope's study gives some insight into the origins of this situation in the 1940s and early 1950s. He stresses the opposition of White labor to the advancement of Blacks, and he repeatedly states that management pursued an equal opportunity policy. However, management's role in this regard consisted primarily of placing some Black workers in semiskilled positions. During the first few years of existence of the Southern plants there was no union representation and management had a relatively free hand in its placement policies. According to Hope, Harvester management made no effort to place Blacks in skilled positions, and, as we have seen, there was virtually no Black representation at the white-collar level (Hope, 1955, pp. 63–64). Hope also mentions that there was a universally recognized taboo against appointing Blacks to positions where they would supervise White workers (ibid., p. 110). It was equally forbidden for Blacks to "bump" or displace a White worker from a job, regardless of seniority or qualifications (ibid., p. 113). Any Black tempted to file a grievance on the basis of discrimination was brought under intense pressure from union and company officials, as well as fellow workers, on the basis that it would be detrimental to good race relations (ibid., p. 124).

One of the most interesting aspects of the Southern International Harvester plants was the use of the public school system to maintain the pattern of Black concentration. Vocational courses were made available to White students which would prepare them to enter the skilled trades at Harvester and other industrial plants. Vocational courses available to Black students did not prepare them to enter such trades. In addition, the schools conducted an adult evening Apprenticeship Training Program. These programs were run by the schools, together with Joint Apprenticeship Committees composed of an equal number of representatives from the unions and the major employers. The program was coordinated by a representative of the U.S. Bureau of Apprenticeship Training (ibid., pp. 32–33). The result was an arrangement where the companies, the unions, the local schools, and the federal government combined to ensure that Black workers were excluded from the training which could gain them entry to skilled occupations.

There is little evidence of the role of minority labor in cushioning White unemployment in the Southern plants. Ozanne, however, notes that

> when layoffs came in 1960 there were more in the assembly and foundry than in the tool room and maintenance. Thus, black layoffs were proportionately greater than white. This occurred at Memphis and Louisville even though the blacks had equal seniority with the whites. In certain older Harvester plants which had been lily-white before World War II the disproportionate decline of black employment was caused by the lesser seniority of blacks. [Ozanne, 1972, p. 36]

Another setting in which we can examine the uses of minority labor at International Harvester is provided by the company's Solar Division, in San Diego. While time-series data for minority employment are not available here, an examination of Solar can provide a look at the contemporary situation in one Harvester plant.

Solar began as an aircraft company during the 1920s and became part of International Harvester in 1960. Since the 1960s its main product has been industrial gas turbines, a line which is currently prospering. Solar employs some 3,000 workers in two San Diego plants and has gross sales of over $100 million. In 1973 minority workers were 13.2 percent of the Solar work force. In the San Diego area as a whole, minorities represented 17.8 percent of the labor force, approximately 12 percent being Chicano, 4 percent Black, and 2 percent other minorities.

As in other Harvester plants, the most obvious minority work pattern is concentration in some occupational categories and underrepresentation in others. In 1973, minorities at Solar were represented in the broad occupational categories used by the census in the following manner (author's data):

Officials and managers	2.8%
Professionals	4.3

Technicians	8.5
Office and clerical	12.6
Craftsmen	11.1
Operatives	23.0
Laborers	46.5
Service Workers	54.8

In line with Ozanne's comments (cited above), we find that minority workers are concentrated at the bottom within each category as well. Thus if the service component is divided into its two constituents, we find that only 4 of the 21 guards are minorities, while fully 19 of the 21 custodians are minority workers. Likewise, 5 of the 8 minority workers listed as officials and managers are foremen. Looking only at the overall pattern, however, it is clear that the Solar minority work force is overrepresented in those occupations listed below the skilled workers, and substantially underrepresented at occupational levels above office and clerical. Of all the occupational categories, the two largest by far were operatives and professionals. There was a relatively small number of laborers.

Judged from a variety of evidence, Solar management attaches little importance to changing this pattern of concentration and underrepresentation. For example, in 1966 Solar was visited by employment specialists from the Department of the Navy to audit Solar's compliance with equal opportunity employment laws and decrees (Solar has important military contracts). The Navy inspectors made a series of recommendations, which were listed along with the suggestions by the Solar EEO (Equal Employment Opportunity) coordinator, at that time a regular member of the management team. This document reads, in part:

> RECOMMENDATION: Explore the possibility of setting up a "field employment office" in some minority populated areas ("poverty pockets") of town, to be staffed one or two days a week by an employment representative with authority to hire in the field.
>
> SUGGESTED ACTION: Do not implement. Any benefit to the company is questionable and the expense would probably not be justified.
>
> RECOMMENDATION: Organize a training program or series of meetings for front-line supervisors and their employees to instill EEO principles firmly in them. Also, make it clear that any individual who does not firmly support EEO should seek employment elsewhere.
>
> SUGGESTED ACTION: Do not implement. A training program would be far too expensive and difficult to organize, and we feel this is hardly an appropriate subject for a formalized training program.

Solar had also been under pressure to develop a Minority Skills Inventory in order to identify promotable minority workers. In 1970 the director of

Industrial Relations wrote a memo indicating that he felt such a Skills Inventory should be developed, and suggesting a procedure. He went on to say:

> Recognizing that this Skills Inventory will not be too useful, disclosure of its existence should be kept to a minimum, on a need to know basis. Expense should also be kept to a minimum. Since we are talking about 472 presently employed minorities plus all the new minority employees this will be a long tedious process. I believe that once a format and official guidelines are developed the O.F.C.C. [Office of Federal Contract Compliance] will be satisfied as long as we press forward. We should, however, all sing the same tune and have several examples of use and success for the Skills Inventory.

Solar, along with all companies which are contractors with the federal government, is required to file an Affirmative Action Plan. This Affirmative Action Plan must describe patterns of minority employment within the company, identify any "underutilization" of minorities, locate barriers to fuller utilization within the company, and propose goals and mechanisms for eliminating any existing patterns of discrimination and underutilization. While Solar's Affirmative Action plans have been approved every year by the federal agency charged with review of the plans, examination of the plans for 1973 and 1974 shows that they are woefully inadequate. Solar's plans make no attempt to locate barriers to equal opportunity within the company, and they set no long-range goals for overcoming existing underutilization. Their analysis of underutilization, the most basic element of the plans, is full of inaccuracies and misleading use of statistics. Short-range (one-year) goals are the only ones that are set, contrary to the provisions of federal law, and these are so lacking in ambition as to call into serious question the company's desire to correct the existing patterns of concentration and underrepresentation. For example, the goals in the 1973 plan called for adding one minority employee in the category of officials and managers, three minority professionals, and one minority technician. These three categories of employment, combined, totaled over 1,200 employees at Solar in 1973. Yet even these insignificant goals were not achieved. In 1974 Solar had the same number of minorities in these three categories as it had in 1973. The 1974 plan made no mention of the fact that the 1973 goals had not been achieved, and proceeded blithely to set other goals.

The responsibility for enforcing equal opportunity and affirmative action within a company is supposed to rest upon a high-level official expressly appointed to that function. In 1973 Solar hired a young Black employee and designated him its EEO coordinator, a position which carried little power. The EEO coordinator took his position seriously and tried to revive the Minority Skills Inventory and to implement other aspects of the Affirmative Action Plan. Within a couple of months he was fired. The reason given for his termination was that he had refused to supply his superiors in the Industrial Relations Department with the names of minority employees who had raised complaints about the company in private meetings held at employees' homes during nonworking hours.

The responsibility for reviewing Solar's Affirmative Action plans and for general monitoring of its minority employment patterns is delegated by the Office of Federal Contract Compliance (OFCC) to the Department of Defense. The failure of the government to take action in this case to correct obvious patterns of unequal opportunity is only a reflection of a virtually universal pattern. As Ozanne states in his review of Black employment in the farm equipment industry:

> In spite of the efforts of OFCC to establish concrete standards for employment integration, the judgment of "in compliance" or "non-compliance" is, to a great extent, a subjective one. The decision is made especially difficult because of the possible dire consequences of the only overt response provided for a ruling of "non-compliance," i.e., the denial or cancellation of a government contract which may put a plant out of business and/or prevent or hinder the government from obtaining necessary armaments or other materials. [Ozanne, 1972, p. 106]

Thus it appears that there will be little remedial action forthcoming from the government to change the patterns of minority employment that are so deeply entrenched at Solar and other branches of International Harvester.

CONCLUSION

From this review of minority employment practices, what can we conclude about the existence of colonial labor at International Harvester?

On the aspect of occupational stratification there is strong and convincing evidence. It is clear that in the present, as in the past, minority workers have in fact disproportionately filled the least desirable jobs in the industry. It is also clear that in many if not in all instances this has been a matter of conscious policy. Management has had definite ideas about what type of work was "suitable" for minorities, and it has consciously excluded them from other types of work. In the case of the South, we noted the manipulation of the educational system for the purpose of maintaining this state of affairs. While there is variation regionally and over time, the patterns remain strong everywhere. Furthermore, the lack of commitment to affirmative action can lead only to the assumption that management today is satisfied with the present arrangements. In this connection, it is well to note that International Harvester has often been lauded as a leader and a "pioneer" in developing equal employment opportunities (Ozanne, 1972, pp. 36–37). In general, then, we can say that the pattern of occupational concentration and exclusion or underrepresentation is an important aspect of colonial labor, at least in this particular company.

On the aspect of wage differentials there is little direct evidence. Wage differentials appear to have had some significance, but not to have been a primary factor. One study of a Southern plant argues for the existence of wage differentials, but it fails to separate out the effect of occupational concentration (Weintraub, 1959, pp. 214–26). Interviews with Solar's minority employees have failed to turn up wage discrimination as a complaint. It appears that unionization has largely eliminated wage differentials as a significant element in large and modern industrial plants. This is not necessarily the case for other types of industries.

Some evidence exists for the use of minority labor as a buffer group. As noted above, severe labor surpluses such as that of the 1930s resulted in the disproportionate laying-off of minority workers. Ozanne (cited above) describes how layoffs in some Harvester plants in 1960 disproportionately affected Blacks, but he sees this as a side effect of their concentration in certain types of jobs and their lower seniority. In the same study, Ozanne presents data for five large firms (unspecified) in the farm equipment and construction machinery industries during a period of layoffs from 1968 to 1970. According to him, in three of these five firms Black blue-collar workers (but not white-collar workers) suffered substantially more job losses than Whites, and did better in only one case. Here again he attributes the pattern to lack of seniority among the Black workers (Ozanne, 1972, pp. 92–93). In the case of Solar, a mild decline in employment in 1973 did not result in minority workers' being laid off disproportionately. What would happen in the case of more severe dislocations remains to be seen.

The use of minority labor as an industrial reserve army is the other aspect of colonial labor. There is no question that minorities have been used as a pool of labor to be drawn upon in times of labor shortage. Minorities performed this function during the 1920s, when minority hiring was clearly seen as an alternative to bidding up the price of labor. The Second World War provides a second clear example of a minority reserve force put to use. While it is not difficult to cite historical examples of minority labor being used in this manner, it is more difficult to determine whether management simply took advantage of an existing situation or whether it consciously contributed to its perpetuation. The existence of a pool of available surplus labor, of course, is something that cannot be determined by the managers of a single company. It is in large part a consequence of the overall level of employment, which is in turn affected by federal government policies and the general state of the economy. While the corporations can have their effect on this through their influence on government policy, this would require a different type of study to determine. However, corporate management can have a direct effect on the existence of a *minority* industrial reserve army through the adoption of a buffer-type policy. The disproportionate laying-off of minority workers in times of labor constriction would help ensure a pool of such workers to be drawn upon when needed. It also reduces the seniority of minority workers and makes them more vulnerable to layoffs. Excluding minorities from non-blue-collar and higher-status jobs would also have this effect, in that it would increase the number of minority unemployed and also concentrate minorities in jobs which are most subject to layoffs. Thus there seems to be an interaction among the various aspects of a racially segmented labor force that needs to be taken into account.

The history of International Harvester's racially segmented labor force bears out the point that while changes have taken place in the twentieth century, racial inequality continues to be an important and institutionalized characteristic. While International Harvester is not *the* typical American corporation, it appears to be generally representative of the large, oligopolistic firms that dominate the American industrial landscape. Thus this case study, while limited to one company, has broader implications for the existence of racial class segmentation in the United States today.

Bibliography

Acuña, Rodolfo. 1972. *Occupied America*. San Francisco: Canfield Press.

Adam, Heribert. 1971. *Modernizing Racial Domination: The Dynamics of South African Politics*. Berkeley: University of California Press.

Allen, Robert. 1969. *Black Awakening in Capitalist America*. Garden City, N.Y.: Doubleday.

Allen, Ruth. 1931. "Mexican Peon Women in Texas." *Sociology and Social Research*, Nov.–Dec. 1931, pp. 131–42.

Almaguer, Tomás. 1975. "Class, Race, and Chicano Oppression." *Socialist Revolution*, July–Sept. 1975, pp. 71–99.

———. 1977. *Interpreting Chicano History: The 'World-System' Approach to Nineteenth-Century California*. Berkeley: University of California, Institute for the Study of Social Change, Working Papers Series, No. 101.

Arrow, Kenneth. 1971. *Some Models of Racial Discrimination in the Labor Market*. Santa Monica, Calif.: Rand.

Baerrensen, Donald. 1971. *The Border Industrialization Program of Mexico*. Lexington, Mass.: D. C. Heath.

Bagú, Sergio. 1952. *Estructura Social de la Colonia*. Buenos Aires: Libreria "El Ateneo" Editorial.

Balandier, G. 1966. "The Colonial Situation: A Theoretical Approach." In Immanuel Wallerstein, ed., *Social Change: The Colonial Situation*, pp. 34–61. New York: Wiley.

Balbus, Isaac. 1971. "Ruling Elite Theory vs. Marxist Class Analysis." *Monthly Review*, May 1971, pp. 36–46.

Bamford, Edwin. 1923–24. "The Mexican Casual Problem in the Southwest." *Journal of Applied Sociology*, Sept. 1923–Aug. 1924, pp. 363–71.

Baran, Paul, and Paul Sweezy. 1966. *Monopoly Capital*. New York: Monthly Review Press.

Barfell, Lawrence. 1937. "A Study of the Health Program among Mexican Children with Special Reference to the Prevalence of Tuberculosis and Its Causes." Master's thesis, University of Southern California.

Barker, Eugene. 1906. "Land Speculation as a Cause of the Texas Revolution." *Texas Historical Association Quarterly*, 1906, pp. 76–95.

Baron, Harold. 1971. "The Demand for Black Labor: Historical Notes on the

Political Economy of Racism.'' *Radical America,* Mar.–Apr. 1971, pp. 1–46.

――――. 1975. ''Racial Domination in Advanced Capitalism: A Theory of Nationalism and Divisions in the Labor Market.'' In Richard Edwards, Michael Reich, and David Gordon, eds., *Labor Market Segmentation,* pp. 173–216. Lexington, Mass.: D. C. Heath.

Barr, Alwyn. 1970. ''Occupational and Geographic Mobility in San Antonio, 1870–1900.'' *Southwestern Quarterly,* Sept. 1970, pp. 396–403.

――――. 1971. *Reconstruction to Reform: Texas Politics, 1876–1906.* Austin: University of Texas Press.

Barrera, Mario, Carlos Muñoz, and Charles Ornelas. 1972. ''The Barrio as Internal Colony.'' In Harlan Hahn, ed., *People and Politics in Urban Society,* pp. 465–98. Los Angeles: Sage Publications.

Barth, Ernest, and Donald Noel. 1972. ''Conceptual Frameworks for the Analysis of Race Relations: An Evaluation.'' *Social Forces,* Mar. 1972, pp. 333–48.

Bean, Walton. 1968. *California: An Interpretive History.* New York: McGraw-Hill.

Beck, Warren. 1962. *New Mexico: A History of Four Centuries.* Norman: University of Oklahoma Press.

Becker, Gary. 1971. *The Economics of Discrimination.* 2d ed. Chicago: University of Chicago Press.

Benedict, Ruth. 1959. *Race: Science and Politics.* New York: Viking Press.

Bernstein, Marvin, ed. 1966. *Foreign Investment in Latin America.* New York: Knopf.

Betts, Raymond. 1968. *Europe Overseas: Phases of Imperialism.* New York: Basic Books.

Billington, Ray. 1974. *Westward Expansion.* 4th ed. New York: Macmillan.

Bishop, C. E. 1967. *Farm Labor in the United States.* New York: Columbia University Press.

Blalock, Hubert J., Jr. 1967. *Toward a Theory of Minority-Group Relations.* New York: Wiley.

Blau, Peter, and Otis Dudley Duncan. 1967. *The American Occupational Structure.* New York: Wiley.

Blauner, Robert. 1972. *Racial Oppression in America.* New York: Harper and Row.

Block, Fred. 1977. ''The Ruling Class Does Not Rule: Notes on the Marxist Theory of the State.'' *Socialist Revolution,* May–June 1977, pp. 6–28.

Block, N. J., and Gerald Dworkin. 1974. ''IQ: Heritability and Inequality.'' *Philosophy and Public Affairs,* pt. 1, Summer 1974, pp. 331–409; pt. 2, Fall 1974, pp. 40–99.

Bogardus, Emory. 1927. ''The Mexican Immigrant.'' *Journal of Applied Sociology,* May–June 1927, pp. 470–88.

――――. 1934. *The Mexican in the United States.* Los Angeles: University of Southern California.

Bonacich, Edna. 1972. "A Theory of Ethnic Antagonism: The Split Labor Market." *American Sociological Review*, Oct. 1972, pp. 547–59.

Bonilla, Frank, and Robert Girling, eds. 1973. *Structures of Dependency*. Stanford, Calif.: Stanford Institute of Politics.

Boucher, Chauncey, 1921. "In Re That Aggressive Slavocracy." *The Mississippi Valley Historical Review*, June–Sept. 1921, pp. 13–79.

Braverman, Harry. 1974. *Labor and Monopoly Capital*. New York: Modern Reader.

Brayer, Herbert. 1974. *William Blackmore: The Spanish-Mexican Land Grants of New Mexico and Colorado, 1863–1878*. Denver: Bradford Robinson, 1949. Reprinted in Carlos Cortés, ed., *Spanish and Mexican Land Grants*. New York: Arno Press.

Bridges, Amy. 1974. "Nicos Poulantzas and the Marxist Theory of the State." *Politics and Society*, Winter 1974, pp. 161–92.

Briggs, Vernon. 1973. *Chicanos and Rural Poverty*. Baltimore: Johns Hopkins University Press.

Briggs, Vernon, Walter Fogel, and Fred Schmidt. 1977. *The Chicano Worker*. Austin: University of Texas Press.

Brody, David. 1972. "Labor and the Great Depression: The Interpretative Prospects." *Labor History*, Spring 1972, pp. 231–44.

Brookshire, Marjorie. 1954. "The Industrial Pattern of Mexican-American Employment in Neuces County, Texas." Ph.D. dissertation, University of Texas.

Broom, Leonard, and Eshref Shevky. 1952. "Mexicans in the United States: A Problem in Social Differentiation." *Sociology and Social Research*, Jan.–Feb. 1952, pp. 150–58.

Brown, Malcolm, and Orin Cassmore. 1939. *Migratory Cotton Pickers in Arizona*. Washington: U.S. Government Printing Office.

Browning, Harley, and S. Dale McLemore. 1964. *A Statistical Profile of the Spanish-Surname Population of Texas*. Austin: University of Texas Bureau of Business Research.

Brunt, P. A. 1965. "Reflections on British and Roman Imperialism." In *Comparative Studies in Society and History*, pp. 267–88.

Bullock, Paul. 1972. *Youth in the Labor Market: Employment Patterns and Career Aspirations in Watts and East Los Angeles*. Los Angeles: UCLA Institute of Industrial Relations.

Burma, John. 1954. *Spanish-speaking Groups in the United States*. Durham, N.C.: Duke University Press.

Burns, James McGregor, and Jack Peltason. 1966. *Government by the People*. 6th ed. Englewood Cliffs, N.J.: Prentice-Hall.

Bustamante, Jorge. 1972. "The Historical Context of the Undocumented Immigration from Mexico to the United States." *Aztlan*, Fall 1972, pp. 257–82.

————. 1976. "Structural and Ideological Conditions of the Mexican Undocumented Immigration to the United States." *American Behavioral Scientist*, Jan.–Feb. 1976, pp. 364–76.

Caldwell, Edwin. 1965. "Highlights of the Development of Manufacturing in

Texas, 1900-1960." *Southwestern Historical Quarterly*, Apr. 1965, pp. 405-31.

California State Relief Administration. 1936. *Migratory Labor in California*. San Francisco: State Printing Office.

Camarillo, Alberto. 1975a. "The Development of the Chicano Working Class: Santa Barbara, 1860-1930." Paper presented at Pacific Coast Branch of American Historical Association, Berkeley.

————. 1975b. "The Making of a Chicano Community: A History of the Chicanos in Santa Barbara, California, 1850-1930." Ph.D. dissertation, UCLA.

Cárdenas, Gilberto. 1973. "Mexican Migration." Paper presented at Conference on Demographic Study of the Mexican American Population, University of Texas, Austin, May 17-19, 1973.

————. 1975. "United States Immigration Policy toward Mexico: An Historical Perspective." *Chicano Law Review*, Summer 1975, pp. 66-89.

Cardoso, Lawrence. 1974. "Mexican Emigration to the United States, 1900-1930: An Analysis of Socio-Economic Causes." Ph.D. dissertation, University of Connecticut.

————. 1975-76. "Labor Emigration to the Southwest, 1916 to 1920: Mexican Attitudes and Policy." *Southwestern Historical Quarterly*, July-Apr. 1975-76, pp. 400-16.

Carmichael, Stokely, and Charles Hamilton. 1967. *Black Power*. New York: Random House.

Cartey, Wilfred, and Martin Kilson, eds. 1970. *The Africa Reader: Colonial Africa*. New York: Vintage.

Caughey, John. 1970. *California*. 3d ed. Englewood Cliffs, N.J.: Prentice-Hall.

Chilcote, Ron, and Joel Edelstein, eds. 1974. *Latin America: The Struggle with Dependency and Beyond*. Cambridge, Mass.: Schenkman.

Charles, Ralph. 1940. "Development of the Partido System in the New Mexico Sheep Industry." Master's thesis, University of New Mexico.

Christoffel, Tom. 1970. "The Permanent Job Shortage." In Tom Christoffel, et al., eds., *Up Against the American Myth*, pp. 259-75. New York: Holt, Rinehart, and Winston.

Clark, Kenneth. 1972. *Dark Ghetto*. New York: Harper and Row.

Clark, Victor. 1908. "Mexican Labor in the United States." *Bureau of Labor Bulletin No. 78*. Washington: U.S. Bureau of Labor Statistics.

Cleland, Robert. 1914-15. "The Early Sentiment for the Annexation of California: An Account of the Growth of American Interest in California, 1835-1846." *Southwestern Historical Quarterly*, July 1914-Jan. 1915.

————. 1947. *California in Our Time: 1900-1940*. New York: Knopf.

————. 1951. *The Cattle on a Thousand Hills*. 2d ed. San Marino, Calif.: Huntington Library.

Clinchy, Everett. 1954. "Equality of Opportunity for Latin-Americans in Texas." Ph.D. dissertation, Columbia University.

Coalson, George. 1952. "Mexican Contract Labor in American Agriculture.'' *Southwestern Social Science Quarterly,* Dec. 1952, pp. 228–38.

————. 1977. *The Development of the Migratory Farm Labor System in Texas, 1900–1954.* San Francisco: R & E Research Associates. (Reprint of a 1955 University of Oklahoma dissertation.)

Coatsworth, John. 1974. ''Railroads, Landholding, and Agrarian Protest in the Early Porfiriato.'' *Hispanic American Historical Review,* Feb. 1974, pp. 48–71.

Cockcroft, James, Andre Gunder Frank, and Dale Johnson. 1972. *Dependence and Underdevelopment.* Garden City, N.Y.: Anchor Books.

Connell, Earl. 1971. *The Mexican Population of Austin, Texas.* San Francisco: R & E Research Associates. (Reprint of a 1925 University of Texas thesis.)

Connor, Seymour. 1971. *Texas: A History.* New York: Crowell.

Copp, Nelson. 1971. *''Wetbacks'' and Braceros: Mexican Migrant Laborers and American Immigration Policy, 1930–1960.* San Francisco: R & E Research Associates. (Reprint of a 1963 Boston University dissertation.)

Cortés, Carlos, ed. 1974. *Mexican Labor in the United States.* New York: Arno Press.

Corwin, Arthur. 1973a. ''Causes of Mexican Emigration to the United States.'' *Perspectives in American History,* 1973, pp. 557–635.

————. 1973b. ''Mexican Emigration History, 1900–1970: Literature and Research.'' *Latin American Research Review,* Summer 1973, pp. 3–23.

————. 1975. ''America's Immigration Dilemma, with Special Reference to Mexico.'' Unpublished paper.

Cotera, Martha. 1976. *Diosa y Hembra: The History and Heritage of Chicanas in the U.S.* Austin, Tex.: Information Systems Development.

Cox, Oliver. 1970. *Caste, Class and Race.* New York: Modern Reader. (Originally published in 1948.)

Craig, Richard. 1971. *The Bracero Program: Interest Groups and Foreign Policy.* Austin: University of Texas Press.

Crain, Forest. 1948. ''The Occupational Distribution of Spanish-Name People in Austin, Texas.'' Master's thesis, University of Texas.

Crawford, Rex. 1942. ''The Latin American in Wartime United States.'' *American Academy of Political and Social Science: Annals,* Sept. 1942, pp. 123–31.

Cross, Ira. 1935. *A History of the Labor Movement in California.* Berkeley: University of California Press.

Crowder, Michael. 1964. ''Indirect Rule—French and British Style.'' *Africa,* July 1964, pp. 197–205.

Cruse, Harold. 1968. *Rebellion or Revolution.* New York: Morrow.

Cumberland, Charles. 1968. *Mexico: The Struggle for Modernity.* London: Oxford University Press.

Dahl, Robert. 1956. *A Preface to Democratic Theory.* Chicago: University of Chicago Press.

————. 1967. *Pluralist Democracy in the United States.* Chicago: Rand McNally.

Dahrendorf, Ralf. 1959. *Class and Class Conflict in Industrial Society.* Stanford, Calif.: Stanford University Press.

D'Antonio, William, and William Form. 1965. *Influentials in Two Border Cities.* Notre Dame, Ind.: University of Notre Dame Press.

D'Antonio, William, and Julian Samora. 1962. "Occupational Stratifications in Four Southwestern Communities." *Social Forces,* Oct. 1962, pp. 17–25.

Davis, Allison, Burleigh Gardner, and Mary Gardner. 1941. *Deep South.* Chicago: University of Chicago Press.

Davis, William Heath. 1929. *Seventy-five Years in California.* San Francisco: J. Howell.

Degler, Carl. 1967. *The Age of the Economic Revolution 1876–1900.* Glenview, Ill.: Scott, Foresman.

De Leon, Arnoldo. 1970. "The Rape of Tio Taco: Mexican Americans in Texas, 1930–1935." *Journal of Mexican American Studies,* Fall 1970, pp. 4–15.

Divine, Robert. 1957. *American Immigration Policy, 1924–1952.* New Haven: Yale University Press.

Doeringer, Peter, and Michael Piore. *Internal Labor Markets and Manpower Analysis.* Lexington, Mass.: D. C. Heath.

Dollard, John. 1957. *Caste and Class in a Southern Town.* 3d ed. Garden City, N.Y.: Doubleday.

Domhoff, William. 1967. *Who Rules America?* Englewood Cliffs, N.J.: Prentice-Hall.

————. 1970. *The Higher Circles.* New York: Vintage.

————. 1974. "State and Ruling Class in Corporate America." *Insurgent Sociologist,* Spring 1974, pp. 3–16.

————. 1976. "I Am Not an 'Instrumentalist.'" *Kapitalistate,* Summer 1976, pp. 221–24.

Dos Santos, Theotonio. 1970. "The Structure of Dependence." *American Economic Review,* May 1970, pp. 231–36.

Dowd, Douglas. 1974. *The Twisted Dream: Capitalist Development in the United States since 1776.* Cambridge, Mass.: Winthrop Publishers.

Dumke, Glenn. 1944. *The Boom of the Eighties in Southern California.* San Marino, Calif.: Huntington Library.

Ebright, Malcolm. 1976. "The San Joaquin Grant." Paper presented at Annual Conference of Southwestern Social Science Association, Phoenix.

Edwards, Richard, Michael Reich, and David Gordon, eds. 1975. *Labor Market Segmentation.* Lexington, Mass.: D. C. Heath.

Ehrenreich, Barbara, and John Ehrenreich. 1977. "The Professional-Managerial Class." *Radical America,* pt. 1, Mar.–Apr. 1977, pp. 7–31; pt. 2, May–June 1977, pp. 7–22.

Eisenstadt, S. N. 1963. *The Political Systems of Empires.* New York: Free Press.

Elac, John. 1972. *The Employment of Mexican Workers in U.S. Agriculture, 1900–1960: A Binational Economic Analysis.* San Francisco: R & E Research Associates. (Reprint of a 1961 UCLA dissertation.)

Emmanuel, Arghiri. 1972. *Unequal Exchange.* New York: Monthly Review Press.

Engels, Frederick. *The Origin of the Family, Private Property and the State.* New York: International Publishers.

Esping-Andersen, Gosta, Roger Friedland, and Erik Wright. 1976. "Modes of Class Struggle and the Capitalist State." *Kapitalistate,* Summer 1976, pp. 186–220.

Fann, K. T., and Donald Hodges, eds. 1971. *Readings in U.S. Imperialism.* Boston: Porter Sargent.

Fanon, Frantz. 1963. *The Wretched of the Earth.* New York: Grove Press.

Fehrenbach, T. R. 1968. *Lone Star: A History of Texas and the Texans.* New York: Macmillan.

Fehrenbacher, Don. 1969. *The Era of Expansion: 1800–1848.* New York: Wiley.

Feldman, Herman. 1931. *Racial Factors in American Industry.* New York: Harper.

Fernández, Raul. 1977. *The United States–Mexico Border.* Notre Dame, Ind.: University of Notre Dame Press.

Fieldhouse, D. K. 1966. *The Colonial Empires.* New York: Delta.

Fisher, Donald. 1973. *A Historical Study of the Migrant in California.* San Francisco: R & E Research Associates. (Reprint of a 1945 University of Southern California master's thesis.)

Fisher, Lloyd. 1953. *The Harvest Labor Market in California.* Cambridge, Mass.: Harvard University Press.

Fite, Gilbert, and Jim Reese. 1973. *An Economic History of the United States.* 3d ed. Boston: Houghton Mifflin.

Flaim, Paul. 1973. "Discouraged Workers and Changes in Unemployment." *Monthly Labor Review,* Mar. 1973, pp. 8–16.

Flores, Estevan. 1978. "The Push-Pull Demographic Approach to Mexican Immigration Policy: Implications and Alternatives." Paper presented at the 1978 annual meeting of the National Association for Chicano Studies, Claremont, California.

Fogel, Walter. 1965. *Education and Income of Mexican-Americans in the Southwest.* Advance Report 1, Mexican-American Study Project. Los Angeles: UCLA Graduate School of Business Administration.

————. 1967. *Mexican Americans in Southwest Labor Markets.* Advance Report 10, Mexican-American Study Project. Los Angeles: UCLA Graduate School of Business Administration.

————. 1968. "Job Gains of Mexican-American Men." *Monthly Labor Review,* Oct. 1968, pp. 22–27.

Foner, Philip, ed. 1970. *The Black Panthers Speak.* Philadelphia: Lippincott.

Frank, Andre Gunder. 1967. *Capitalism and Underdevelopment in Latin America.* New York: Monthly Review Press.

Franklin, Raymond and Solomon Resnik. 1973. *The Political Economy of Racism.* New York: Holt, Rinehart and Winston.

Frazier, E. Franklin. 1957. *Race and Culture Contacts in the Modern World.* Boston: Beacon Press.

Freedman, Francesca. 1975. "The Internal Structure of the American Proletariat: A Marxist Analysis." *Socialist Revolution,* Oct.-Dec. 1975, pp. 41-83.

Freeman, Richard. 1973. "Changes in the Labor Market for Black Americans, 1948-1972." *Brookings Papers on Economic Activity,* Summer 1973, pp. 67-120.

Fuller, John. 1969. *The Movement for the Acquisition of All Mexico, 1846-1848.* New York: Da Capo Press.

Fuller, Roden. 1928. "Occupations of the Mexican-born Population of Texas, New Mexico and Arizona, 1900-1920." *Journal of the American Statistical Association,* Mar. 1928, pp. 64-67.

Fuller, Varden. 1940. "The Supply of Agricultural Labor as a Factor in the Evolution of Farm Organization in California." In *Violations of Free Speech and Rights of Labor,* hearings before a Subcommittee of the Committee on Education and Labor of the U.S. Senate, pt. 54, Agricultural Labor in California. Washington: U.S. Government Printing Office.

Furnivall, J. S. 1948. *Colonial Policy and Practice.* Cambridge: Cambridge University Press.

Galarza, Ernesto. 1964. *Merchants of Labor.* Charlotte, N.C.: McNally and Loftin.

————. 1970. *Spiders in the House and Workers in the Field.* Notre Dame, Ind.: University of Notre Dame Press.

————. 1977. *Farm Workers and Agri-business in California, 1947-1960.* Notre Dame, Ind.: University of Notre Dame Press.

Gallagher, John, and Ronald Robinson. 1953. "The Imperialism of Free Trade." *Economic History Review,* Aug. 1953, pp. 1-15.

Gamio, Manuel. 1971a. *The Life Story of the Mexican Immigrant.* New York: Dover Publications. (Originally published in 1931.)

————. 1971b. *Mexican Immigration to the United States.* New York: Dover Publications. (Originally published in 1930.)

Ganaway, Loomis. 1974. *New Mexico and the Sectional Controversy, 1846-1861.* Albuquerque: University of New Mexico Press.

García, Mario. 1975a. "Merchants and Dons: San Diego's Attempts at Modernization, 1850-1860." *Journal of San Diego History,* Winter 1975, pp. 52-77.

————. 1975b. "Obreros: The Mexican Workers of El Paso, 1900-1920." Ph.D. dissertation, University of California at San Diego.

————. 1975c. "Racial Dualism in the El Paso Labor Market, 1880-1920." *Aztlan,* Summer 1975, pp. 197-218.

Gates, Paul. 1958. "Adjudication of Spanish-Mexican Land Claims in California." *Huntington Library Quarterly,* May 1958, pp. 213-36.

———. 1962. "California's Embattled Settlers." *California Historical Society Quarterly,* 1962, pp. 99–130.

———. 1975. "Public Land Disposal in California." *Agricultural History,* 1975, pp. 158–78.

Gellner, Christopher. 1975. "Enlarging the Concept of a Labor Reserve." *Monthly Labor Review,* Apr. 1975, pp. 20–28.

Genovese, Eugene. 1968. "Class and Nationality in Black America." In *Red and Black.* New York: Vintage.

Gerth, H. H., and C. Wright Mills. 1948. *From Max Weber: Essays in Sociology.* New York: Oxford University Press.

Geschwender, James. 1978. *Racial Stratification in America.* Dubuque, Iowa: Wm. C. Brown.

Gibson, Charles. 1966. *Spain in America.* New York: Harper Torchbooks.

Gilmore, N. Ray, and Gladys Gilmore. 1963. "The Bracero in California." *Pacific Historical Review,* Aug. 1963, pp. 265–82.

Gold, David, Clarence Y.H. Lo, and Erik Wright. 1975. "Recent Developments in Marxist Theories of the Capitalist State." *Monthly Review,* pt. 1, Oct. 1975, pp. 29–43; pt. 2, Nov. 1975, pp. 36–51.

Gómez-Quiñones, Juan. 1972. "The First Steps: Chicano Labor Conflict and Organizing, 1900–1920." *Aztlan,* Spring 1972, pp. 13–49.

González, Nancie. 1967. *The Spanish Americans of New Mexico.* Albuquerque: University of New Mexico Press.

González, Rosalinda. 1976. "The Chicana in Southwest Labor History, 1900–1975: A Preliminary Bibliographic Analysis." Unpublished paper.

González Casanova, Pablo. 1965. "Internal Colonialism and National Development." *Studies in Comparative International Development,* 1, no. 4: 27–37.

Gordon, David. 1972. *Theories of Poverty and Underemployment.* Lexington, Mass.: D.C. Heath.

Gossett, Thomas. 1965. *Race: The History of an Idea in America.* New York: Schocken.

Graebner, Norman. 1955. *Empire on the Pacific.* New York: Ronald Press.

Grebler, Leo. 1966. *Mexican Immigration to the United States.* Mexican-American Study Project Advance Report 2. Los Angeles: UCLA Graduate School of Business Administration.

Grebler, Leo, Joan Moore, and Ralph Guzmán. 1970. *The Mexican-American People.* New York: Free Press.

Greer, Scott. 1959. *Last Man In.* Glencoe, Ill.: Free Press.

Griswold del Castillo, Richard. 1974. "La Raza Hispano Americana: The Emergence of an Urban Culture among the Spanish Speaking of Los Angeles, 1850–1880." Ph.D. dissertation, UCLA.

———. 1975. "Myth and Reality: Chicano Economic Mobility in Los Angeles, 1850–1880." *Aztlan,* Summer 1975, pp. 151–71.

Gross, Bertram, and Stanley Moses. 1972. "Measuring the Real Work Force: 25 Million Unemployed." *Social Policy,* Sept.–Oct. 1972, pp. 5–10.

Gutiérrez, José Angel. 1968. "La Raza and Revolution: The Empirical Conditions of Revolution in Four South Texas Counties." Master's thesis, St. Mary's University, San Antonio.

Gutman, Herbert. 1973. "Work, Culture and Society in Industrializing America, 1815–1919." *American Historical Review*, Fall 1973, pp. 531–88.

Handman, Max. 1926. "The Mexican Immigrant in Texas." *Southwestern Political and Social Science Quarterly*, June 1926, pp. 33–41.

————. 1930. "Economic Reasons for the Coming of the Mexican Immigrant." *American Journal of Sociology*, Jan. 1930, pp. 601–11.

Harper, Allan, Andrew Córdova, and Kalervo Oberg. 1943. *Man and Resources in the Middle Rio Grande Valley*. Albuquerque: University of New Mexico Press.

Hawley, Ellis. 1966. "The Politics of the Mexican Labor Issue, 1950–1965." *Agricultural History*, July 1966, pp. 157–76.

Hayden, Tom. 1968. "Colonialism and Liberation in America." *Viet-Report*, Summer 1968, pp. 32–39.

Hechter, Michael. 1975. *Internal Colonialism: The Celtic Fringe in British National Development, 1536–1966*. Berkeley: University of California Press.

Heller Committee for Research in Social Economics of the University of California and Constantine Panunzio. 1933. *How Mexicans Earn and Live: A Study of the Incomes and Expenditures of One Hundred Mexican Families in San Diego, California*. University of California Publications in Economics, 13, no. 1. Berkeley: University of California Press.

Hernández, José, Leo Estrada, and David Alvírez. 1973. "Census Data and the Problem of Conceptually Defining the Mexican American Population." *Social Science Quarterly*, Mar. 1973, pp. 671–87.

Hernández-Alvarez, José. 1966. "A Demographic Profile of the Mexican Immigration to the United States, 1910–1950." *Journal of Inter-American Studies*, July 1966, pp. 472–96.

Hobsbawm, Eric. 1976. "The Crisis of Capitalism in Historical Perspective." *Socialist Revolution*, Oct.–Dec. 1976, pp. 77–96.

Hoffman, Abraham. 1972. "Mexican Repatriation Statistics: Some Suggested Alternatives to Carey McWilliams." *Western Historical Quarterly*, Oct. 1972, pp. 391–404.

————. 1974. *Unwanted Mexican Americans in the Great Depression: Repatriation Pressures, 1929–1939*. Tucson: University of Arizona Press.

Hogan, William. 1946. *The Texas Republic: A Social and Economic History*. Norman: University of Oklahoma Press.

Hope, John. 1955. "Negro Employment in Three Southern Plants of International Harvester Company." In NPA Committee of the South, *Selected Studies of Negro Employment in the South*. Washington, D.C.: National Planning Association.

Horsman, Reginald. 1973. "Origins of Racial Anglo-Saxonism in Great Britain before 1850." *Journal of the History of Ideas*, July–Sept. 1973, pp. 387–410.

Hufford, Charles. 1971. *The Social and Economic Effects of the Mexican Migration into Texas*. San Francisco: R & E Research Associates. (Reprint of a 1929 thesis.)

Hughes, Charles. 1975. "The Decline of the Californios: The Case of San Diego, 1846–1856." *Journal of San Diego History*, Summer 1975, pp. 1–27.

Hutchinson, E. P. 1956. *Immigrants and Their Children, 1850–1950*. New York: Wiley.

International Migration Review. 1971. Special issue on Mexican and Mexican-American migrants, Fall 1971.

Jamieson, Stuart. 1945. *Labor Unionism in American Agriculture*. Bureau of Labor Bulletin No. 836. Washington: Government Printing Office.

Jensen, Arthur. 1969. "How Much Can We Boost IQ and Scholastic Achievement?" *Harvard Educational Review*, Winter 1969, pp. 1–123.

———. 1973. *Educability and Group Differences*. New York: Harper and Row.

Jiménez, Andres. 1977. *Political Domination in the Labor Market: Racial Division in the Arizona Copper Industry*. Berkeley: University of California, Institute for the Study of Social Change, Working Papers Series, No. 103.

Jones, Lamar. 1965. "Mexican-American Labor Problems in Texas." Ph.D. dissertation, University of Texas.

———. 1970. "Labor and Management in California Agriculture, 1864–1964." *Labor History*, 1970, pp. 23–40.

Jones, Robert. 1945. *Mexican War Workers in the United States: The Mexico-United States Manpower Recruiting Program and Its Operation*. Washington, D.C.: Pan American Union.

Jordan, Winthrop. 1968. *White over Black: American Attitudes toward the Negro, 1550–1812*. Baltimore: Penguin Books.

Kane, Tim. 1973. "Structural Change and Chicano Employment in the Southwest, 1950–1970: Some Preliminary Observations." *Aztlan*, Fall 1973, pp. 383–98.

Katz, Friedrich. 1974. "Labor Conditions on Haciendas in Porfirian Mexico: Some Trends and Tendencies." *Hispanic American Historical Review*, Feb. 1974, pp. 1–47.

Keleher, William. 1964. *Maxwell Land Grant*. New York: Argosy-Antiquarian. (Originally published in 1942.)

Key, V. O. 1961. *Public Opinion and American Democracy*. New York: Knopf.

Kibbe, Pauline. 1946. *Latin Americans in Texas*. Albuquerque: University of New Mexico Press.

Kiser, George. 1972. "Mexican American Labor before World War II." *Journal of Mexican American History*, Spring 1972, pp. 122–42.

Kluckholn, Florence, and Fred Strodtbeck. 1961. *Variations in Value Orientations.* Evanston, Ill.: Row, Peterson.

Knowlton, Clark. 1967. "Land Grant Problems among the State's Spanish Americans." *New Mexico Business,* 1967, pp. 1–13.

————. 1970. "Changing Spanish-American Villages of Northern New Mexico." *Journal of Mexican American Studies,* Fall 1970, pp. 31–43.

————. 1973. "Patron-Peon Pattern among the Spanish Americans of New Mexico." In Renato Rosaldo et al. eds., *Chicano: The Evolution of a People,* pp. 232–37. Minneapolis: Winston Press.

————. 1975. "The Neglected Chapters in Mexican-American History." In Gus Tyler, ed., *Mexican-Americans Tomorrow.* Albuquerque: University of New Mexico Press.

Knox, William. 1971. *The Economic Status of the Mexican Immigrant in San Antonio, Texas.* San Francisco: R & E Research Associates. (Reprint of a 1927 University of Texas thesis.)

Kohn, Hans. 1958. "Reflections on Colonialism." In Robert Strausz-Hupe and Henry Hazard, eds., *The Idea of Colonialism,* pp. 2–16. New York: Praeger.

Kolko, Gabriel. 1967. *The Triumph of American Conservatism.* Chicago: Quadrangle Books.

Kuper, Leo, and M. G. Smith, eds. 1971. *Pluralism in Africa.* Berkeley: University of California Press.

Kushner, Sam. 1975. *Long Road to Delano.* New York: International Publishers.

Lamar, Howard, 1970. *The Far Southwest, 1846–1912.* New York: Norton.

Landoldt, Robert. 1965. "The Mexican-American Workers of San Antonio, Texas." Ph.D. dissertation, University of Texas.

Larson, Robert. 1968. *New Mexico's Quest for Statehood, 1846–1912.* Albuquerque: University of New Mexico Press.

Lawrence, Anne. 1977. "The Formation of Labor Market Boundaries: A Comparative Analysis of the Bracero Program in Agriculture and the Railroad Industry in the American Southwest, 1942–1964." Unpublished paper.

Lea, Tom. 1957. *The King Ranch.* Boston: Little, Brown.

Lenin, V. I. 1975. *The State and Revolution.* Reprinted in Robert Tucker, ed., *The Lenin Anthology.* New York: Norton.

Leonard, Olen. 1943. *The Role of the Land Grant in the Social Organization and Social Processes of a Spanish-American Village in New Mexico.* Ann Arbor, Mich.: J. W. Edwards.

Leonard, Olen, and Helen Johnson. 1967. *Low-Income Families in the Spanish-Surname Population of the Southwest.* Agricultural Economic Report No. 112. Washington: U.S. Department of Agriculture.

Leonard, Olen, and C. P. Loomis. 1941. *Culture of a Contemporary Rural Community: El Cerrito, New Mexico.* Washington: U.S. Department of Agriculture, Bureau of Agricultural Economics, Rural Life Studies 1, November 1941.

Levy, Jacques. 1975. *César Chávez*. New York: Norton.

Lieberson, Stanley. 1961. "A Societal Theory of Race and Ethnic Relations." *American Sociological Review*, Dec. 1961, pp. 902–10.

Lingenfelter, Richard. 1974. *The Hardrock Miners*. Berkeley: University of California Press.

Loehlin, John, Gardner Lindzey, and J. N. Spuhler. 1975. *Race Differences in Intelligence*. San Francisco: W. H. Freeman.

London, Joan, and Henry Anderson. 1970. *So Shall Ye Reap*. New York: Thomas Crowell.

Longmore, T. Wilson, and Homer Hitt. 1943. "A Demographic Analysis of First and Second Generation Mexican Population of the United States: 1930." *Southwestern Social Science Quarterly*, Sept. 1943, pp. 138–49.

Loomis, Charles. 1942. "Wartime Migration from the Rural Spanish Speaking Villages of New Mexico." *Rural Sociology*, Dec. 1942, pp. 384–95.

———. 1958. "El Cerrito, New Mexico: A Changing Village." *New Mexico Historical Review*, 1958, pp. 53–75.

Loomis, Charles, and Nellie Loomis. 1942. "Skilled Spanish-American War-Industry Workers from New Mexico." *Applied Anthropology*, Oct.–Nov.–Dec. 1942, pp. 33–36.

López, Olibama. 1942. "The Spanish Heritage in the San Luis Valley." Ph.D. dissertation, University of Denver.

López, Ronald. 1970. "The El Monte Berry Strike of 1933." *Aztlan*, Spring 1970, pp. 101–14.

Lowi, Theodore. 1969. *The End of Liberalism*. New York: Norton.

Lyle, Jerolyn. 1973. "Factors Affecting the Job Status of Workers with Spanish Surnames." *Monthly Labor Review*, Apr. 1973, pp. 10–16.

McConnell, Grant. 1966. *Private Power and American Democracy*. New York: Knopf.

McKay, Roberta. 1976. "Americans of Spanish Origin in the Labor Force: An Update." *Monthly Labor Review*, Sept. 1976, pp. 3–6.

McLean, Robert. 1929. "Mexican Workers in the United States." *Proceedings*, National Conference on Social Welfare, 1929, pp. 531–38.

———. 1930. "Tightening the Mexican Border." *Survey*, Apr. 1, 1930.

———. 1932. "The Mexican Return." *The Nation*, Aug. 24, 1932, pp. 165–66.

McWilliams, Carey. 1942. *Ill Fares the Land*. Boston: Little, Brown.

———. 1968. *North from Mexico*. New York: Greenwood Press. (Originally published in 1948.)

———. 1971. *Factories in the Field*. Santa Barbara, Calif.: Peregrine Publishers. (Originally published in 1939.)

Maloney, Thomas. 1964. "Recent Demographic and Economic Changes in Northern New Mexico." *New Mexico Business*, 1964, pp. 2–14.

Manuel, Herschel. 1934. "The Mexican Population of Texas." *Southwestern Social Science Quarterly*, June 1934, pp. 29–51.

————. 1965. *Spanish-speaking Children of the Southwest*. Austin: University of Texas Press.

Marshall, F. Ray. 1971. "Some Reflections on Labor History." *Southwestern Historical Quarterly*, Oct. 1971, pp. 137–57.

Martínez, John. 1972. *Mexican Emigration to the U.S., 1910–1930*. San Francisco: R & E Research Associates. (Reprint of a 1957 University of California Ph.D. dissertation [Berkeley]).

Martínez, Oscar. 1975. "On the size of the Chicano Population: New Estimates, 1850–1900." *Aztlan*, Spring 1975, pp. 43–68.

Marx, Karl. 1967. *Capital*. Vol. 1. New York: International Publishers.

Meador, Bruce. 1973. *"Wetback" Labor in the Lower Rio Grande Valley*. San Francisco: R & E Research Associates. (Reprint of a 1951 University of Texas thesis.)

Meier, Matt, and Feliciano Rivera. 1972. *The Chicanos*. New York: Hill and Wang.

Meinig, D. W. 1969. *Imperial Texas*. Austin: University of Texas Press.

————. 1971. *Southwest: Three Peoples in Geographical Change, 1600–1700*. New York: Oxford University Press.

Memmi, Albert. 1965. *The Colonizer and the Colonized*. Boston: Beacon Press.

Menefee, Selden. 1941. *Mexican Migratory Workers of South Texas*. Washington: Government Printing Office. (Reprinted in Carlos Cortés, ed., *Mexican Labor in the United States*. New York: Arno Press, 1974.)

Menefee, Selden, and Orin Cassmore. 1940. *The Pecan Shellers of San Antonio*. Washington: Government Printing Office. (Reprinted in Carlos Cortés, ed., *Mexican Labor in the United States*. New York: Arno Press, 1974.)

Merk, Frederick. 1963. *Manifest Destiny and Mission in American History*. New York: Knopf.

Metzler, William, and Afife Sayin. 1950. *The Agricultural Labor Force in the San Joaquin Valley, California: Characteristics, Employment, Mobility, 1948*. Washington: U.S. Department of Agriculture.

Mexicans in California. 1930. Report of Governor C. C. Young's Mexican Fact-finding Committee. San Francisco: State Building, Oct. 1930.

Meyers, Frederic. 1951. *Spanish-Name Persons in the Labor Force in the Manufacturing Industry in Texas*. Inter-American Education Occasional Papers 8. Austin: University of Texas Press.

Miliband, Ralph. 1965. "Marx and the State." *Socialist Register*, 1965, pp. 278–96.

————. 1969. *The State in Capitalist Society*. New York: Basic Books.

————. 1972. "Reply to Nicos Poulantzas." In Robin Blackburn, ed., *Ideology in Social Science*, pp. 253–62. Glasgow: Fontana.

————. 1973. "Poulantzas and the Capitalist State." *New Left Review*, Nov.–Dec. 1973, pp. 83–92.

Mills, C. Wright. 1956. *The Power Elite.* New York: Oxford University Press.

Mollenkopf, John. 1975. "Theories of the State and Power Structure Research." *Insurgent Sociologist,* Spring 1975, pp. 245–64.

Montejano, David. 1977. *Race, Labor Repression, and Capitalist Agriculture: Notes from South Texas, 1920–1930.* Berkeley: University of California, Institute for the Study of Social Change, Working Papers Series, no. 102.

Moore, Barrington, Jr. 1967. *Social Origins of Dictatorship and Democracy.* Boston: Beacon Press.

Morefield, Richard. 1956. "Mexicans in the California Mines. 1848–1853." *California Historical Society Quarterly,* 1956, pp. 37–46.

———. 1971. *The Mexican Adaptation in American California, 1846–1875.* San Francisco: R & E Research Associates. (Reprint of a 1955 University of California thesis.)

Mörner, Magnus. 1967. *Race Mixture in the History of Latin America.* Boston: Little, Brown.

Moynihan, Daniel, 1965. *The Negro Family: The Case for National Action.* Washington: U.S. Department of Labor, Mar. 1965.

Murguía, Edward. 1975. *Assimilation, Colonialism and the Mexican American People.* Mexican American Monograph Series 1. Austin: University of Texas Press.

Myrdal, Gunnar. 1962. *An American Dilemma.* New York: Pantheon. (Originally published in 1944.)

Nadel, George, and Perry Curtis. 1964. *Imperialism and Colonialism.* New York: Macmillan.

Nance, Joseph. 1963. *After San Jacinto: The Texas-Mexican Frontier, 1836–1841.* Austin: University of Texas Press.

Nash, Gerald. 1964. *State Government and Economic Development: A History of Administrative Policies in California, 1849–1933.* Berkeley: University of California Press.

———. 1973. *The American West in the Twentieth Century.* Englewood Cliffs, N.J.: Prentice-Hall.

Nelson, Eastin, and Frederic Meyers. 1950. *Labor Requirements and Labor Resources in the Lower Rio Grande Valley of Texas.* Inter-American Education Occasional Papers 6. Austin: University of Texas Press.

Nelson, Jack. 1974. "The Changing Economic Position of Black Urban Workers." *Review of Black Political Economy,* Winter 1974, pp. 35–48.

Nelson Cisneros, Victor. 1975. "La Clase Trabajadora en Tejas, 1920–1940." *Aztlan,* Summer 1975, pp. 239–65.

Nkrumah, Kwame. 1966. *Neo-Colonialism: The Last State of Imperialism.* New York: International Publishers.

North, David. 1970. *The Border Crossers.* Washington, D.C.: TransCentury Corp.

North, David, and Marion Houstoun. 1976. *The Characteristics and Role of*

Illegal Aliens in the U.S. Labor Market: An Exploratory Study. Washington: Employment and Training Administration, U.S. Department of Labor, Mar. 1976.

North, Douglass C. 1966. *The Economic Growth of the United States, 1790–1860.* New York: Norton.

Nostrand, Richard. 1968. "The Hispanic-American Borderland: A Regional, Historical Geography." Ph.D. dissertation, UCLA.

Nun, José. 1969. "Superpoblación relativa, ejército industrial de reserva y masa marginal." *Revista Latinoamericana de Sociología,* July 1969, pp. 178–236.

O'Connor, James. 1973. *The Fiscal Crisis of the State.* New York: St. Martin's Press.

Offe, Claus. 1973. "The Abolition of Market Control and the Problem of Legitimacy." *Kapitalistate,* nos. 1 and 2, 1973.

————. 1974 "The Theory of the Capitalist State and the Problem of Policy Formation." Mimeo.

Officer, James. 1960. "Historical Factors in Interethnic Relations in the Community of Tucson." *Arizoniana,* Fall 1960, pp. 12–16.

Omvedt, Gail. 1973. "Towards a Theory of Colonialism." *Insurgent Sociologist,* Spring 1973, pp. 1–24.

Oxman, G. Bromely. 1921. "The Mexican in Los Angeles from the Standpoint of the Religious Forces in the City." *American Academy of Political and Social Science Annals,* Jan. 1921, pp. 130–33.

Ozanne, Robert. 1967. *A Century of Labor-Management Relations at McCormick and International Harvester.* Madison: University of Wisconsin Press.

————. 1968. *Wages in Practice and Theory: McCormick and International Harvester, 1860–1960.* Madison: University of Wisconsin Press.

————. 1972. *The Negro in the Farm Equipment and Construction Machinery Industries.* Racial Policies of American Industry, Report No. 26. Philadelphia: University of Pennsylvania Press.

Padfield, Harland, and William Martin. 1965. *Farmers, Workers and Machines: Technological and Social Change in Farm Industries of Arizona.* Tucson: University of Arizona Press.

Parigi, Sam. 1964. "A Case Study of Latin American Unionization in Austin, Texas." Ph.D. dissertation, University of Texas.

Park, Joseph. 1961. "The History of Mexican Labor in Arizona during the Territorial Period." Master's thesis, University of Arizona.

Parkes, Henry Bamford. 1970. *A History of Mexico.* Boston: Houghton Mifflin.

Paul, Rodman. 1963. *Mining Frontiers of the Far West, 1848–1880.* New York: Holt, Rinehart and Winston.

————. 1971. "The Spanish-Americans in the Southwest, 1848–1900." In John Clard, ed., *The Frontier Challenge: Responses to the Trans-Mississippi West,* pp. 31–56. Lawrence: University of Kansas Press.

Peñalosa, Fernando. 1963. "Class Consciousness and Social Mobility in a

Mexican-American Community.'' Ph.D. dissertation, University of Southern California.

Peñalosa, Fernando, and Edward McDonagh. 1966. "Social Mobility in a Mexican-American Community.'' *Social Forces,* June 1966, pp. 498–505.

Pendleton, Edwin. 1950. "History of Labor in Arizona Irrigated Agriculture.'' Ph.D. dissertation, University of California at Berkeley.

Perlo, Victor. 1975. *Economics of Racism U.S.A.* New York: International Publishers.

Perrigo, Lynn. 1960. *Texas and Our Spanish Southwest.* Dallas: Banks Upshaw.

Perry, Louis, and Richard Perry. 1963. *A History of the Los Angeles Labor Movement, 1911–1941.* Berkeley: University of California Press.

Pesotta, Rose. 1944. *Bread upon the Waters.* New York: Dodd, Mead.

Peterson, Herbert. 1974. "Twentieth-Century Search for Cibola: Post–World War I Mexican Labor Exploitation in Arizona.'' In Manuel Servín, ed., *The Mexican-Americans,* 2d ed., pp. 113–32. Beverly Hills, Calif.: Glencoe Press.

Pitt, Leonard. 1970. *The Decline of the Californios.* Berkeley: University of California Press.

Piven, Frances, and Richard Cloward. 1971. *Regulating the Poor: The Functions of Public Welfare.* New York: Pantheon.

Poston, Dudley, and David Alvírez. 1973. "On the Cost of Being a Mexican American Worker.'' *Social Science Quarterly,* Mar. 1973, pp. 697–709.

Poulantzas, Nicos. 1972. "The Problem of the Capitalist State.'' In Robin Blackburn, ed., *Ideology in Social Science,* pp. 238–53. Glasgow: Fontana.

———. 1973a. "On Social Classes.'' *New Left Review,* Mar.–Apr. 1973, pp. 27–54.

———. 1973b. *Political Power and Social Classes.* London: New Left Books.

———. 1975. *Classes in Contemporary Capitalism.* London: New Left Books.

———. 1976. "The Capitalist State: A Reply to Miliband and Laclau.'' *New Left Review,* Jan.–Feb. 1976, pp. 63–83.

Prager, Jeffrey. 1972–73. "White Racial Privilege and Social Change: An Examination of Theories of Racism.'' *Berkeley Journal of Sociology,* 1972–73, pp. 117–50.

President's Commission on Migratory Labor. 1951. *Migratory Labor in American Agriculture.* Washington: Government Printing Office.

Price, Glenn. 1967. *Origins of the War with Mexico: The Polk-Stockton Intrigue.* Austin: University of Texas Press.

Pumpelly, Raphael. 1871. *Across America and Asia.* 5th ed., rev. New York: Leypodt and Holt.

Rainwater, Lee, and William Yancey. 1967. *The Moynihan Report and the Politics of Controversy.* Cambridge, Mass.: MIT Press.

Reich, Michael. 1972. "The Economics of Racism." In Richard Edwards, Michael Reich, and Thomas Weisskopf, eds., *The Capitalist System,* pp. 313–21. Englewood Cliffs, N.J.: Prentice-Hall.

Reisler, Mark. 1973. "Passing through Our Egypt: Mexican Labor in the United States, 1900–1940." Ph.D. dissertation, Cornell.

————. 1976. *By the Sweat of Their Brow: Mexican Immigrant Labor in the United States, 1900–1940.* Westport, Conn.: Greenwood Press.

Report of the National Advisory Commission on Civil Disorders. 1968. New York: Bantam Books.

Rex, John. 1970. *Race Relations in Sociological Theory.* London: Weidenfeld and Nicolson Press.

Rhodes, James Ford. 1907. *History of the United States from the Compromise of 1850,* vol. 1. New York: Macmillan.

Rhodes, Robert, ed. 1970. *Imperialism and Underdevelopment.* New York: Monthly Review press.

Richardson, Rupert. 1958. *Texas: The Lone Star State.* Englewood Cliffs, N.J.: Prentice-Hall.

Riegel, Robert. 1926. *The Story of the Western Railroads.* Lincoln: University of Nebraska Press.

Ríos, Antonio, ed. 1977. *Immigration and Public Policy: Human Rights for Undocumented Workers and Their Families.* Los Angeles: UCLA Chicano Studies Center Document No. 5.

Robinson, W. W. 1948. *Land in California.* Berkeley: University of California Press.

Rochín, Refugio. 1973. "Economic Deprivation of Chicanos—Continuing Neglect in the Seventies." *Aztlan,* Spring 1973, pp. 85–102.

Rock, Michael. 1976. "The Change in Tenure New Mexico Supreme Court Decisions Have Effected Upon the Common Lands of Community Land Grants in New Mexico." *The Social Science Journal,* Oct. 1976, pp. 53–63.

Romano, Octavio. 1968. "The Anthropology and Sociology of the Mexican-Americans: The Distortion of Mexican-American History." *El Grito,* Fall 1968, pp. 13–26.

Romo, Ricardo. 1975a. "Mexican Workers in the City: Los Angeles, 1915–1930." Ph.D. dissertation, UCLA.

————. 1975b. "Responses to Mexican Immigration, 1910–1930." *Aztlan,* Summer 1975, pp. 173–94.

————. 1977. "The Urbanization of Southwestern Chicanos in the Early Twentieth Century." *New Scholar,* 1977, pp. 183–207.

Rose, Arnold. 1967. *The Power Structure.* Oxford: Oxford University Press.

Ruiz, Ramon, ed. 1963. *The Mexican War.* New York: Holt, Rinehart and Winston.

Ryan, William. 1971. *Blaming the Victim.* New York: Vintage.

Ryscavage, Paul, and Earl Mellor. 1973. "The Economic Situation of Spanish Americans." *Monthly Labor Review,* Apr. 1973, pp. 3–9.

Samora, Julian. 1971. *Los Mojados: The Wetback Story.* Notre Dame, Ind.: University of Notre Dame Press.

———. 1975. "Mexican Immigration." In Gus Tyler, ed., *Mexican-Americans Tomorrow.* Albuquerque: University of New Mexico Press.

Sánchez, George. 1967. *Forgotten People.* Albuquerque: Calvin Horn, 1967. (Originally published in 1940.)

Sardei-Biermann, Sabine, Jens Christiansen, and Knuth Dohse. 1973. "Class Domination and the Political System: A Critical Interpretation of a Recent Contribution by Claus Offe." *Kapitalistate,* no. 2, 1973, pp. 60–69.

Saunders, Lyle, and Olen Leonard. 1951. *The Wetback in the Lower Rio Grande Valley of Texas.* Inter-American Educational Occasional Papers 7. Austin: University of Texas Press.

Schermerhorn, Richard. 1970. *Comparative Ethnic Relations.* New York: Random House.

Schmidt, Fred. 1970. *Spanish Surnamed American Employment in the Southwest.* Los Angeles: UCLA Institute of Industrial Relations.

Schmidt, Fred, and Kenneth Koford. 1975. "The Economic Condition of the Mexican-American." In Gus Tyler, ed., *Mexican-Americans Tomorrow,* pp. 81–106. Albuquerque: University of New Mexico Press.

Schwartz, Harry. 1945. *Seasonal Farm Labor in the United States.* New York: Columbia University Press.

Scott, Florence. 1965. *Historical Heritage of the Lower Rio Grande.* Rio Grande City, Tex.: La Retama Press.

Scott, Robin F. 1971. "The Mexican-American in the Los Angeles Area, 1920–1950: From Acquiescence to Activity." Ph.D. dissertation, University of Southern California.

Scruggs, Otey. 1961. "The United States, Mexico, and the Wetbacks, 1942–1947." *Pacific Historical Review,* May 1961, pp. 149–64.

———. 1963. "Texas and the Bracero Program, 1942–1947." *Pacific Historical Review,* Aug. 1963, pp. 251–64.

Shapiro, Harold. 1925. "The Pecan Shellers of San Antonio, Texas." *Southwestern Social Science Quarterly,* Mar. 1925, pp. 229–44.

———. 1952. "The Workers of San Antonio, Texas, 1900–1940." Ph.D. dissertation, University of Texas, Austin.

Shibutani, Tamotsu, and Kian Kwan. 1965. *Ethnic Stratification.* New York: Macmillan.

Shockley, John. 1974. *Chicano Revolt in a Texas Town.* Notre Dame, Ind.: University of Notre Dame Press.

Simmons, Ozzie. 1952. "Anglo Americans and Mexican Americans in South Texas: A Study in Dominant-Subordinate Group Relations." Ph.D. dissertation, Harvard University. (Reprinted by Arno Press, 1974.)

Simpson, George, and J. Milton Yinger. 1958. *Racial and Cultural Minorities.* Rev. ed. New York: Harper.

Slobodek, Mitchell. 1964. *A Selected Bibliography of California Labor History*. Los Angeles: UCLA Institute of Industrial Relations.

Snowden, Frank. 1970. *Blacks in Antiquity*. Cambridge, Mass.: Harvard University Press.

Snyder, Louis. 1939. *Race: A History of Modern Ethnic Theories*. New York: Longmans, Green.

Special Report of the 1970 San Bernardino County Grand Jury. *Fair Employment Practices Investigation, 1970*.

Spratt, John. 1955. *The Road to Spindletop: Economic Change in Texas, 1875-1901*. Dallas: Southern Methodist University Press.

Stambaugh, J. Lee, and Lillian Stambaugh. 1954. *The Lower Rio Grande Valley of Texas*. San Antonio: Naylor.

Staples, Robert. 1976. "Race and Colonialism: The Domestic Case in Theory and Practice." *Black Scholar*, June 1976, pp. 37-48.

Stavenhagen, Rodolfo. 1965. "Classes, Colonialism, and Acculturation." *Studies in Comparative International Development*, 1, no. 6: 53-77.

Stein, Stanley, and Barbara Stein. 1970. *The Colonial Heritage of Latin America*. New York: Oxford University Press.

Stoddard, Ellwyn. 1976a. "A Conceptual Analysis of the 'Alien Invasion': Institutionalized Support of Illegal Mexican Aliens in the U.S." *International Migration Review*, Summer 1976, pp. 157-89.

―――. 1976b. "Illegal Mexican Labor in the Borderlands." *Pacific Sociological Review*, Apr. 1976, pp. 175-210.

Sturdivant, Frederick. 1969. "Business and the Mexican-American Community." *California Management Review*, Spring 1969, pp. 73-80.

Sullivan, Mary Loretta, and Bertha Blair. 1936. *Women in Texas Industries*. U.S. Department of Labor, Women's Bureau, Bulletin No. 126. Washington: Government Printing Office.

Swadesh, Frances. 1974. *Los Primeros Pobladores: Hispanic Americans of the Ute Frontier*. Notre Dame, Ind.: University of Notre Dame Press.

Szymanski, Albert. 1972. "Trends in the American Working Class." *Socialist Revolution*, July-Aug. 1972, pp. 101-22.

―――. 1975. "Trends in Economic Discrimination against Blacks in the U.S. Working Class." *Review of Radical Political Economics*, Fall 1975, pp. 1-21.

Taylor, Paul. 1928. *Mexican Labor in the United States: Imperial Valley*. Berkeley: University of California Publications in Economics (vol. 6, no. 1).

―――. 1929. *Mexican Labor in the United States: Valley of the South Platte, Colorado*. Berkeley: University of California Publications in Economics (vol. 6, no. 2).

―――. 1930. *Mexican Labor in the United States: Dimmit County, Winter Garden District, South Texas*. Berkeley: University of California Publications in Economics (vol. 6, no. 5).

―――. 1932. *Mexican Labor in the United States: Chicago and the Calumet*

Region. Berkeley: University of California Publications in Economics (vol. 7, no. 2).

———. 1937. "Migratory Farm Labor in the United States." *Monthly Labor Review*, Mar. 1937, pp. 537–49.

———. 1945. "Foundations of California Rural Society." *California Historical Society Quarterly*, Sept. 1945, pp. 193–228.

———. 1971. *An American-Mexican Frontier: Nueces County, Texas*. New York: Russell and Russell. (Originally published in 1934.)

Taylor, Paul, and Tom Vasey. 1936. "Historical Background of California Farm Labor." *Rural Sociology*, Sept. 1936, pp. 281–95.

Taylor, Ronald. 1973. *Sweatshops in the Sun: Child Labor on the Farm*. Boston: Beacon Press.

Taylor, William, and Elliott West. 1975. "Patron Leadership at the Crossroads: Southern Colorado in the Late Nineteenth Century." In Norris Hundley, ed., *The Chicano*, pp. 73–95. Santa Barbara, Calif.: Clio Books.

Thomas, Howard, and Florence Taylor. 1951. *Migrant Farm Labor in Colorado*. National Child Labor Committee. (Reprinted in Carlos Cortés, ed., *Mexican Labor in the United States*. New York: Arno Press, 1974.)

Thompson, Albert. 1956. "The Mexican Immigrant Worker in Southwestern Agriculture." *American Journal of Economics and Sociology*, Oct. 1956, pp. 73–82.

Tomasek, Robert. 1957. "The Political and Economic Implications of Mexican Labor in the United States under the Non Quota System, Contract Labor Program, and Wetback Movement." Ph.D. dissertation, University of Michigan.

Torres, Rudy. 1978. "Political Economy of U.S. Class Structure: Notes on Dual Labor Market Theory." Claremont, Calif.: Claremont Working Papers in Public Policy, Spring 1978.

Tuck, Ruth. 1946. *Not with the Fist*. New York: Harcourt Brace.

Twitchell, R. E. 1911. *Leading Facts of New Mexican History*. Cedar Rapids, Ia.: Torch Press.

Tyler, Gus, ed. 1975. *Mexican-Americans Tomorrow*. Albuquerque: University of New Mexico Press.

U.S. Commission on Civil Rights. 1974. *Counting the Forgotten: The 1970 Census Count of Persons of Spanish Speaking Background in the United States*. Washington: Government Printing Office.

———. 1978. *Improving Hispanic Unemployment Data*. Washington: Government Printing Office, May 1978.

Vaca, Nick. 1970. "The Mexican-American in the Social Sciences: 1912–1970." *El Grito*, pt. 1, Spring 1970, pp. 3–24; pt. 2, Fall 1970, pp. 17–51.

van den Berghe, Pierre. 1965. *South Africa: A Study in Conflict*. Berkeley: University of California Press.

————. 1967. *Race and Racism: A Comparative Perspective.* New York: Wiley.

Vander Zanden, James W. "Sociological Studies of American Blacks." *Sociological Quarterly,* Winter 1973, pp. 35–52.

Walker, Helen. "Mexican Immigrants as Laborers." *Sociology and Social Research,* Sept. 1928, pp. 55–62.

Walker, Kenneth. "The Pecan Shellers of San Antonio and Mechanization." *Southwestern Historical Quarterly,* July 1965, pp. 44–58.

Walter, Paul. 1938. "A Study of Isolation and Social Change in Three Spanish Speaking Villages of New Mexico." Ph.D. dissertation, Stanford University.

————. 1939. "The Spanish-speaking Community in New Mexico." *Sociology and Social Research,* Nov.–Dec. 1939, pp. 150–57.

Walton, John. 1975. "Internal Colonialism: Problems of Definition and Measurement." In Wayne Cornelius and Felicity Trueblood, eds., *Latin American Urban Research,* vol. 5: 29–50. Beverly Hills, Calif.: Sage Publications.

Warburton, Amber, Helen Wood, and Marian Crane. 1943. *The Work and Welfare of Children of Agricultural Laborers in Hidalgo County, Texas.* U.S. Department of Labor, Children's Bureau, Publication 298. (Reprinted in Carlos Cortés, ed., *Mexican Labor in the United States.* New York: Arno Press, 1974.)

Warner, W. Lloyd. 1936. "American Caste and Class." *American Journal of Sociology,* Sept. 1936, pp. 234–37.

Waters, Laurence. 1941. "Transient Mexican Agricultural Labor." *Southwestern Social Science Quarterly,* June 1941, pp. 49–66.

Webb, John. 1937. *The Migratory-Casual Worker.* Washington: Government Printing Office.

Weber, Devra. 1972. "The Organization of Mexicano Agricultural Workers, the Imperial Valley and Los Angeles, 1928–1934: An Oral History Approach." *Aztlan,* Fall 1972, pp. 307–47.

Weber, Max. 1968. *Economy and Society.* Ed. Guenther Roth and Claus Wittich. New York: Bedminster Press.

Weinstein, James. 1968. *The Corporate Ideal in the Liberal State: 1900–1918.* Boston: Beacon Press.

Weintraub, Robert. 1959. "Employment Integration and Racial Wage Differences in a Southern Plant." *Industrial and Labor Relations Review,* Jan. 1959, pp. 214–26.

Westphall, Victor. 1965. *The Public Domain in New Mexico, 1854–1891.* Albuquerque: University of New Mexico Press.

————. 1973. *Thomas Benton Catron and His Era.* Tucson: University of Arizona Press.

Willhelm, Sidney. 1971. *Who Needs the Negro?* Garden City, N.Y.: Doubleday Anchor.

Williams, Dean. 1973. *Some Political and Economic Aspects of Mexican*

Immigration into the United States since 1941. San Francisco: R & E Research Associates. (Reprint of a 1950 UCLA thesis.)

Wilson, William. 1973. *Power, Racism, and Privilege*. New York: Macmillan.

Wolfe, Alan. 1973. *The Seamy Side of Democracy*. New York: David McKay.

————. 1974. "New Directions in the Marxist Theory of Politics." *Politics and Society,* Winter 1974, pp. 131–60.

Wollenberg, Charles. 1975. "Working on El Traque: The Pacific Electric Strike of 1903." In Norris Hundley, ed., *The Chicano,* pp. 96–107. Santa Barbara, Calif.: Clio Books.

Womack, John. 1968. *Zapata and the Mexican Revolution*. New York: Vintage.

Wright, Erik Olin. 1974–75. "To Control or to Smash Bureaucracy: Weber and Lenin on Politics, the State, and Bureaucracy." *Berkeley Journal of Sociology,* 1974–75, pp. 69–108.

————. 1976. "Class Boundaries in Advanced Capitalist Societies." *New Left Review,* July–Aug. 1976, pp. 3–41.

Wyllys, Rufus. 1950. *Arizona: The History of a Frontier State*. Phoenix: Hobson and Herr.

Zamora, Emilio. 1975. "Chicano Socialist Labor Activity in Texas, 1900–1920." *Aztlan,* Summer 1975, pp. 221–36.

Zeleny, Carolyn. 1944. "Relations between the Spanish Americans and Anglo-Americans in New Mexico." Ph.D. dissertation, Yale University.

Zwelling, Shomer. 1970. *Expansion and Imperialism*. Chicago: Loyola University Press.

Index